CONTENTS

ABOUT THE AUTHORS

Emma Wincup is a Senior Lecturer in Criminology and Criminal Justice at the University of Leeds. Prior to taking up her current post she held lectureships at the University of Kent and Cardiff University. In both of these she set up undergraduate Criminology degree programmes.

Throughout her career Emma has been keen to enhance student education. She is the author of three textbooks, and editor of a further two. She is currently writing an introductory book with her colleague, Henry Yeomans, entitled *Thinking Criminologically*.

Emma is particularly committed to supporting students to become independent researchers and has extensive experience of delivering research training and supervising individual students to complete projects. Her approach is practically-based whilst encouraging students to engage with wider theoretical and methodological debates.

To find out more about Emma's work please visit www.law.leeds.ac.uk/people/staff/wincup/or follow her on Twitter @dselawleeds

Kathy Hampson completed her PhD in youth justice through Leeds University. After working in a busy Youth Offending Team (YOT), during which she authored several books about working with young people, she is now North Wales Resettlement Broker Co-ordinator, for the Welsh charity Llamau. In this role she has continued to conduct research focused on the resettlement of young people coming out of custody and on YOT working practice, resulting in several publications. She has worked at Aberystwyth University as a criminology lecturer, is a criminology tutor for the University of Essex Online, and regional tutor for Birmingham University.

Ella Holdsworth is currently a PhD student at the University of Leeds, under the supervision of Professor Anthea Hucklesby and Dr Emma Wincup. Her research interests include female offenders and community sentences. She completed her LLB in Law in 2004, also at the University of Leeds, followed by an MA in Criminology. Ella developed an interest in her PhD by focusing on the use of electronically monitored curfews as a community sentence with women. Her most recent work includes being involved in a comparative European project on the use of electronic monitoring as an alternative to imprisonment in EU Member States.

Jo Large is a Senior Lecturer in Criminology and Sociology at Teesside University, UK. Jo teaches research methods at undergraduate and postgraduate level and also teaches on the Inside Out Prison Exchange Program. Jo's research interests include illicit criminal markets such as counterfeit goods – in particular examining the relationship between demand and supply within a broader context of consumer culture. This also includes analysis of debates around ethics, harm and the overlapping nature of licit and illicit economies. More recently, Jo has been developing work within the field of deviant leisure examining the relationship between volunteer and charity based tourism and harm.

PREFACE AND ACKNOWLEDGEMENTS

The first edition of *Criminological Research: Understanding Qualitative Methods* was published over a decade ago and the backdrop to it is outlined in the preface which has been reprinted from the first edition. In that my co-author and I identified a gap in the market which we appear to have filled successfully. Published book reviews have been overwhelming positive and informal feedback equally so. We were delighted to receive an invitation to produce a second edition and were convinced that a text on qualitative research aimed specifically at criminologists was still needed despite the voluminous amount of 'methods' texts which have been published in the intervening years. This one is sole-authored: my co-author from the first edition is now retired but still enjoys being an occasional criminologist! I am grateful to Lesley for allowing me to develop the second edition as I saw fit but writing a second edition was so much harder without her.

I've often picked up a second edition of a textbook and felt short-changed as only minor revisions have been made. I was determined that I would not do the same. Whilst the basic structure is broadly similar, all chapters have been substantially rewritten and three new case studies have been added. In the first edition, I reflected on my own research experiences. This time I have included those of my PhD students (two have now successfully completed with one to go). I hope you enjoy reading their candid accounts of the research process as much as I have enjoyed supporting them with their doctoral studies.

Even if I felt making minor tweaks was desirable, it was certainly not a realistic option. So much has changed since the first edition manuscript was submitted in Easter 2003. Then ethical scrutiny of research was in its infancy, the political climate allowed for more generous funding of criminological research – albeit quantitative approaches were preferred – and relatively little use had been made of new technological developments in qualitative research contexts. My career has also moved on and since the first edition was published I have spent a great deal of time providing research training, particularly to postgraduate students. I have tried to incorporate these new insights into this new edition.

The second edition has been a long time in the making and I am grateful to everyone at SAGE for their seemingly endless patience as I struggled to fit writing into a busy academic schedule (you know you've been working on a book too long when you see editors come and go!). A particular thanks to Mila Steele for her encouragement in the final stage of the marathon when I had come too far to give up but finishing was far in the distance.

The second edition, like the first, owes a great deal to my time at Cardiff as both a research student and lecturer. Attending an event to celebrate 40 years of ethnography at Cardiff, and specifically the work of Paul Atkinson, reminded me of what had sparked my interest in qualitative research in the first instance and encouraged me to continue working on the second edition for the final few months. At Cardiff, I was fortunate to be nurtured as I embarked upon a journey to become an independent qualitative researcher by Paul, Sara Delamont, Mike Maguire, Amanda Coffey and Ian Shaw in particular. This, and the first edition, is part of my attempt to do the same for future generations.

Emma Wincup
Leeds
October 2016

PREFACE AND ACKNOWLEDGEMENTS FROM THE PREVIOUS EDITION

Qualitative research in criminology has a long-established history dating back to the ethnographic studies of crime and deviance carried out by the Chicago School in the 1920s and 1930s. Despite the fact that qualitative techniques have been employed for almost a century, there has been little systematic attention to the use of different types of qualitative methods in criminological research, or consideration of the particular issues surrounding their usage. Consequently we were particularly pleased to be asked to write this contribution to the *Introducing Qualitative Methods* series. Having agreed to take up the challenge, our first task was to prepare a proposal for the publishers. This included an assessment of the likely market for the book. There are now a vast number of books on qualitative research. It is no longer possible to read everything published on the topic, and it is sometimes barely possible to keep up with even a narrowly defined area of interest within it. The question as to whether another text on qualitative research was needed had to be asked. Unsurprisingly our answer to this question was yes. Despite the growing literature, we felt that criminologists interested in qualitative research still struggle to find suitable texts.

Criminologists do not have their own set of methods but conducting criminological research raises numerous difficulties and dilemmas. Those embarking on a criminological study are more likely than not to have chosen a sensitive topic, particularly a politically sensitive one. Undoubtedly, they will face a whole range of ethical dilemmas, not least through being party to knowledge about illegal acts. Principally for those who choose an ethnographic approach, conducting fieldwork often means having to cope with the ongoing presence of risk and danger. Of course, other qualitative researchers face such difficulties and dilemmas but there are some important differences because the subject matter of criminology gives them a particular accent.

Having examined available texts we felt that criminologists could make good use of either the numerous generic texts available on qualitative research or specialist volumes that provide reflexive accounts of the research process (see for example, Jupp et al., 2000; King and Wincup, 2000). However what was missing from the literature was an authoritative text that provided an introduction to qualitative methods and methodological debates, which was grounded in the realities of conducting criminological research. The book fulfils this role and is intended to complement those referred to above. In many respects a book along these lines is long overdue. However, it is also timely because problems of law and order have received unprecedented political attention since the final decade of the twentieth century, at least in England and Wales (see Chapter 2), and this has led to increased government funding for criminological research. At the time of writing such research funding appears not to be so readily available, but law and order issues continue to dominate political debates.

The growth of political interest in crime and criminal justice is mirrored by an ever-expanding range of courses on offer at all levels in universities. More people than ever before are involved in criminological research or are trained in its methods. King and Wincup (2000) argue that if criminological problems are to be properly understood and appropriately addressed, they must be effectively researched in ways that are theoretically grounded, methodologically secure and practically based. Our aim in this book is to support this task through offering comprehensive coverage of the qualitative approaches used by criminologists, and the issues they face when they attempt to put these principles into practice. Throughout the book, we make extensive use of illustrative examples and include both classic and contemporary studies. By drawing upon the research experiences of established criminologists we hope that new generations of criminologists can learn from what has gone on before.

This book is also informed by our own teaching and research experience. Both of us have considerable experience of conducting research on a range of criminological concerns. We have worked together on studies of remand prisoners and the risk management of sex offenders, and separately on projects concerned with female offenders, probation practice and drug use (Wincup) and fear of crime, policing and crime prevention (Noaks). We have always used qualitative approaches, although have sometimes combined these with the use of quantitative techniques. These research experiences inform our teaching of research methods at undergraduate and postgraduate level, including the supervision of doctoral students. Teaching these courses has made us aware that most students struggle when they have to put their learning of qualitative research methods into practice by developing a workable research design. More often than not, students are too ambitious and suggest studies with ill-focused research questions and/or unrealistic data collection plans. Consequently, we have always tried to convey to our students some sense of the reality of conducting criminological research. In so doing we take care to point out that research is always more difficult than anyone envisages but at the same time it offers enjoyment and intellectual challenges. We also inform our students that it is not sufficient to read about how to do interviews or analyse documents in one of the many 'cook book' style research textbooks that are now available and then go off and collect their data. Instead they should try to prepare themselves by building up familiarity with the debates that surround the use of the method, and by reading criminological studies that have used the same method. This book follows in the same vein.

We wrote this book with undergraduate and postgraduate criminology students in mind but it will also be relevant to students studying related disciplines such as forensic psychology, sociology, social policy and socio-legal studies. The book will also be of interest to a wider range of groups. These include researchers at different stages in their careers, lecturers with responsibility for research methods courses, practitioners involved in research and those who fund criminological research.

STRUCTURE OF THE BOOK

The contents of this book are set out in three sections. In Part One we begin by offering an account of the development of the qualitative research tradition within criminology. Two chapters are then devoted to issues which are pertinent to criminological research: the ways in which the political context shapes the research process and the ethical issues which arise when researchers choose to focus on crime and criminal justice. Collectively they provide a backdrop for understanding the discussions which follow in the remainder of the book. In Part Two are a series of chapters that explore the different elements of the research process. We begin with negotiating and sustaining access, move on to consider the main data collection techniques used by qualitative researchers and end with a discussion of qualitative data analysis. Finally, in Part Three we present two case studies which draw upon our own experiences as criminological researchers. The first (written by Emma Wincup) discussess research conducted for the Home Office, and the second (written by Lesley Noaks) is an example of doctoral research.

Each chapter contains references to both methodological and criminological literature and an annotated guide to further reading with full publication details given in the References. Exercises that can be used to form the basis of seminars or workshops on research methods courses also accompany each chapter.

During the course of writing this book we are grateful for the support and advice from a large number of people. Paul Atkinson, Ros Beck, Fiona Brookman, Amanda Coffey, Sara Delamont and a number of anonymous reviewers read the proposal and offered helpful suggestions. We would also like to thank David Silverman for being a supportive and encouraging series editor and Patrick Brindle, Zoë Elliott and Michael Carmichael at SAGE for their enthusiasm, encouragement and advice.

PART I
FOUNDATIONS OF QUALITATIVE RESEARCH IN CRIMINOLOGY

QUALITATIVE APPROACHES TO CRIMINOLOGICAL RESEARCH

1

Qualitative research has a long and distinguished history in the social sciences, arising in part from dissatisfaction with quantitative approaches. The ethnographic studies conducted by the Chicago School in the 1920s and 1930s established the importance of qualitative research for the study of crime and deviance (see Chapter 7). In this chapter, a brief history is given of the origins of criminology and the development of the empirical research tradition within it. This provides a backdrop for considering the growth of qualitative approaches to criminological research, and for pinpointing the pragmatic utility and methodological desirability of qualitative approaches for researching crime and criminal justice. Before exploring the development of qualitative criminological research, we need to pause for a moment and consider first what we understand by qualitative approaches.

WHAT DO WE MEAN BY QUALITATIVE APPROACHES?

There is now a vast methodological literature on qualitative research but too often it obscures rather than clarifies what the term refers to. Curiously it often defines qualitative research with reference to what it is not, i.e. quantitative research, thus contributing to the polarisation of the two approaches (an issue we will return to later in this chapter) and underplaying both the strengths of qualitative research and the diversity of approaches which can produce qualitative data in many forms. The term 'qualitative approaches' is used consciously to recognise that whilst there are common features of qualitative research studies as we outline in Box 1.1, qualitative data are gathered by researchers from a range of disciplines and theoretical backgrounds using a multiplicity of methods. Traditionally this has included observation, interviews and documentary analysis but as we will explore later in the chapter, qualitative researchers are becoming more innovative. These methods can also be deployed, albeit in different ways, to gather quantitative data rendering the frequently deployed concept of qualitative methods a misnomer.

Box 1.1   What is a qualitative approach? Delineating key features

1   Qualitative approaches explore the social construction of reality

Qualitative research recognises the role of individuals and groups in creating a social world. The task for qualitative researchers is to understand everyday life which comprises, for example, of customs and routines, norms and values, roles and responsibilities; all of which have meaning attached to them by social actors.

2   Qualitative approaches seek to understand the subject's point of view

Qualitative researchers are influenced by the work of Max Weber (1949) who developed the theoretical concept 'verstehen'. This refers to the interpretative process in which an 'outsider' seeks to understand empathetically the social world of the research participant. In this way, qualitative researchers seek to give a 'voice' to those they are 'studying' which is seen as particularly important when conducting research with marginalised groups.

3   Qualitative researchers emphasise the need for reflexivity

Reflexivity refers to the need to reflect upon the role of the researcher and recognise how they can influence the construction of knowledge at all stages of the research process. This is particularly important when gathering data via human interaction and requires the researcher to reflect upon how their characteristics (for example, in terms of gender, age and ethnic origin) might have influenced the data collection process.

4   Qualitative approaches emphasise the importance of depth of understanding

Reflecting the emphasis placed on uncovering meaning, qualitative researchers prioritise the collection of rich and detailed data. Consequently, qualitative studies are often small-scale, and make use of case studies which might be an individual institution or a particular locality.

5   Qualitative research values context and aims to collect data in 'natural' settings

Since qualitative research is typically associated with researching social life it follows that researchers should conduct research in settings familiar to the research participants.

6   Flexibility is integral to qualitative approaches

This is an important feature of qualitative research and applies throughout the research process. It is particularly important at the data collection stage when researchers need to reflect upon the data gathered and use it to guide future data collection.

Given these unique characteristics, it follows that studies which make use of qualitative approaches should not be judged on the typical evaluative criteria for assessing the quality of qualitative research but instead more meaningful criteria should be used. The features listed above, which represent the strengths of qualitative approaches, have often been used to argue (using evaluative criteria which should be reserved for studies which adopt a purely quantitative approach) that qualitative research is too subjective, difficult to replicate, produces findings which are limited in scope and lacks transparency. These issues are explored in more detail in the final chapter.

THE ORIGINS OF CRIMINOLOGY AND CRIMINOLOGICAL RESEARCH

There is considerable debate about how best to define criminology. For Garland (2002: 7), criminology is 'a specific genre of discourse and inquiry about crime that has developed in the modern period and that can be distinguished from other ways of talking and thinking about criminal conduct'. Criminologists will no doubt be aware that virtually everyone has 'commonsense' knowledge about crime, and correspondingly many ideas about the causes of crime and the best ways to tackle it. However, what characterises criminologists is that they subject these ideas to rigorous enquiry using either quantitative or qualitative research conducted by themselves or other researchers. Defining criminology as a discipline with an emphasis on empirically grounded, scientific study, Garland proposes that criminology grew out of a convergence between a governmental project and a Lombrosian project. The former were a series of empirical studies beginning in the nineteenth century that have sought to map patterns of crime and monitor the workings of the criminal justice system. Such work aims to ensure that justice is delivered effectively, efficiently and fairly. The latter was a contrasting project based on the notion that it is possible to 'spot the difference' (Coleman and Norris, 2000: 26) between those who offend and those who do not by using scientific means. This paved the way for a tradition of inquiry seeking to identify the causes of crime through empirical research, beginning with the use of quantitative methods but later supplemented by qualitative ones.

The legacy of this historical development can still be felt and produces continued tension within the discipline between policy-oriented criminological research, with its emphasis on the management and control of crime, and a theoretically oriented search for the causes of crime. For Garland (2002) the combination of the two projects is sufficient if criminology is to continue to claim to be a useful and scientific state-sponsored academic discipline. Whilst this aspect of his view is not widely challenged, the implication that classicism 'becomes the criminology that never was' (Coleman and Norris, 2000: 16), in the sense that it does fit Garland's definition of criminology, has been disputed. Others, for instance Hughes (1998), would argue that with the benefit of hindsight the Classical School is the first clearly identifiable school of criminology, distinctive because it marks a shift away from explaining crime in terms of religion or superstition. Even a cursory glance through the main texts available on criminological theory – both established 'classics' and contemporary – indicate at least implicit support for this view (see for example, Lilly et al., 2014; Taylor et al., 1973).

The Classical School, a term used retrospectively to describe the work of philosophers such as Beccaria and Bentham, refers to late eighteenth century theorising about crime which grew out of the Enlightenment project with its focus on reason. The Classical approach to the study of crime was underpinned by the notion of rational action and free will. These notions were neither subjected to empirical testing nor had they been developed from exploratory research. Hence, they do not meet Garland's definition of criminology. The debate presented here relates to the question 'Is criminology a science?' – a question that has also plagued closely related disciplines such as sociology. In relation to criminology, Coleman and Norris (2000: 176) argue this is a 'difficult question that has taken up a lot of energy over the years, often to little effect'. We can certainly say with confidence that the empirical criminological research tradition dates back over 300 years, although those conducting it may not have identified themselves as criminologists.

The debate outlined above is one of many that criminologists continue to have on fundamental issues. This is unsurprising in many respects. Criminology, as an academic discipline, is held together by a substantive concern: crime (Walklate, 2007). Consequently, it is multi-disciplinary in character rather than being dominated by one discipline. For this reason, it is helpful to view criminology as a 'meeting place' for a wide range of disciplines including sociology, social policy, psychology and law amongst others. Individual criminologists frequently adhere more closely to one social science discipline than others. Hence, to understand fully what they are attempting to articulate, it is important to note the conceptual apparatus they are utilising (Walklate, 2007). For instance, my own research – broadly defined in terms of links between crime and social problems – draws heavily upon sociology, social policy and political science. As a consequence of the diverse theoretical frameworks upon which 'criminologists' (defined broadly as researchers with an interest in crime and its control rather than those who identify themselves in this way) can draw, they frequently disagree with one another. Walklate (2007) argues that despite such disagreements there is some consensus (and we would argue that it is tenuous) in that criminologists aspire to influence crime control policy. However, there is much less consensus around features of what constitutes the crime problem.

We will now explore the development of both quantitative and qualitative traditions within criminology, and to locate their emergence and development within their social and political context. We include the former because it provides a backdrop to understanding the emergence of qualitative techniques which have been used by researchers who adopt a wide range of theoretical perspectives. Whilst we will demonstrate linkages between different theoretical traditions and the use of qualitative and quantitative approaches, we wish to emphasise that the relationship between theory and research is not a straightforward one.

Before moving on it is important to note that not all criminological research is empirical but that some takes a theoretical form. Both forms require different skills and training but it is not appropriate for a 'pragmatic division of labour' (Bottoms, 2008: 79) to be fully adopted. All empirical researchers need to acknowledge that theory is an essential element of the data collection and analysis process (see Chapter 8). Similarly, theorists need to draw upon, and understand, empirical research as one means of testing the ability of their theoretical ideas to explain the social world.

THE QUANTITATIVE TRADITION

The quantitative tradition is closely allied to a theoretical perspective known as positivism, which has been adopted to study a wide range of social phenomenon. Researchers who adhere to this approach aim to explain crime and predict future patterns of criminal behaviour. Emulating the analysis by natural scientists of causal relationships, positivists are concerned with developing objective knowledge about how criminal behaviour was determined by either individual or social pathology. As Muncie (2013) notes, identifying the exact moment when positivist criminology became apparent is difficult but it is typically associated with the work of French and Belgian 'moral' statisticians in the 1820s. The publication of national crime statistics, beginning in France in 1827, provided these scholars with a dataset to be analysed. Quetelet's (1842) work is well-known. He was concerned with the propensity to commit crime, which he used to refer to the greater or lesser probability of committing a crime. The potential causes of crime he concerned himself with were the influence of season, climate, sex and age. Based on his analysis of these variables, he concluded that crime patterns are regular and predictable, reaffirming his view that the methods of the natural sciences are wholly appropriate for understanding the causes of crime. For positivists such as Quetelet, the search for the causes of crime emphasised the role of social contexts external to the individual, thus the role of social, economic and environmental factors. Other important sociological positivist work includes Durkheim's (1895) analysis of crime rates and the Chicago School studies of crime patterns within the city of Chicago (Shaw and McKay, 1942). All these studies made use of official crime data in the form of police statistics or court records.

Both positivism and the quantitative tradition have been subjected to fierce criticism, particularly since the 1960s. Critics have argued that it is highly dubious to translate statistical association into causality. Quantitative work in criminology continues to be conducted but no longer adheres to a narrow positivist research tradition. Instead, quantitative work seeks to understand the complexity of social behaviour through examining a wide range of factors. For example, Jennings et al. (2015) combined a number of large datasets to situate explanations of crime in the changing social, economic and political contexts of the 1980s, 1990s and 2000s. In addition, quantitative research techniques have also been used to explore the workings of the criminal justice system, often evaluating new interventions. A recent example is an outcome evaluation of two domestic violence interventions delivered by the National Probation Service (Bloomfield and Dixon, 2015). Quantitative data were collected to examine whether the interventions were successful in reducing reoffending over a two year follow up period.

THE QUALITATIVE TRADITION

The qualitative tradition in criminology developed in the United States. It owes a great deal to the work of the Chicago School. This school made important contributions to criminological theory, namely through developing 'social disorganisation' theory and their 'ecological model' of the development of cities and patterns of crime within them (see Downes et al., 2016). Whilst many aspects of their work, particularly the 'ecological model', have been discredited, they left behind a tradition of linking urban social problems to crime and provided the inspiration for the development of environmental criminology. Some of this work was based on quantitative research but the Chicago School also bequeathed a tradition of conducting criminological research which was distinctive in that they used ethnographic techniques to explore groups on the margins of urban industrial society in the United States in the 1920s and 1930s. They focused, in particular, on the 'dispossessed, marginal and the strange' (Brewer, 2000: 12) and included in the long list of Chicago School ethnographies (see Deegan, 2007) are studies of gangs, prostitution and homelessness.

Drawing their inspiration from developments within sociological theory, Chicago School researchers pursued innovative qualitative work making use of participant observation, life histories and documents. This work began to influence British criminologists in the 1960s (see Chapter 7 for a more detailed discussion). The qualitative tradition is now firmly established in criminology. Part of the explanation for this is the growth of new theoretical perspectives, which are broadly compatible with qualitative approaches to criminological research. Positivism has been subjected to fierce criticism by advocates of symbolic interactionism. As a result, they turned their attention away from the causes of crime to explore the process by which crimes are created and social reactions to crime. Advocates of the interactionist position see the social world as a product of social interactions, emphasising the socially constructed nature of crime and deviance. The basic principles of positivism were called into question as symbolic interactionists emphasised the importance of human agency, consciousness and meaning in social activity, and highlighted the plurality of norms and values relating to 'normal' and 'deviant' behaviour. Symbolic interactionism inspired the development of the labelling perspective and the work of 'deviancy theorists' in the UK (Downes et al., 2016). Criminologists working within these theoretical frameworks were anti-statistical. Whilst their work has been subjected to vehement criticism for paying insufficient attention to the exercise of power by Marxists and critical criminologists in particular, these theoretical approaches have continued to support the use of qualitative methods.

The history of criminology we have presented so far is characterised by male criminologists studying male offenders whose contribution to the problem of crime far exceeds women's whether measured via official crime data or self-report studies (Smith and Wincup, 2009). From the late 1960s feminists began to draw attention to the tendency for female offenders to be ignored or on the rare occasions they were included to be misrepresented as mad rather than bad (see Heidensohn, 1996 for an overview of the feminist critique of criminology). Whilst arguably criminology has yet to embrace fully the gendered nature of crime, it has made females visible as offenders, victims and criminal justice professionals. Feminist criminologists have also posed epistemological and methodological questions, questioning the nature of criminological knowledge and the most appropriate ways of gathering it (see

Heidensohn and Gelsthorpe, 2007). For some feminists, particularly those who would describe themselves as radical or socialist feminists and therefore concerned with women's oppression by men (see Renzetti, 2013 for a more detailed discussion of different perspectives within feminist criminology), research should always be from the standpoint of women, giving a voice to those who have traditionally been silent. Often this has led to a preference for qualitative data but as we will explore in Chapters 6 and 7, there has been considerable debate about whether there is a natural fit between feminism and particular research methods. Moreover, there has been extensive discussion about whether it is appropriate to talk about a woman's voice or whether this fails to recognise how women are divided by social class, ethnic origin, sexual orientation and so on.

In many respects, the qualitative tradition is alive and well. Increasingly qualitative researchers are using more innovative methods which Wiles et al. (2010) categorise as inception (using new settings for research), adaptation (altering or expanding an existing method) or adoption (using a method in a different discipline or sphere). Criminological examples of these three types of intervention are listed in Box 1.2. The 'cultural turn' in criminology has also been influential in supporting the qualitative tradition. Cultural criminologists, who emphasise the importance of locating crime and its control within broader cultural dynamics, have favoured qualitative approaches, ranging from the collection and analysis of media images of youth subcultures to ethnographic research with 'deviant' subcultures (see Ferrell et al., 2008). Whilst there is much to be optimistic about, there are also threats to the health of qualitative criminological research, not least due to the political context which for a period of time after the turn of the millennium explicitly favoured quantitative research. We explore this recent history in the next chapter.

Box 1.2   Thinking outside the box: Innovation and qualitative criminological research

INCEPTION: Williams (2007) used online methodologies, replicating methods used to study the 'real' world in virtual settings which included a graphical online community (cyberworlds), associated newsgroups, web pages and an email distribution list.

ADAPTATION: Hollway and Jefferson (2008) used free association narrative interview to research fear of crime. Applying psychoanalytic principles to the research context, they emphasise the importance of allowing interviewees to structure their own narratives in order to understand the unconscious connections people make when they have the freedom to do so. The focus here is on the account as a whole rather than a series of questions and answers.

ADOPTION: Anderson (2016) used creative methods, specifically 'collage as inquiry' (Butler-Kisber, 2007) to explore meaning and interlinked processes of recovery for people with complex needs including drug and alcohol dependence and offending. This approach is 'borrowed' from arts and humanities.

COMBINING TRADITIONS

Whilst we have just presented quantitative and qualitative traditions within criminology separately, we are mindful of the dangers of too sharp a distinction between the two traditions. As Silverman (1998) argues, it is absurd to push too far the qualitative/quantitative distinction. He suggests that the qualitative/quantitative research dichotomy is acceptable as a pedagogical device to aid understanding of a complex topic but such dichotomies are dangerous because they tend to locate researchers in oppositional groups. For some criminological researchers this is not problematic because they adhere strictly to either qualitative or quantitative methodology. However, many, including those who identify themselves as qualitative researchers, make use of quantitative measures where appropriate. This might take many forms. Firstly, it is possible to derive some quantitative data from techniques typically associated with the generation of qualitative data. It is feasible that a study involving qualitative interviews will produce some basic quantitative data such as counts of interviewees who fit into particular categories. Secondly, we might use the same data collection method such as the face-to-face interview to generate both qualitative and quantitative data by including a range of questions, some open-ended, others fixed-choice. Thirdly, we might use two different methods, one that will produce qualitative data (for example, focus groups) and another quantitative data (for example, structured observation). The case studies included in Chapters 10 and 11 illustrate how different forms of data can be used to answer research questions, although the discussion prioritises the collection of qualitative data.

The process of combining both qualitative and quantitative methodologies is one aspect of triangulation. Triangulation can be defined simply as 'the use of different methods of research, sources of data or types of data to address the same research question' (Jupp, 2013b: 474). For Hoyle (2000), the term shrouds in mystery straightforward and sensible means of looking at the social world and obfuscates the role of the social researcher. However, the concept is widely used in a number of ways and these are defined in Table 1.1.

The term 'triangulation' was first used in the context of social research by Campbell and Fiske (1959) but was used more frequently following the publication of Webb et al.'s text on unobtrusive measures and social research in 1966.

Table 1.1   Forms of triangulation

Form of triangulation	Alternative names (if any)	Definition
Data triangulation		Collection of different types of data on the same topic using the same method or different methods
Investigator triangulation	Researcher triangulation, team triangulation	Collection of data by more than one researcher
Method triangulation	Technique triangulation	Collection of data by different methods
Theoretical triangulation		Approaching data with multiple perspectives and hypotheses in mind

Whilst Webb et al. (1966: 174) are keen to point out that single measures are not 'scientifically useless' they propound that 'the most fertile search for validity comes from a combined set of different measures'. Triangulation as a social science concept derives from a loose analogy with navigation and surveying (Hammersley and Atkinson, 2007). The term was used in these professional fields to refer to the use of two or more landmarks to pinpoint a position more accurately than if one were used.

Applied to social research, arguments have been advanced for combining methods. The use of different methods can be an implicit or explicit decision. It may also be built in to the research strategy adopted. Brewer (2000) argues that combining methods is a routine feature of ethnographic research (see also Chapter 7). Most research projects in the social sciences are in a general sense multi-method because alongside the main method of choice, subsidiary techniques are used, even if this is not explicit in the research design. For example, conducting interviews in a prison will always involve some degree of observation of the social setting, which may impact on the research even if the data are not formally recorded or analysed. Similarly, a study relying mainly on participant observation within a youth centre for children at risk of offending is likely to begin with reading published documents about the centre, for instance bids for funding, annual reports and media coverage.

Numerous advantages are advanced in the literature to persuade researchers to adopt a multi-method approach, and the overarching theme is that combining methods increases the validity of the findings. Reflecting on his own criminological research career, Maguire (2000) argues for utilising as many diverse sources of evidence as feasible to answer a research question. His rationale is that criminological research often involves working with information that is unreliable to varying extents. By bringing together different methods with their own blend of strengths and weaknesses, it is hoped that the weaknesses of one method can be countered by the strengths of the others. If the data gathered using the different methods offer similar conclusions, criminologists can be more confident that the conclusions offered are valid in the sense that they are plausible and credible.

Denzin (1970) also advocates a strong case for triangulation, suggesting that this is the basic theme of his book entitled *The Research Act in Sociology*. He argues that his definition of each method implies a triangulated perspective. Denzin notes that the shifting nature of the social world and the biases that arise from the sociologist's choice of theories, methods and observers provide difficulties that a researcher working in the natural sciences does not face. For Denzin, the solution is to recognise these difficulties and to use multiple strategies of triangulation (data, investigator, methodological and theoretical) as the preferred line of action. He suggests that triangulation is the key to overcoming intrinsic bias that stems from single method, single observer and single theory studies. Despite Denzin's claim in the preface that he subscribes to a symbolic interactionist perspective, Silverman (1985) highlights how Denzin's prescriptions can be seen to mesh with the positivist desire to seek an ultimate 'truth' about the social world through cross-validation. In his later writings, Denzin (1990, 1994) no longer subscribes to his earlier view, favouring an approach which gives precedence to the subjective world-view of research participants as the only reliable vantage point.

THINKING CRITICALLY ABOUT TRIANGULATION

Substantial support can be found for Hammersley and Atkinson's (2007) argument that triangulation is not a simple test. Even if the findings do accord, this cannot be interpreted as 'fact'. It is plausible that the results tally due to systematic or random error. For this reason, Hammersley and Atkinson (2007) suggest researchers need to avoid naïve optimism, and resist the temptation to assume that the aggregation of data from different sources will produce a more complete picture. For the majority of qualitative research studies, the goal of establishing 'truth' is actively rejected and multiple versions of reality are acknowledged. Consequently, differences between data are as significant and enlightening as similarities. As King (2000: 306) argues, it is incumbent on the researcher to report the conflicts as far as possible so that the reader may also try to form a judgement. We can add here that the role of the researcher is also to explain different findings.

Jupp's (2013b) suggestion that a much less bold and precise claim for triangulation can be made is helpful. He argues that different methods can be used to examine different aspects or dimensions of the same problem. Deliberately avoiding the term 'triangulation' and replacing it with 'methodological pluralism', Walklate (2007: 325) advances a similar view.

> Methodological pluralism ... reflects a view of the research process which privileges neither quantitative nor qualitative techniques. It is a position which recognizes that different research techniques can uncover different layers of social reality and the role of the researcher is to look for confirmation and contradictions between those different layers of information.

Best practice is for researchers to adopt a pragmatic and theoretically coherent approach to data collection, using appropriate methods to answer their research questions. The latter is important because researchers need to guard against the tendency to keep adding research techniques to their research design in an eclectic manner with the blind hope that it will produce a better thesis, report or other publication. A multi-method approach should only be pursued if it adds value to the study by enhancing understanding of the criminological issue of interest. Sometimes there may be little to be achieved by using different methods. As Jupp (2013b) argues, some combinations of methods do not work well because they are founded on different assumptions about the nature of the social world and how it can be explained. Hence, combining methods does not automatically enhance validity. There are often pragmatic reasons for considering carefully whether a number of methods should be utilised. Maguire (2007: 276) shares the useful advice he received as a novice researcher: 'the best tip is to imagine the final report and work backwards'. This should not be interpreted as a rigid approach to criminological research. Instead it requires the researcher to consider what they have been asked to produce both in terms of focus and also length.

WHY CONDUCT QUALITATIVE RESEARCH ON CRIMINOLOGICAL TOPICS?

In the remainder of this chapter we provide some of the more common responses to the question above in order to persuade the reader to employ qualitative methods for future research projects.

QUALITATIVE RESEARCH PROVIDES A MEANS OF RESEARCHING THE 'DARK FIGURE OF CRIME'

The 'dark figure of crime' can be defined as 'the figure for unrecorded crime or undetected offenders, that is to say those not included in official statistics' (Coleman and Moynihan, 1996: 146). There are other ways of collecting information on offences which do not appear in official crime statistics using quantitative techniques. The most obvious example is the Crime Survey for England and Wales, a victimisation study involving interviews with 50,000 individuals aged 16 and over living in private households, complemented by a separate survey of young people aged 10 to 15 (see www.crimesurvey.co.uk/index.html). Maguire (2002: 322) suggests that a 'data explosion' took place at the end of the twentieth century, and he goes further to argue that there is no longer a strong demand in late-modern societies for a crude general 'barometer' (2002: 361) of crime; a role traditionally fulfilled by official crime statistics. Criminologists are streetwise enough to realise that combining the different data sources will never reveal the full extent of the 'dark figure of crime'. More realistically the hope is that combining different sets of quantitative data will build up a more complete understanding of the nature and extent of crime. However, as Coleman and Moynihan (1996) argue, there are some areas of criminological enquiry that are difficult to investigate using official data and survey methods. Hence they suggest qualitative techniques could be used as a means of researching these areas. Whilst these techniques need to be subjected to critical assessment, they should not be seen as a second best or a kind of fall-back to be employed where there are no quantitative data available. The use of qualitative techniques offers the opportunity to make a distinct contribution by elucidating the context in which offending takes place and the meanings attached to such behaviour.

One example of a form of crime which is difficult to research using quantitative approaches is white-collar crime. The definition of white-collar crime has been contentious since it was first coined by Sutherland (1949), and it remains a contested concept. We will not attempt to open up this debate here but instead direct the reader to Payne (2016) for an accessible introduction to this complex area of crime. As our working definition, we will adopt the following:

> a heterogeneous group of offences committed by people of relatively high status or enjoying relatively high levels of trust, and made possible by their legitimate employment. (Tombs and Whyte, 2013: 492)

It would be misleading to suggest that qualitative research on white-collar crime is unproblematic. Explanations as to why it is rarely detected, reported and prosecuted also serve as explanations for the lack of research in this area. They include the invisibility of such offences, their complex nature, the difficulties of identifying victims and the limited number of convicted individuals. Offences are hidden in occupational routines, and for this reason, often the only strategy researchers can employ is to conduct covert participant observation (see Chapter 4). A dated but excellent example of this form of research is Ditton's (1977) study, which he describes as an ethnography of fiddling and pilferage. His setting was a medium-sized factory-production bakery. Croall (2001) remarks that researchers are rarely in a position to conduct overt research on the more serious forms of white-collar crime, especially within financial and commercial enterprises. There are, however, some notable exceptions. Levi's (1981) study of long-firm fraud is described by Hobbs (2000: 171) as 'as close to an ethnography of fraud as we are ever likely to get'. Levi conducted an intensive study of court records from the Old Bailey and Manchester Crown Court, interviewed credit controllers and business-men, criminal justice and legal professionals, observed four trials at the Old Bailey and interviewed offenders within prison and the community. The latter aspect of the research was limited due to lack of time but also because the places frequented by white-collar offenders were beyond the budget of a doctoral student! Where access to the extent enjoyed by Levi has not been possible, qualitative researchers have been creative in their use of data sources. In addition to the sources of data used by Levi, qualitative researchers have also made use of individual case studies, investigative journalism, court reports, media reports of cases and interviews with enforcers (Croall, 2001). For Hobbs (2000) multiple methods have become the norm, and researchers inevitably have to compromise but with a preference for qualitative approaches.

> The covert, non-institutionalized base from which professional and organised crime operates favours the use of a range of largely interpretive approaches. Until gangsters, armed robbers, fraudsters and their ilk indicate their enthusi-asm for questionnaires or large-scale social surveys, ethnographic research, life histories, oral histories, biographies, autobiographies and journalistic accounts will be at a premium. (Hobbs, 1994: 442)

Given the difficulties of pursuing this line of research, as long as researchers remain cognisant of the limits of their data, they can help to illuminate the 'dark figure of crime'.

We could have selected many other forms of crime as illustrative examples. As argued in the extensive literature on crime data (see for example, Hope, 2013), the 'dark figure of crime' includes a wide range of behaviours which, for varying reasons, are not counted in official crime statistics. Qualitative research has shed light on many of these including illicit drug use, domestic violence, hate crime and sexual offences.

QUALITATIVE RESEARCH LEADS TO AN 'APPRECIATION' OF THE SOCIAL WORLD FROM THE POINT OF VIEW OF THE OFFENDER, VICTIM OR CRIMINAL JUSTICE PROFESSIONAL

Matza (1969) first used the term 'appreciative studies' to refer to specific studies of deviant subcultures. This work was based on observation, sometimes involving par-ticipation, of the social world of deviants. In this respect the influence of symbolic interactionism is apparent. Criminologists often talk about appreciative criminology, referring to 'an approach that seeks to understand and appreciate the social world from the point of view of the individual or category of individual, with particular reference to crime and deviance' (Jupp, 2013a: 16).

There are numerous examples of criminological studies which have attempted to 'appreciate' the social world from the point of view of the criminal justice professional, and one example is included in Box 1.3. It would be fair to say that some criminal justice professions have attracted more attention than others, with studies of police officers receiving the greatest consideration. There are a number of explanations for this imbalance, and the more obvious ones relate to the ease at which access can be negotiated, the appeal of the professional group and its work to criminological researchers and the priorities of funding bodies. These issues are explored in the next chapter.

Box 1.3   Understanding occupational culture: Qualitative interviews with electronic monitoring officers

Hucklesby's (2011) research with electronic monitoring officers is an example of how qualitative research can shed light on the occupational culture of criminal justice professionals. Whilst not our focus here it is worth noting that increasingly those engaged in crime control are employed by the private sector. Her study involved interviews with 20 monitoring officers employed by G4S, one of the contracted providers at the time, coupled with observation of over 50 shifts. The research found that whilst there was a loosely defined shared working orientation it did not represent a clearly defined occupational culture. Instead, the officers could be categorised into three working credos (the technician, the probation worker and the pragmatist). The credos the officer was most closely aligned to influenced how they managed concerns about their personal safety which shaped the working practices of all officers.

Before moving on, a few brief comments need to be offered about appreciative research with offenders and victims. Hoyle's (2012) review of research on victims demonstrates that a great deal of criminological attention is now focused on victims. Alongside the long-established quantitative surveys of victimisation and fear of crime, there are numerous examples of qualitative work on experiences of victimisation and criminal justice responses. Feminists have played an important contribution with studies of hidden victimisation including domestic violence, sexual violence and child abuse. The scope of work on victimisation continues to grow and challenge conventional understanding about victimisation, through exposing 'new' forms, for example at the hands of the State or corporations, or in 'new' settings such as cyberspace. In this field of criminology, there is considerable scope for a 'mixed economy' using different forms of data. Hoyle (2012) argues that qualitative approaches can make a particular contribution to understanding victimisation experiences.

Alongside the growing interest with victims, research on offenders continues. It is, however, different from the past; it is less concerned with understanding offending behaviour and more focused on how best to address the problem of crime, looking for guidance on how best to prevent crime or to reduce reoffending. Criminologists, as Maguire (2007) notes, have been guilty for some time of focusing their research efforts on convicted offenders rather than meeting them in their 'natural' settings. He argues that without the correcting influence of ethnographic work (see Chapter 7), it becomes too easy for criminologists to see offenders as 'problems' or 'numbers' rather than individuals (Maguire, 2007: 285). There are important exceptions to this trend, for example, the work of cultural criminologists which we referred to earlier in the chapter.

QUALITATIVE RESEARCH CAN COMPLEMENT QUANTITATIVE RESEARCH

Qualitative research can complement quantitative research in a number of ways. Firstly, using qualitative approaches can help to inform the design of research instruments for the collection of quantitative data. King (2000) has used this strategy to conduct research in prisons. He suggests beginning with observation and records, then moving on to interviews and ending with questionnaires. The latter can be used to test the generality of the findings in the wider population. By administering questionnaires at the end of the fieldwork the response rate is also boosted as the researcher has established rapport with the research participants.

Secondly, qualitative studies can contribute to our understanding of the context in which crime occurs and criminal justice is administered through providing rich and detailed data to flesh out the bare skeleton provided by quantitative data (Coleman and Moynihan, 1996). Regardless of the size of the dataset or the number of variables contained within it, quantitative data can only represent abstractions from complex interactions, and as Bottomley and Pease (1986: 170) remind us 'we should not allow statistics to make us forget the people behind the numbers'. A burglary offence, which appears in official crime statistics, is the outcome of negotiation processes between the victim and/or witness and the police. It tells us nothing about decisions to report and record the crime. These decision-making processes can be researched using qualitative techniques such as semi-structured interviews with victims, witnesses and police officers or observation within a police station.

Thirdly, Mhlanga (2000) argues that statistical correlations in quantitative research require further explication using qualitative research techniques. Mhlanga's study of the role of ethnic factors in decisions made by the Crown Prosecution Service (CPS) to prosecute young offenders (Mhlanga, 1999) included an examination of case files of just over 6000 offenders. These files were used to collect statistical data on a number of key variables including ethnic origin, gender, age and previous convictions. The data gathered were analysed using multivariate techniques, which control for other variables in order to identify the actual impact of ethnic factors. Noting that it is 'always hazardous to move from correlation to explanation' (Mhlanga, 2000: 414), and even more so when the topic of interest is a sensitive one, Mhlanga made a decision to present preliminary findings to CPS lawyers and managers to gain feedback. This took the form of a discussion group (he does not describe it as a focus group). The finding that the CPS were more likely to discontinue cases involving ethnic minority defendants was explored. The discussion group came up with two explanations for this: firstly, the police were 'getting it wrong' by charging ethnic minority defendants without sufficient evidence, and secondly, the CPS 'could be using positive discrimination' in favour of ethnic minority defendants (Mhlanga, 2000: 415). Mhlanga suggests that in any further research on this topic, it would be highly desirable to conduct individual face-to-face interviews with CPS lawyers.

QUALITATIVE RESEARCH HELPS TO INFORM THE DEVELOPMENT OF POLICIES OF CRIME CONTROL

There are multiple ways in which qualitative research, conducted either by researchers or practitioners, can assist the policy development process. Research can fulfil the role of evaluating current policy. It may also serve as an instrument for generating ideas for policy development. Finally, research may take the form of action research, which integrates the processes of research and action. In so doing the typical model of academics or other researchers generating knowledge to be applied by practitioners is rejected. We will concentrate on action research here and leave the broader discussion of the relationship between qualitative research and criminal justice policy to the next chapter.

Action research was first developed in the US and the UK in the late 1940s by social scientists who advocated closer ties between social science and solving current social problems (Denscombe, 2014), often relating to health, education and social welfare (Banks, 2012). It describes a form of research, which is often evaluative in nature, which sets out to impact upon policy and practice (Crow, 2013). This evidently practical approach to research is typically associated with small-scale research studies and promotes practitioner involvement and thus their professional development. Action research can be perceived as a dynamic model based upon ongoing dialogue (Crow, 2013). To begin the process, critical reflection on professional practice is required to identify a problem, which is then researched and the findings are translated into a plan for change. The plan is then implemented and evaluated. It is envisaged that the process is ongoing with a rolling programme of research, with research continually informing practice in a cyclical way. The reality is that action research often involves discrete, one-off pieces of research (Denscombe, 2014). Action researchers are not limited to qualitative techniques but can use different techniques for data collection. However, qualitative methods are particularly suited to exploratory, small-scale studies. A criminological example of action research is provided in Box 1.4. This example illustrates some of the challenges of action research (see Denscombe, 2014) relating to objectivity (since the researcher is far from impartial), ethics (since research and practice are indistinguishable) and ownership (which partner takes control over the research and its outcomes?). It also exemplifies what can be achieved when all parties have a shared commitment to a goal (see Crow, 2013).

Box 1.4   Action research in challenging cultural contexts: Establishing alternatives to custody for juveniles in Bangladesh

Banks (2012) describes her experiences of working on a juvenile justice reform project in Bangladesh which was funded by the Canadian government and designed to develop the capacity of local officials through, for example, training and mentoring. She argues that action research is uniquely placed to provide culturally sensitive 'bottom up' support rather than imposing a reform agenda. It also allows resources to be devoted to research when otherwise none would be available. One of her first steps was to establish a 'micro policy network' (Banks, 2012: 480) to conduct baseline research initially and then provide ongoing monitoring and evaluation once a juvenile diversion project was established so that operational issues could be identified and resolved quickly. This was followed up with a workshop on practice in juvenile diversion where research findings were shared and perspectives on the project were gleaned. For Banks (2012) action research helped to appreciate the prevailing cultural norms, for example that children should not be 'spoilt' and that confinement is necessary for children deemed 'uncontrollable'. Recognising these enhanced the legitimacy of the diversion project in a country which still bears the imprint of its colonial past and might therefore resist the imposition of allegedly superior cultural norms. Banks (2012) argues that action research allows participants to be 'knowing agents' rather than objects of research.

CHAPTER SUMMARY AND CONCLUSION

In this chapter we have explored, albeit briefly, the maturation of criminology as an academic discipline and we have drawn the reader's attention to competing interpretations of the past. As Coleman and Norris (2000: 24) note in relation to criminology, 'there has been some confusion over both its birthday and parentage'. Exploring this debate included an analysis of the emergence of both qualitative and quantitative research traditions within criminology. We focused predominantly, but not exclusively, on the growth of qualitative approaches to researching crime and criminal justice. Whilst it may at first glance appear out of place to reflect on quantitative approaches in a text on qualitative research, such reflections were needed for two reasons. Firstly, by exploring the strengths and weaknesses of quantitative approaches we can elucidate the reasons why qualitative approaches developed. Secondly, researchers frequently use both quantitative and qualitative methods in their studies.

By combining both qualitative and quantitative approaches, criminological researchers are avoiding 'methodological pigeonholing' (Bottoms, 2008: 81). This can be defined as 'the tendency to assume that certain sorts of research methods "go with" particular kinds of theoretical approach, to the exclusion of other kinds of data' (Bottoms, 2008: 81). Bottoms (2008) suggests that some qualitative researchers have set up mental barriers against the use of quantitative data, and similarly some quantitative researchers have been reluctant to make use of qualitative data. He argues that these unjustifiable mental barriers have been some of the most unhelpful features of the British criminological landscape in the last quarter of the twentieth century. He proposes that these barriers are now being overcome, leading to a healthier approach to criminological research. Many criminologists would concur with his view. Crucially it is important to select an approach suited to the research question being posed. Just as it might be considered flawed to insist on only using either qualitative or quantitative approaches, it is equally problematic to always assume that combining approaches is appropriate. There are many examples of criminological projects which rely wholly on qualitative approaches and which make a significant contribution to theory, knowledge, policy and practice.

Exercises

1   Identify ONE form of crime which makes up part of the 'dark figure'. A contemporary example is supplying psychoactive substances to friends following their criminalisation (in the UK) in May 2016. Whilst illegal, this type of crime is unlikely to be detected. Consider how you might use qualitative approaches to shed light on this form of crime.

2   What do you think makes a good qualitative study? Keep a note of your key characteristics and revisit them when you have read the discussion of quality criteria for qualitative research in the final chapter.

3   Look at a recent issue of a criminological journal which publishes empirical research, for example *Criminology and Criminal Justice*. Choose ONE article which is based solely upon qualitative research. Reflect upon why you think they chose a purely qualitative approach.

FURTHER READING

- Cresswell, J. (2015) *A Concise Introduction to Mixed Methods Research*. Thousand Oaks, CA: Sage.

  This brief overview of mixed methods research takes the reader through the different stages of the research process and offers a foundation for understanding mixed methods methodology.

- Mason, J. (2002) *Qualitative Researching*, 2nd edn. London: Sage.

  Despite being published some time ago, this well-established text provides excellent guidance on the practice of social research. It is organised around three stages of the research process: questions of strategy, generating qualitative data and analysing qualitative data.

- Miller, J. and Palacios, R. (eds) (2015) *Qualitative Research in Criminology*. New Jersey: Transaction Publishers.

  Compiled by two experienced American qualitative researchers, this edited collection contains 17 chapters written by criminologists from across the globe including some referenced in this chapter (Hobbs, Ferrell). It explores the significant role of qualitative research in expanding and refining understandings of crime and justice.

- Silverman, D. (2013) *A Very Short, Fairly Interesting and Reasonably Cheap Book about Qualitative Research*, 2nd edn. London: Sage.

  Written by one of the leading authors on qualitative approaches to research this book seeks to demonstrate how qualitative research can be methodologically inventive, empirically rigorous, theoretically alive and practically relevant.

- Tewksbury, R. (2009) 'Qualitative versus quantitative methods: Understanding why qualitative methods are superior for criminology and criminal justice', *Journal of Theoretical and Philosophical Criminology*, 1(1): 38–58.

  This controversial article makes the bold claim that qualitative approaches offer a superior means for conducting meaningful research in criminology and criminal justice.

THE POLITICS OF RESEARCHING CRIME AND JUSTICE

Our starting point for this chapter is that all forms of criminological research are inherently bound up with wider political contexts that, ultimately, shape the research process. Most criminological researchers are willing to acknowledge, sometimes reluctantly, the inevitability that their research can never be free from political influences. An unwillingness relates to the desire of some criminologists, arguably those who adopt methods more closely aligned to the natural sciences, to maintain that their research is objective.

In this chapter, we begin by exploring the different meanings attached to the term 'political'. We then move on to offer a brief account of the increasing politicisation of research on crime and criminal justice (particularly from 1979 onwards), and alongside this present a chronological account of the politicisation of criminological theory (especially in the 1960s and 1970s) which demonstrates how some criminologists have actively embraced the political dimension of research. For these criminologists, the political nature of crime and justice is their starting point, and their research is a form of politics. Developing the argument that the political context influences the conduct of criminological research in multiple ways, we reflect upon these influences throughout the research process from design through to dissemination. Within the chapter I will draw upon my own research experiences, as well as the accounts available in which researchers have shared their own views of conducting criminological research in a highly politicised world. This commitment to reflexivity is one of the strengths of qualitative research.

TOWARDS A DEFINITION OF 'POLITICAL'

The term 'political' has multiple meanings attached to it in both lay and academic discourse, and this is apparent by exploring dictionary definitions. For example,

1. Relating to the ideas or strategies of a particular party or group in politics;
2. Interested in or active in politics;
3. Motivated by a person's beliefs or actions concerning politics;
4. Chiefly derogatory, done or acting in the interests of status or power within an organisation rather than a matter of principle.

(www.oxforddictionaries.com/definition/english/political)

In academic discourse, the term 'political' is traditionally compared against the term 'civil' (Tonkiss, 1998). The former is conceived as concerned with public affairs and the formal process of government. In contrast, the latter is understood as related to essentially private and freely chosen activity. Together they make up what is commonly understood by social scientists as 'society'. However, this dichotomy can be rendered problematic by exploring the interface between the civil and the political. Some of the most influential voices in this respect have been feminist ones. Summarised in the slogan 'the personal is political', feminists have drawn political attention to crimes within the home, encouraging State incursion into the private sphere (see Delamont, 2003 for a more detailed discussion of feminist work). Tonkiss' definition of the term 'political' captures feminist and other debates surrounding the civil/political dualism.

> The political realm is that which brings together social relations into focus but specifically in terms of their direction, control, management and adjustment to the demands of the state. The social is rarely, if at all, ever apolitical but the politics are not always those mediated by state and party. (Tonkiss, 1998: 259)

Reviewing debates in the methodological literature about competing definitions of 'political' (see for example, Hammersley, 1995; Hughes, 2011), it becomes apparent that definitions vary tremendously in terms of how all-encompassing they are. Narrow definitions tend to focus on 'the processes relating to the work and influence of explicit political ideologies, political parties, and the legitimate and organised coercive institutional power of the modern nation state' (Hughes, 2011: 309) whilst others are much broader and note that *all* human interactions are micro-political processes (Hammersley, 1995). Helpfully, Hammersley identifies two distinct, but closely related, ways in which research may be seen as political. The first acknowledges that research is implicated in power relations. The key questions here are the extent to which researchers are autonomous from the State or other powerful interests in society, and the extent to which researchers exercise power. The second way relates to the question of whether value judgements are implicated in the research process. We are at risk of devoting the whole chapter to the debate about the meaning of the term 'political', and rather than continuing in detail we recommend that interested readers consult Hammersley's (1995) text. Cognisant of the difficulties of reaching an authoritative definition, a working definition of the term 'political' is offered below.

Criminological research is a political endeavour in two senses. Firstly, the political context inevitably shapes, to varying extents, all stages of the research process because criminologists are researching a social problem, which politicians seek to control, although sometimes they deny its existence. Secondly, criminological researchers inevitably become embroiled in micro-political processes because research often seeks to understand the standpoints of different, sometimes opposing, groups.

Our focus in this chapter is on the first sense, what is often referred to colloquially as politics with a 'big P'. The second is important and discussed in the next chapter on research access.

THE POLITICISATION OF LAW AND ORDER

Through being explicit about the ways in which criminological research can be perceived as a political endeavour, we have already drawn attention to the politicisation of the problem of crime. We develop briefly this discussion here, focusing on England and Wales. Surprisingly law and order has only been a topic contested by different political parties since the mid-1960s, gaining dominance in the 1979 election campaign (Downes and Morgan, 2012). Public spending, according to the Conservatives, needed to be reduced. The only exception to this was in the law and order sphere. The approach adopted during the Thatcher (1979–1990) and Major (1990–1997) governments varied. It began with a highly punitive approach, embodying 'law and order ideology' (Cavadino et al., 2013: 6). In the four years leading up to the 1991 Criminal Justice Act, this rhetoric continued to colour policy but a 'less dogmatic and more pragmatic' approach was taken (Cavadino et al., 2013: 7). The 1991 Criminal Justice Act was a radical piece of legislation but some of its central provisions were hastily repealed in 'the law and order counter-reformation' immediately followed (Cavadino et al., 2013: 7). They were replaced by measures which marked the revival of a highly punitive approach. For example, the pledge to reduce the prison population through the use of community sanctions was overridden by a commitment to the use of custodial sentences. The Conservative government portrayed themselves as *the* party of law and order, leaving the opposition with the task of challenging them.

Following their victory in the 1997 General Election, Labour (now packaged as New Labour) sought to live up to its manifesto promise to be 'tough on crime, tough on the causes of crime'. This promise was an attempt to assure voters that they could be successful on law and order issues. These had been successfully portrayed by previous Conservative governments as Labour's Achilles Heel (Morgan and Hough, 2007: 46). Labour passed a deluge of legislation through Parliament, including some measures initially put in place by the Conservatives. As the new millennium drew closer a 'new second-order consensus' had been reached by the major political parties, and this resulted in persistent jostling for political advantage (Downes and Morgan, 2012: 185), although when Ken Clarke was (briefly) Justice Secretary (2010–2012) he made 'vain attempts' to move penal policy in a less punitive direction (Cavadino et al.,

2013: 7). Downes and Morgan (2012) observe that crime has been overtaken by other government and public concerns, for example the economy and public services in the 1997, 2001 and 2005 General Election campaigns. When law and order issues were discussed they focused on immigration and political asylum. Similarly, in 2010, law and order did not feature significantly as an election issue and the main political parties promised remarkably similar policies (Downes and Morgan, 2012). This trend has continued, although with an increased focus on terrorism in the 2015 General Election campaign. A shift in political emphasis away from crime, coupled with over-all reductions in public spending, has had a significant impact on the amount of funding now available for research; an issue we will return to after exploring the relationship between criminology and politics.

THE POLITICISATION OF CRIMINOLOGICAL THEORY

The politicisation of law and order has mirrored developments in academic crimi-nology. In this section we offer a loose chronological account of the politicisation of criminological theory. The term 'loose' in this context should not be taken to imply that we will present it in a careless way. Rather we simply wish to draw the reader's attention to some of the difficulties of following a strictly chronological and linear account. Attempts to periodise the development of criminological theory are super-ficially attractive. Such simplification is inherent in the abundance of texts that outline the range of criminological perspectives. These texts tend to introduce the dominant perspective at a particular point in time, note how it was subjected to intense criticism by an emerging perspective, report its decline and then move on to discuss the new perspective which they now treat as the dominant one. The pattern continues. The best texts note that adopting this structure is a pedagogic device, and attempt to convey some sense of the complexities that lie beneath the development of criminological theory. For instance, noting that seemingly 'new' perspectives often draw upon the influences of earlier ones.

Bottoms (2008) distinguishes between five approaches to criminology: classicism, natural-science positivism, active-subject socially oriented criminologies, active-subject individually oriented criminologies and political-activist criminologies. We will focus here on the latter approach. For Bottoms, political-activist criminologies include Marxist-oriented criminologies, feminist criminologies and the theoretical movement known as 'Left realism'. Gaining dominance within British criminology since 1970, these perspectives have been somewhat openly political. The combina-tion of political activism and theorising challenges traditional conceptions of the relationship between theory and research. As Bottoms suggests, the legacy of positiv-ism has left criminology suspicious about political engagement for fear that their research may be perceived as unscientific. Political-activist criminology makes explicit that criminological theory and research are inseparable from the political landscape. However, there is a danger that political goals can override the pursuit of knowledge. We provide a necessarily brief, and hopefully not too crude, summary of the main political-activist criminologies below.

Marx himself wrote little about crime but his theoretical framework has been applied by others to the study of it. One of the key elements of Marxism is that all social phenomena, including crime, can be explained in terms of each society's economic relations. In capitalist society, the private ownership of the means of production allows the bourgeoisie to exploit the proletariat, and thus crime can be seen as part of the struggle in which the economically powerless proletariat attempts to cope with the exploitation and poverty imposed on them. Bonger (1916) was the first to apply Marxist principles to crime but the Marxist tradition had little impact on criminology until the 1970s. At that time, a growing number of criminologists offered Marxist-inspired analyses of the problem of crime (see for example, Chambliss, 1975). They also went further to suggest that the solution to the crime problem lies in revolution, bringing about major social, economic and political change. Other criminologists were reluctant to adopt a pure form of Marxism, and instead attempted to fuse elements of interactionism (with its focus on the social reaction to crime) with the fundamentals of Marxism. The result was the publication of *The New Criminology* by Taylor and colleagues (1973). With the benefit of hindsight, this text is widely cited as the genesis of critical criminology. Taylor and colleagues endeavoured to develop a criminological theoretical framework and to endorse a variety of radical politics through their insistence that a society based on principles of socialist diversity and tolerance would be free of crime.

By the mid-1970s criminology was highly politicised. A growing concern with the process of criminalisation provided the backdrop for critical criminologists to explore the ways in which power associated with the capitalist State asserts itself in relation to crime. The influence of Marx was joined by that of Foucault and Gramsci. In simple terms, critical criminology seeks to explore the ways in which the variables of class, ethnicity and gender are played out in relation to crime and criminal justice. The concern of critical criminologists is not only with discriminatory practices but the ways in which structural inequalities are perpetuated. For instance, critical criminologists seek to understand the ways in which State practices seek to marginalise, and consequently criminalise, certain groups. The influence of feminism is apparent in critical criminological work. The second wave of the women's movement in the late 1960s and early 1970s introduced a new dimension to criminological debates. It began by noting the misrepresentation, or more commonly neglect, of women in criminological theory, and attempted to redress the balance by focusing their attention on women as victims, offenders and criminal justice professionals. An important dimension to their work is the blurring of the boundary between theory and practice. Feminist criminologists have been active in campaigning for law reform, changes to criminal justice policy and providing a range of support services for female victims of crime.

In the mid-1980s, Left realism emerged in the UK as a response to both the utopianism of earlier Marxist-inspired criminologies and the punitive and exclusionary character of right realist policies in the US. Left realism still claimed to be radical in its criminology but combined this with a commitment to offer effective solutions to the crime problem. Rather than seeking to challenge the State, criminologists on the political Left now sought to work with the State as part of an attempt to take crime seriously. Not all critical criminologists engaged in this work. Some, as we will explore later, actively chose not to conduct government funded research whilst others have focused their efforts on broadening our understanding of the problem of crime through exposing the most harmful behaviours which are not necessarily those which are routinely dealt with by criminal justice agencies (Dorling et al., 2008).

We make no attempt to reflect on the current state of criminological theory here or to debate its future. Reviewing the final chapters of the many available texts on criminological theory will provide divergent views on this topic. Suffice to say here that contemporary criminology is characterised by multiple perspectives, and some might describe it as 'fragmented' (Ericson and Carriere, 1994). Supporters of these different perspectives vary in terms of how explicitly political their views on crime are. They also differ in the type of research strategies they generate, hence look to different sources of funding. We develop this issue below.

WHO CONDUCTS CRIMINOLOGICAL RESEARCH?

The vast majority of criminological research is undertaken by those working or studying in higher education institutions. Given the interdisciplinary nature of criminology, these academic researchers may be based in different departments across a university campus and may not identify themselves as criminologists. Researchers conducting criminological research can also be found in a wide range of other organisations including central government departments, criminal justice agencies, private sector organisations and voluntary sector organisations.

Criminological research may also be carried out by practitioners working in the criminal justice sphere. Reiner and Newburn (2007: 355) term this group 'inside insiders'. Research may be done as part of a postgraduate degree or as part of a programme of work. Criminal justice professionals can sometimes apply for dedicated fellowships. For example, The Griffins Society, which gives practitioners who work with females who offend or are at risk of offending an opportunity to conduct research which can influence practice. These fellowships are rare and too often practitioners end up conducting research in addition to their 'day job', sometimes for an educational qualification. The growth of practitioner research is not peculiar to criminology, and there is a growing literature on the subject (see for example, Costley et al., 2010; Fox et al., 2007; Fuller and Petch, 1995; Robson and McCartan, 2015). Chapter 11 provides a reflexive account of conducting research with young offenders whilst working as a practitioner in the same youth offending team.

There are multiple sources of funding available to criminological researchers, although as we will explore in this chapter it is increasingly difficult to secure research funding. The opportunities available are fewer than in the past and place constraints on the type of research project which can be undertaken. The process of bidding for funds is also fiercely competitive. The organisation which employs the researcher will determine the sources of funding they are eligible to compete for, and consequently the type of research that they can undertake. We elaborate on the main types of funding for criminological research below.

DIRECT GOVERNMENT FUNDING

Direct funding refers to financial support for research provided by government agencies. The most relevant ones for the study of crime and criminal justice are the Home Office and the Ministry of Justice. Both have a wide range of responsibilities and criminology students should familiarise themselves with their respective remits. Of particular relevance for criminologists is the responsibility of the Home Office for policing and drugs and the Ministry of Justice for the criminal courts and the management of offenders, both in the community and custody. Additionally, the Youth Justice Board, a non-departmental public body, oversees the Youth Justice System in England and Wales. None of these agencies have large research budgets and commission external research on an infrequent basis. In the past the Home Office has provided a major source of government funding for criminological research (the Ministry of Justice was only established in 2007), and we explore the history of its involvement below because it is revealing about the changing relationship between research and politics.

Home Office research dates back to the early 1950s. The Criminal Justice Act 1948 authorised the Home Secretary to conduct, or support financially, research into the causes of delinquency and the treatment of offenders. Initially research grants were made to universities and in 1957 a dedicated Home Office Research Unit was established to increase the support provided for research it funded and to carry out its own projects (see Home Office, 1974 for a more detailed account of its early history). It became a major locus of criminological research but did not always enjoy an easy relationship with politicians. The Conservative government of 1979–1990 was deeply phobic about criminological research. Michael Howard carefully scrutinised research during his term as Home Secretary (1993–1997) and his junior minister (David Maclean) went as far as proposing closure of the research section of the Home Office. Before that date Home Office research was shifting towards an 'administrative criminology' agenda. This term, coined by Jock Young in the 1980s, refers to criminological research which abandons the search for the causes of crime and focuses its efforts on strategies and policies to prevent and deter crime. The inclusion of the word 'planning' to create the Home Office Research and Planning Unit in 1981 was more than symbolic. As Maguire (2000) notes, the Home Office moved towards a position where funding decisions were almost exclusively driven by narrow short-term policy concerns, and where the research questions, methods and timescale were ever more tightly established in advance by civil servants. This has the effect of losing sight of the broader academic debates, and runs the risk of neglecting more fruitful and innovative ideas. Increased Home Office control over the research agenda has been described as the inevitable corollary of the party politicisation of law and order (Morgan and Hough, 2007).

We have noted already the significant influence of the Home Office on the type of criminological research undertaken, both in terms of subject matter but also methodological approach. In contrast to the early experience of the Home Office in inviting researchers to suggest possible projects, research opportunities became available in response to an invitation to tender for a project which is often quite tightly prescribed. The majority of government funding continues to be allocated in this way and concerns about the process have been aired elsewhere (Crace and Plomin, 2001; Morgan and Hough, 2007). The influence of the Home Office on criminological research became particularly apparent in the early years of the New Labour government. Tony Blair (Prime Minister from 1997–2007) emphasised his commitment to be 'tough on crime, tough on the causes of crime' and his government established the Crime Reduction Programme which is described in Box 2.1.

Box 2.1   The Crime Reduction Programme

In April 1999, the Crime Reduction Programme was launched as a ten-year programme but it only ran for three. Described by Morgan and Hough (2007: 46) as 'the largest programme of criminological research ever undertaken in the United Kingdom', it had an overall budget of £400 million (£25 million of which was dedicated to research). The programme comprised of a series of diverse initiatives, dealing with a wide range of offences and every aspect of the criminal justice process. The aim of the programme was to establish *what works* in reducing crime as part of a commitment to evidence-based policy and practice. As a result, funding was made available for independent evaluation, always leading to the collection of quantitative data but sometimes qualitative data. The latter were typically gathered at the early stages of an evaluation to shed light on implementation issues from the perspective of stakeholders (see, for example, Lewis et al., 2003).

The Crime Reduction Programme raises a series of issues about the politics of criminological research. The first is the question about whether criminologists should undertake this work. Whilst large numbers of criminologists were involved in the Crime Reduction Programme as either grant holders or researchers, criminological researchers were divided in their response to the increased funding. Some sought to avoid involvement, suggesting that the work was theoretically impoverished and too closely allied to the interests of the State. Others welcomed the opportunity to have some degree of involvement with the development of crime policy but were streetwise enough to recognise the political nature of the work. No doubt others were more pragmatic and opportunistic, unable to resist the large sums of money on offer. Those who did get involved were often disappointed about their inability to influence policy in the way they intended. A number of criminologists have written at some length about their personal experiences of being involved (Hope, 2004; Maguire, 2004; Raynor, 2004). More generally it has provided fuel for a fierce critique of government-funded research (see for example, Hope and Walters, 2008) with calls to boycott such funding because it inevitably engages criminologists in 'a form of intellectual collusion that is akin to corruption' (Walters, 2008: 23).

The second issue is the implication for qualitative research. Increasingly research was expected to answer the question 'what works?'. The Crime Reduction Programme was unable to do so which is one of the reasons why it was terminated early (Maguire, 2004). Poorly implemented projects led to few conclusive results at a time when politicians were under pressure to reduce crime rates (Wincup, 2013). In the aftermath of the Crime Reduction Programme 'the solution' was to invest resources in so-called 'gold standard' research designs; namely the randomised controlled trial which is the method of choice in medicine and health care. Against this backdrop qualitative approaches were seen as the 'poor relation', judged harshly using criteria most appropriately deployed for quantitative approaches (see Chapter 12). Their role in evaluating policy – for example, to appreciate the complexity of the implementation process from the perspective of different stakeholders – was overshadowed by their inability to provide simple – and some might argue simplistic answers – to the question 'what works?' (see Wincup, 2013). Fortunately, other funders have been more accommodating of qualitative approaches.

INDIRECT GOVERNMENT FUNDING

As opportunities for direct government funding have declined, criminologists have become reliant on other sources. An important one in this respect is research council funding, not least because of the prestige attached to this source of funding. Criminological research comes largely under the remit of the Economic and Social Research Council (ESRC) but some criminological work may fall under the Arts and Humanities Research Council (AHRC), for example, historical research. Research councils are independent non-departmental public bodies of the Department for Business, Innovation and Skills. The ESRC was established in 1965 but the AHRC is a far more recent creation (since 2005). Overall, there are seven research councils and it is conceivable that criminologists could, perhaps as part of multi-disciplinary teams, apply for funds from all of them. Searching for the term 'crime' in the Research Councils UK database (which covers the period from 2007) returns details of 373 projects but only 211 of these were funded by the ESRC or AHRC. Increasingly research councils are pooling resources. For example, at the time of writing (Summer 2016), the ESRC and AHRC are seeking to commission cross-disciplinary and innovative research projects that will extend understanding of transnational organised crime. We will focus on the ESRC as the most obvious funder of criminological research.

ECONOMIC AND SOCIAL RESEARCH COUNCIL

The ESRC is the largest organisation for funding research on economic and social issues, supporting over 4000 researchers (including postgraduate students). Whilst the majority of its funding – £192 million in 2016/17 – comes from government, it emphasises its role in supporting *independent* research which is 'high quality', 'vigorous' and 'authoritative' and impacts upon business, the public sector and civil society (ESRC, 2016). Not all of this funding is for research projects but used to discharge its wider responsibilities to lead and support the social sciences, for example through research training and public engagement (ESRC, 2015). Qualitative researchers are potentially well-served by the ESRC in that it has a stated commitment to support social and economic research in its entirety. Alongside support for new qualitative empirical work there is scope to apply for funding to conduct methodological research or make use of existing qualitative data (see Chapter 8). However, at the time of writing (Summer 2016), browsing the list of active ESRC funded projects on the Research Councils UK database does suggest that successful projects on 'crime' are more likely to adopt a quantitative approach.

Whilst the ESRC supports a wide range of research increasingly it has had to prioritise social and economic issues which require social science evidence in order to address the challenges they present. The five priority areas announced for 2016–2020 include three which are of obvious interest to criminologists. These are listed below with suggested areas for further exploration:

- *Mental health*: the mental health of drug-using offenders; impact of police work on mental health
- *Housing*: hate crime against rough sleepers; resettlement of older prisoners
- *Ways of being in the digital age*: cyberbullying; hate speech and social media.

The government also funds research indirectly via the British Academy, an independent national body for the humanities and social sciences. It is a registered charity which also has access to additional funding including donations from members of the public but in 2015/16 four-fifths of its income was from central government departments.

OTHER SOURCES OF FUNDING

It would be overly ambitious to try to cover all the sources of funding available to criminological researchers. The CVs of many criminologists, particularly those who began their careers when research funding was more plentiful, typically reveal a wide range of funders including the ones already mentioned but potentially charitable foundations, criminal justice agencies, and funders from across the public, private and voluntary sectors (see Morgan and Hough, 2007). The funding landscape is complex. For example, sometimes the funding I have received for research has involved collaborations between different organisations (for example, the probation areas in the East of England region commissioned a project on the housing needs of female offenders). It may also be a requirement for organisations to commission research when requesting funds to deliver a new initiative (see Wincup and Hucklesby, 2007 for a discussion of this in relation to research on the resettlement of prisoners).

Our review is inevitably selective and we will focus on charitable foundations and local criminal justice agencies. Before we do so, it is worth noting the changing funding landscape. As greater swathes of the criminal justice process are 'contracted out', the private sector may decide to dedicate more funds to research. We return to the issue of private sector funding in the next section because arguably this is one of the most controversial forms of research funding. The future of EU funding is under threat following the UK's decision to leave the EU in 2016.

CHARITABLE FOUNDATIONS

There are a number of charitable foundations that are willing to fund criminological research, although none of them have crime as their exclusive focus. In the UK, the major players are the Leverhulme Trust (dating back to 1933), the Nuffield Foundation (founded in 1943) and the Joseph Rowntree Foundation (which has funded research from 1959). The Leverhulme Trust distributes approximately £80 million a year, funding research across all subjects, predominantly in the form of research centres, project grants and fellowships (The Leverhulme Trust, 2016a). Given its scope, it makes a modest contribution to funding criminological research but in 2015 supported research on victims, prison suicide and penal history (Leverhulme Trust, 2016a). It operates in a responsive mode, placing emphasis on allowing applicants to choose the topic they wish to research provided that it is 'of outstanding merit', 'original', 'important' and 'has significance beyond a single field' (Leverhulme Trust, 2016a: 5). There are relatively few exceptions, and the one most relevant to criminologists is policy-driven research where the principal objective is to assemble an evidence base for immediate policy initiatives (Leverhulme Trust, 2016b). In contrast, the Joseph Rowntree Foundation focuses solely on research which seeks 'to change policy, practice and public debate on poverty' (Joseph Rowntree Foundation, 2016). In 2015, it spent almost £6.5 million pounds on research on its three programmes of work. Whilst none appeared to be directly relevant to criminological research, in the past it has funded relevant research, for example, on drugs and alcohol. The Nuffield Foundation operates in a similar way, awarding research grants of approximately £5 million in 2014 (Nuffield Foundation, 2015) across a range of social and educational policy areas, alongside other research-related activities such as capacity building and engaging with policy-makers and practitioners. Research funding is allocated under grant programmes, including an 'open door' one. Those most obviously relevant to criminologists include child protection and law in society.

LOCAL CRIMINAL JUSTICE AGENCIES

Local criminal justice agencies rarely have sufficient funds to conduct their own research or to contract others to do so. Whilst in the past some criminal justice agencies (for example, local probation areas) have been able to employ researchers, few are now able to do so, and if research (defined broadly) is conducted at all it tends to be focused on monitoring and evaluation. Consequently, it tends to be quantitative rather than qualitative. Criminal justice agencies who want to get involved in research need to look for alternatives to employing researchers or commission one-off projects (see the example described in Box 2.2). As we will explore later in this chapter they are helped in this task by the emphasis now placed upon ensuring research has impact (discussed later in this chapter). One outcome of this is that researchers are more likely to view criminal justice agencies as research partners, involving them in a meaningful way from the outset.

Box 2.2   The N8 Policing Research Partnership

The N8 is a collaboration of the eight most intensive research universities in the North of England (www.n8research.org.uk). There are a number of research themes, one of which is policing. This research partnership involves 11 police forces and is focused on the challenges of policing in the twenty-first century. It promotes opportunities for research collaboration, with academics co-producing research with their policing partners, as well as mechanisms for knowledge exchange to increase the impact of academic research. Funding comes from the Higher Education Funding Council, policing partners and universities.

DOES (S)HE WHO PAYS THE 'PIPER' CALL THE TUNE?

Having described the various sources of funding available to criminological researchers (the 'pipers'), we will now attempt to answer this question.

As we have seen funders have their own preferences for the research they would like to support. They vary in their specificity and can include a series of individual project programmes, a set of research priorities, a series of programmes, and exceptionally a general sense of the types of research which they would like to support. These preferences are the end product of a series of interactions between key stakeholder groups. For government departments, the main players are ministers, civil servants and research commissioners. Research councils each have a Council which includes representatives from academia, business and the public sector with responsibility for strategic direction. For charitable bodies, the trustees are influential in determining the research they are able to fund. All these players will have to work within the parameters of their organisation's role, and in the case of charitable trusts the original wishes of the benefactor.

The extent to which funding bodies influence the actual conduct of research varies considerably. Those who enter in a 'customer-contract' relationship with organisations experience the greatest level of interest, and this is typically when researchers have been commissioned to work on a specific project. This can take many forms including the submission of regular progress reports (linked to payments) and steering group meetings. Critics might interpret them as compromising the independent nature of the research that has been commissioned. A more balanced view is to recognise the need to be cautious when money is being invested in research, and to appreciate the support that can be offered, even if the level of involvement feels intrusive at times. The issues explored here are brought into sharp relief when the funder is a private sector organisation and therefore has a vested outcome in the research. This does raise important political and ethical questions as explored in Box 2.3 but these issues may also apply in other contexts. For example, whilst conducting research for both public and voluntary sector organisations, I have been aware that the funders were hoping that the research would produce particular results, for example, providing evidence that a project was successful.

Box 2.3 Should the alcohol industry fund research?

In the July 2016 issue of the *Journal of Studies on Alcohol and Drugs*, a range of perspectives were published on whether researchers should accept funding from the alcohol industry. There was strong support for researchers not accepting monies from this source. It was suggested that by using such funds researchers were implicitly supporting the view held by the alcohol industry that alcohol-related harm is an individual rather than a social problem; that the industry seeks to promote responsible drinking; and that accordingly public health interventions (for example, minimum pricing) to reduce alcohol-related harm are not needed (see Adams, 2016). Adams (2016) draws attention to the complexity of the situation and the need to understand the relationship between government and the alcohol industry. At the very least, the alcohol industry provides the government with revenue which can be used to fund research. The debate opens up a series of interesting political and ethical questions, for example, should the alcohol industry bear responsibility for funding research into some of the harms it has caused?

This debate is new to the social sciences but is established in other areas – whether researchers should accept funding from tobacco companies or the pharmaceutical industry are parallel examples.

We return to the debate about the ways in which conducting funded research, especially for government bodies, impinges upon academic autonomy when we discuss the politics of publication and dissemination below.

THE POLITICS OF PUBLICATION AND DISSEMINATION

There are numerous ways in which criminologists can disseminate their findings, which we will explore in Chapter 8. Written forms of dissemination tend to be favoured by academics and these typically include journal articles, research monographs, book chapters and research reports but there is scope to be far more creative. We focus here on the political dimensions of publication and dissemination. As we will see these impact differently depending on whether a researcher is based in an academic institution or elsewhere. These dimensions influence the type of research outputs which are published, whether they are published and if so, when they are published.

For researchers based in universities, the Research Excellence Framework (REF) and its predecessors which date back to 1986 (see Stern, 2016) have had a profound impact on publishing practices, which we will explore below, and research more generally (see HEFCE, 2011). These audits take place periodically (approximately every six years). Research outputs, alongside other dimensions of research practice (currently, the research environment and evidence of impact, which we will consider in the next main section), are subject to scrutiny to allow higher education funding bodies to distribute public funds for research selectively on the basis of quality. These exercises place particular importance on the production of peer-reviewed articles, ideally placed in the highest ranking journals although the significance attached to the choice of journal is the focus of some debate. Consequently, there is little incentive for academics to contribute to edited collections which can prove useful in bringing together a body of work on a particular topic. There is anecdotal evidence that early career researchers are being advised that writing a journal article is more efficient than producing a research monograph, although this is still highly valued in many disciplines, including criminology. These can be difficult to secure contracts for as there are now few publishers who are willing to commission such books, understandably favouring textbooks which sell in far greater numbers. Journal articles are not particularly accessible as most require expensive subscriptions. There are significant developments to make them more so, increasing the reach of research which is especially important when it is funded with public monies. Across the globe there is a push to make research outputs open access, that is, removing the restrictions on access and reducing the restrictions on their use. Research funders increasingly expect the outcomes of research they fund to be accessible to all. The logic is that increasing the access to research findings will have a positive impact on research utilisation. Whilst this is a laudable aim, providing physical access to research outputs does not necessarily mean they will be read widely as they may be inaccessible for other reasons, for example, because they assume background knowledge.

There are, of course, other opportunities to publish work beyond the standard academic fare. The REF has led to what might be termed 'research output bifurcation', expecting academics to write articles which are original, significant and rigorous alongside producing outputs which contribute to enhancing the impact of research outside academia. As we will explore shortly, it is not sufficient for academics to simply disseminate their research to policy-makers and practitioners but also to contribute to the broader strategy of ensuring research makes a difference. Potential outlets include practitioner journals (for example, *Prison Service Journal*), professional magazines (for example, *Police Review, The Magistrate*), newspapers (particularly broadsheets), political magazines (for example, *New Statesman*) and journals produced by voluntary sector organisations (for example, *Criminal Justice Matters*). Reaching out to this audience is not a new practice for criminologists. As a consequence of the applied nature of criminological research and the desire of many criminologists to make a difference, writing for these audiences is well-established.

Rapid technological development has provided a far wider range of opportunities to reach a diverse audience: social media can be used to publicise research outputs; reports can be uploaded to websites; and bespoke content can be created for websites such as *The Conversation* (www.theconversation.com/uk) and *Discover Society* (www.discoversociety.org) which have extensive public reach. Criminologists frequently contribute to these with recent articles in the former on the policing of hate crime and cyberattacks and the latter on prostitution and racial violence.

Despite the scope for innovation a research report of some kind is a requirement of all funders of criminological research. What happens next varies. It may be sent to academics with specialist expertise in the area to review and/or be scrutinised by research commissioners. The authors may be asked to respond to the comments, and sometimes this process is repeated. Receiving constructive comments on a draft often leads to a more polished report, even if the feedback is a little painful to read at first. Similarly, observations from policy-makers can produce a more user-friendly, policy-relevant publication. However, the whole process can also be frustrating, not least because it can lead to immoderate delays. It can also produce contradictory feedback and suggested changes to the research design, which are of little use once the data have been collected. Until the final report has been accepted, funded researchers often need to ask permission to publish findings. A 'publish and be damned' attitude is unwise if researchers wish to receive future funding, not least because researchers are often expressly forbidden in their legal contracts to make public any findings prior to the publication of the final report without permission.

Below we consider the politics of publication in relation to government funded research but it is worth emphasising that even if research is not funded by the State, publishing research findings is not a politically neutral act. Whyte (2000) notes that presenting a paper on the findings of his critical criminological research on the oil industry to an industrial audience led to an abrupt end to his access to the Health and Safety Executive Offshore Safety Division. Hoyle (2000) shares her experience of publishing a book based on her PhD on policing domestic violence. She experienced extensive media publicity because of her unwillingness to support right-wing feminist calls for blanket arrest and prosecution policies and custodial sentences for all convicted abusers. For Hoyle, the criticisms (described as politically driven denunciation) stemmed from her failure to support political orthodoxy on domestic violence.

CENSORSHIP, CONTROVERSY AND CRIMINOLOGICAL RESEARCH

The publication of government funded research has recently been subject to scrutiny. Sir Stephen Sedley was commissioned to explore specifically the delayed publication of government-commissioned research, reporting in June 2016 (Sedley, 2016). The inquiry's focus was on research conducted by external organisations with government funding, although it recognised that research is sometimes conducted in-house. Recognising that the government has a responsibility to 'account' for the use of public monies on research by publishing research findings, the starting point for the inquiry was recognition that results have not always been published in time for them to be useful, and also that in some instances politically awkward findings have been held back. The inquiry examined nine examples, including a criminological one: delayed publication of an international comparison of drug laws. Allegations of delays were predominantly made by MPs and the media, although one author of a study was brave enough to do so. The report in some respects was reassuring, uncovering little evidence that the government routinely delays politically unpalatable research. But as Brown (2016) notes in the afterword to the report, the Sedley inquiry found evidence of weak rules and chaotic systems; at its worst government departments had no clear sense of what research had been commissioned never mind what had happened to it! This is inexcusable and the report makes a number of recommendations to rectify this as outlined in Box 2.4 overleaf. The inquiry included a call for evidence and it is regrettable that few academics responded to the call. It is unsurprising that many did not. It might be considered foolish to 'bite the hand that feeds you' and it is not always made clear to researchers why reports have been delayed or are not published at all – the latter happened to a number of criminologists, including myself, during the mid-2000s.

Box 2.4   Increasing the impact of government-funded research: Recommendation of the Sedley Inquiry (2016)

1   A standardised central register of all externally commissioned government research
2   Clarity on what constitutes externally commissioned government research
3   A clear commitment to prompt publication in research contracts
4   Routine publication of research the government has considered in policy formulation with, if applicable, reasons for rejecting it
5   A clear statement of the current requirements for prompt publication and adherence to them
6   Training in research for policy communicators

At the extreme, State-funded research may be subjected to censorship. Drawing on his considerable experience as a Home Office researcher (now working in a university), Mair (2007) reveals that he felt his work was never subjected to censorship. Anticipating his critics, he is keen to defend himself against the charge that his work was self-censored through gradual acceptance of repressive practices. However, he does concede that he felt under indirect pressure to produce the 'right' results from his study of electronic monitoring. This illustrates that political pressures may not be explicit but form part of the social milieu in which the researcher works. There are, however, some examples of censorship. We consider two examples here, which might be described as infamous.

The first is Baldwin and McConville's (1977) Home Office funded study on the outcome of jury trials in Birmingham Crown Court. This was conducted in the mid-1970s. Drawing on the data gathered from over 100 interviews with defendants, they found repeated evidence of plea-bargaining. Since little had been written on the topic in the UK, the researchers hoped to publish a book in the area. The reaction to the findings has been presented in-depth elsewhere (Baldwin, 2007), and we will summarise it here. A confidential draft of the report was leaked to the media. The controversy caused led the Senate of the Bar to contact the Home Secretary urging him to discourage publication. The university put in place an inquiry after being warned by the Home Secretary about possible implications should the book be published. The book was eventually published in 1977. The same year, Cohen and Taylor published an account of their attempts to publish research on long-term imprisonment, going as far as to suggest that their research was 'sabotaged' (Cohen and Taylor, 1972: 68) by the Home Office. The study employed qualitative methodology – an approach for which they received a great deal of critical comment – and focused on how prisoners talked about their experiences of coping with lengthy custodial sentences. Despite their protests that the study was 'not particularly radical' (Cohen and Taylor, 1977: 85) and constituted an important piece of independent sociological inquiry, they found themselves 'trapped in a complex web of social and political restrictions' (Cohen and Taylor, 1977: 76). They note that official bodies such as the Home Office are able to exercise a high degree of control of research through five forces which they term as the 'centralisation of power', 'legalisation of secrecy', 'standardisation of research', 'mystifying the decision structure' and 'appealing to the public interest' (Cohen and Taylor, 1977: 77). Ultimately these forces led to the decision to abandon the research rather than collude with the Home Office agenda.

MAKING USE OF CRIMINOLOGICAL RESEARCH: UNDERSTANDING THE LINKAGES BETWEEN CRIMINOLOGICAL RESEARCH AND CRIME POLICY

The relationship between research and policy had been subjected to ongoing academic debate by social scientists (see Hammersley, 1995 for an overview), often leading to the establishment of typologies of the different forms the relationship can take (see Young et al., 2002). We concern ourselves here specifically with criminological research and crime policy, which leads us to the depressing conclusion that criminological research has little direct, immediate impact on crime control policy or practice. Of course research need not always have a direct recompense in this way. Travers (2001: 13) argues that research might be done 'entirely for its own sake!'. In contrast, King (2000) implies that it is not sufficient for research to attempt to address challenging intellectual questions. Instead, researchers should aim to have at least some modest impact on society. This may not be immediate. As Hughes (2011) notes, research may have a long-term influence on both the policy and political process by generating controversy and providing evidence to counter the dominant political discourses on law and order. One study alone is unlikely to change policy but a coherent and cumulative body of knowledge on a criminological issue might have an impact. This body of knowledge might consist of what has been termed 'basic' (concerned with producing theory) and 'applied' (concerned with influencing policy and/or practice) research (Janowitz, 1972).

Criminologists have dedicated little attention to understanding the policy process, although there is now a small literature dedicated to this (Barton and Johns, 2012; Hobbs and Hammerton, 2014; Wincup, 2013). The area is ripe for qualitative studies of the micro-politics of policy-making and we will consider two of the few available which, in different ways, challenge the simplistic view that policy-makers dismiss evidence in favour of political expediency and instead reflect upon how they handle evidence. Monaghan (2011) carried out semi-structured interviews with 'elite' policy actors including MPs, civil servants, senior representatives of drug agencies, NGOs and law enforcement agencies. Combined with documentary analysis his work sheds light on the use of evidence in relation to the highly politicised area of drug policy-making, particularly in relation to drug classification. He argues that it is too simplistic to argue that policies are evidence-free or based only upon favourable evidence. He found a picture of 'complexity and opacity' (Monaghan, 2011: 155) and the task of the (qualitative) researcher is to unpick the mechanisms by which evidence comes to be embedded in policy-making – particularly challenging in heavily politicised areas. Stevens' (2011) ethnographic study drew upon his time on a research placement in a crime policy-making section of the civil service. Both, somewhat depressingly for readers of this volume, reveal that in the hierarchy of evidence that derived from qualitative research is relegated towards the bottom. For example, Stevens (2011) found that civil servants faced with a mass of inconclusive evidence sought to tell policy stories through selecting evidence that would add certainty and enable action, underplaying the uncertain and imprecise nature of knowledge.

Despite the complexities of the relationship, those seeking funding are required to demonstrate how their research will make an impact. Research Councils UK defines this broadly referring to academic impact, plus economic and societal impact. It advises applicants to draft what it refers to as a 'pathways to impact' statement early on so that it can guide the design of the research, challenging the linear model of the research process. In contrast, the REF definition of impact is narrower, although a recent review has called for a more expansive definition (Stern, 2016). The REF defines impact as 'an effect on, change or benefit to the economy, society, culture, public policy or services, health, the environment or quality of life, beyond academia' (HEFCE, 2011). Each unit of assessment (typically an academic department within a higher education institution) was required to submit impact case studies in proportion to the number of academics whose publications (usually four) were submitted for review. Overall, almost 7000 impact case studies were submitted (http://impact.ref.ac.uk/CaseStudies/About.aspx). These are published online (www.impact.ref.ac.uk/CaseStudies/) and criminological examples (on electronic monitoring, terrorism and anti-social behaviour) can be found by looking up those submitted by the School of Law at the University of Leeds. A recent review of the REF (Stern, 2016) argued that impact was one of the success stories of REF2014 (when it was introduced for the first time) with high financial costs balanced by a developing culture of wider engagement to enhance the impact of research. However, there is a danger that this approach oversimplifies the relationship between research and policy through seeking to make direct connections between the two. Each case study was required to demonstrate – with supporting evidence – how the work of a researcher, or a small number of researchers working together – had influenced policy and practice. This runs the risk of privileging some forms of research more than others, for example, 'applied' over 'basic' research. Moreover, given the findings of Monaghan (2011) and Stevens (2011), there is also a risk that qualitative criminological researchers might find it more difficult to demonstrate a direct link with changes to policy and practice, although some of the impact case studies demonstrate it is possible.

CHAPTER SUMMARY AND CONCLUSION

In this chapter we have explored the different ways in which criminological research can be perceived as political. The nature and extent of political influences will vary from project to project, and are dependent on a wide range of factors including the subject matter, the theoretical framework adopted, funding arrangements and the timing of the research. How one defines the term 'political' is crucial and we have opened up this debate for readers to explore further. We adopted an inclusive and catholic definition. We have found support for Hughes' (2011: 325) view that 'criminological research does not occur in a metaphorical germ-free antiseptic zone' and can never be anything put political. Recognising the political nature of criminological research leads us to emphasise the importance of reflexivity; in other words, to be aware of the ways in which the political context shapes our research. Whilst this will add incalculable value to our understanding of the development of knowledge, criminologists often seem reluctant to do this, perhaps fearing that it will detract from the credibility of their findings.

Exercises

1   Select a contemporary criminal justice policy issue (for example, high levels of drug use in the prison population) or a form of crime which appears to be rising (for example, hate crime). Reflect critically on how the political context may support and/or hinder the research questions and design.

2   Focus on the same research topic and reflect upon who might be willing to fund it and why. How might the funding source influence the research process?

3   Focus on the same research topic and design a strategy for influencing policy and practice. Think carefully about your intended audience and the challenges of engaging them. What strategies would you deploy?

FURTHER READING

- Downes, D. and Morgan, R. (2011) 'Overtaking on the Left? The politics of law and order in the "Big Society"', in M. Maguire, R. Morgan and R. Reiner (eds), *The Oxford Handbook of Criminology*, 5th edn. Oxford: Oxford University Press.

  This is the fifth in a series of essays concerned with the public contestation of crime and disorder. Its broad brush approach aims to chart the politicisation of law and order in the post-World War Two period. The other essays can be found in earlier editions of *The Oxford Handbook of Criminology*.

- Hammersley, M. (1995) *The Politics of Social Research*. London: Sage.

  Despite a growing literature on the politics of social research this still provides the best overview of the debate about whether social research is, or indeed should be, political.

- Hughes, G. (2011) 'Understanding the politics of criminological research', in P. Davies, P. Francis and V. Jupp (eds), *Doing Criminological Research*, 2nd edn. London: Sage.

  This chapter offers a comprehensive overview of the varying political contexts and related ethical dilemmas which are intrinsic to criminological research.

- Loader, I. and Sparks, R. (2011) *Public Criminology?* London: Routledge.

  This slim volume explores how criminologists understand their craft and position themselves in relation to social and political controversies.

- Morgan, R. and Hough, M. (2007) 'The politics of criminological research', in R. King and E. Wincup (eds), *Doing Research on Crime and Justice*, 2nd edn. Oxford: Oxford University Press.

  Written by two academics who have both spent extensive periods of time working within government, this chapter muses on the development of the criminological enterprise and the infrastructure of criminological research.

ETHICS IN CRIMINOLOGICAL RESEARCH

3

Conducting research which is ethical is always important, regardless of the subject matter or the disciplinary orientation of researchers; yet given the nature of criminological research ethical issues are brought to the fore. In recent years there has been a growth of theoretical interest in research ethics (for example, specialist journals such as *Research Ethics* which criminologists have contributed to – see the further reading section at the end of this chapter). This has led to a proliferation of publications which we draw upon in this chapter.

In this chapter, our aim is to explore two dimensions of ethical criminological research. The first relates to the ethical governance of criminological research and the policies and procedures in place to ensure that it is carried out in an ethical manner. The second adopts a micro-perspective, exploring the key ethical principles which in most cases will underpin criminological research and reflecting upon exceptional cases when, for justifiable reasons, researchers divert from standard practice. These two dimensions are, of course, related. The role of research governance is not only to scrutinise research proposals and practice in order to ensure research is designed in an ethical manner but also to provide guidance on what constitutes ethical research. Practical guidance for students conducting research projects for the first time is included throughout the chapter.

THE GOVERNANCE OF RESEARCH

Over the past two decades, the ethical conduct of research has been subject to far greater levels of scrutiny than before; a practice which Johnstone (2005) describes as 'ethical policing'. More so than in the past researchers have to demonstrate that their research is ethically sound. The rise of research governance has taken place against a backdrop of increased legislation which impacts upon research but has a much wider reach. The main pieces of legislation are described in Box 3.1. This helps to explain why ethical issues are often caught up with other concerns, for example, data storage and management.

Box 3.1   Contextualising the rise of research governance: The legislative framework for criminological research

***Data Protection Act 1998* (applies to England, Northern Ireland, Scotland, Wales)**

This Act regulates the use of personal information. The definition of personal information is complex and the safest interpretation is to regard it as any data relating to a living, identifiable individual. The provisions of the Act give individuals a right of access to personal data held about them. This is relatively unproblematic for interview-based studies when the interviewee is aware of what has been recorded. Indeed, sometimes qualitative researchers share their transcripts with the interviewee (see Chapter 6). It is more problematic for observation-based studies when participants do not know what has been recorded and may disagree with the researcher's interpretation of events. The Act no longer applies once data cannot be linked to an individual. For some forms of qualitative criminological research this requires more than removing names. Even if anonymous, some individuals may still be identifiable, for example, due to their social position or the nature of their crimes. The most significant implications for researchers are the need to ensure that research data are kept secure, only retained for the length of time necessary and are disposed of appropriately when no longer required.

***Freedom of Information Act* 2000 (applies to England, Northern Ireland, Wales; equivalent legislation was introduced in Scotland in 2002)**

This gives people a general right of access to information held by or on behalf of public authorities (which includes universities) subject to a number of exemptions. The sections most relevant to criminological research are section 40 (which relates to personal information) and section 41 (which relates to information provided in confidence).

***Human Rights Act 1998* (applies to England, Northern Ireland, Scotland, Wales)**

This Act incorporates the rights and freedoms guaranteed under the European Convention on Human Rights into domestic law. Article 8 is most directly relevant to criminological research; it guarantees the right to respect for private and family life, home and correspondence.

***Mental Capacity Act 2005* (applies to England, Northern Ireland, Wales; equivalent legislation was already in place in Scotland: *The Adults with Incapacity Act* (Scotland) 2000)**

This piece of legislation – which applies to those aged 16 and over – states that research with individuals who lack the capacity to consent must have their research design scrutinised and approved by a specialist ethics committee which is independent of the organisation which is conducting the research – either a NHS Medical Ethics Committee or a Social Care Research Ethics Committee. Examples of qualitative criminological studies which might require such approval include projects involving mentally disordered offenders, dependent drug or alcohol users and individuals with learning disabilities. Crucially each case should be judged individually; assuming that an individual has capacity unless there is evidence to the contrary. Researchers are required to put plans in place to support those who may lack capacity to decide whether to participate in a research project.

An important development in relation to research governance is the proliferation of research ethics committees. Given that the intended audience for this book is primarily students we will focus on ethical governance within universities but it is important to emphasise that researchers may need to either seek approval from external ethics committees (for example, if their research involves access to NHS patients) or be prepared to subject their research plans to ethical scrutiny as a condition of gaining access to organisations (see Chapter 4). There are also research ethics committees within learned societies which tend to have a strategic rather than operational focus. For example, the British Society of Criminology has one comprising of six members of the society from a range of academic institutions. Their role is not to scrutinise research proposals, rather to take responsibility for 'maintaining' the code of ethics, to offer professional research ethics training, to organise conferences on ethical issues and to provide advice to members. It is not particularly active in these respects. The *Code of Ethics* was last updated in 2006 and relevant training and events are at best offered on an infrequent basis so novice criminological researchers need to look for training locally or regionally, usually provided by one or more universities. The extent to which the committee offers advice to members is unclear as annual reports are not made available to members. The latest version of the code includes a 'question and answer' section but there are only five included and the answers are brief.

Practice varies across universities but some multi-level ethics governance is typical. For example, at the University of Leeds a University Research Ethics Committee has responsibility for matters of general principle and policy, delegating the task of scrutinising all studies except those with significant ethical dimensions to 'local' committees. Its role is to ensure that research is conducted in accordance with the law and with the highest standards of academic and professional integrity. Situated beneath this high-level committee are five research ethics committees which operate at faculty level, or in some instances are joint faculty committees. Committee members (who are not necessarily subject specialists) act as peer reviewers, examining closely the detail provided on a standard form and associated documentation which includes copies of research instruments, information sheets and consent forms. The level of scrutiny depends upon the nature of the project. For example, a light-touch process operates for projects which are not deemed to be 'high risk'. Many qualitative criminological research projects would not quality for the light-touch process, for example, due to the sensitive nature of the topics being discussed, because participants are considered vulnerable or because of the potential risks to the researchers.

It would be impractical for all research projects to be submitted to these faculty committee levels for approval given the scale of the institution (over 30,000 students and almost 8000 staff). Few research projects now escape some form of scrutiny since all research involving research participants requires ethical approval and this is interpreted broadly as research involving humans, their data or their tissue. This certainly covers many of the projects which criminologists interested in qualitative methods might design. Ethical approval is sometimes devolved to a local level. For example, as a dissertation supervisor – undergraduate and postgraduate – I have responsibility for ensuring that any empirical research projects carried out by students under my supervision are conducted in an ethical manner. Block approval has to be secured for the 'standard' qualitative projects which typically involve the use of interviews or focus groups on non-sensitive topics. Exceptions to this require students to seek full approval. In contrast, all PhD students – whose projects are larger in scope and more likely to influence policy – are required to seek formal approval from the relevant committee.

Similar practices are likely to operate elsewhere so an important first stage when developing a qualitative research project is to familiarise yourself with the sometimes complex ethical governance arrangements to avoid unnecessary delays (see Box 3.2). Ethical scrutiny can take time (for example, applicants at the University of Leeds are advised to allow up to six weeks for a decision to be made) and this needs to be factored into research timetables, particularly for projects which might be contentious (you will have a better sense of which ones might by the end of the chapter). Other research preparations may hinge upon securing ethical approval, for example, being granted research access.

Box 3.2   Seeking ethical approval: A checklist for student researchers

- What are the ethical review processes you need to participate in?
- Is there a health dimension to your research? If so, this might require an application to the NHS Health Research Authority.
- Can you outline the main aims of your research and the chosen research design in a manner accessible to individuals without specialist criminological knowledge?
- Is your research likely to include groups who might be defined as 'vulnerable'? This might include children under the age of 16, prisoners, young offenders, or adults with learning disabilities, other forms of mental incapacity or mental illness.
- Who will be included in the study and who will be excluded? How will you recruit them?
- What information will you provide to potential research participants?
- What type of data will you collect and how will it be stored?
- Are there any conflicts of interest? For example, are you a volunteer or a staff member in the organisation you would like to participate in the research (see Chapter 11 for an example of how the potential conflict can be managed).
- Is the research likely to pose risks for anyone involved?

The introduction of research ethics committees has been the source of much debate among social science researchers who have expressed grave concerns about the ways these institutional bodies have assumed a powerful role as gatekeepers within the research process (Truman, 2003), seeking to protect 'vulnerable' and 'dependent' research subjects from researchers (Johnstone, 2005: 63). We concern ourselves here with the implications for qualitative research. A frequently expressed concern among social scientists is that ethics committees tend to adopt a medical model of research leading to the inappropriate application of quality criteria developed for quantitative research to qualitative designs (Truman, 2003), an issue we will return to in Chapter 12. For Johnstone (2005: 60), the ethical issues encountered by criminologists cannot be considered by deploying a medical model, in part due to the distinctive political and ethical terrain in which criminological research is conducted but also because of the greater use of qualitative methods. He also makes the point that medical research has a more direct relationship with practice than social science research. Although the latter seeks to influence policy it does not always do so directly. By focusing on the utility of knowledge, there is a danger that particular forms of research are squeezed out. We explored these issues in more detail in Chapter 2.

Concerns have also been expressed about the bureaucratic nature of ethical governance. A heavy emphasis is placed upon the completion of lengthy forms and supplying associated documentation including consent forms, information sheets and sometimes research instruments. The latter can cause particular difficulties for qualitative researchers, particularly those undertaking ethnographic work or conducting unstructured interviews who at best may have a list of topics they wish to explore. The requirement to produce research instruments is less problematic in some respects for qualitative researchers who have chosen to conduct semi-structured interviews but it undermines the flexibility associated with qualitative research which allows for the focus of data collection to shift as data are gathered and themes emerging from the initial analysis are explored (see Chapter 8). For Dixon (1997) the current system promotes paper compliance, requiring researchers to demonstrate that they will follow appropriate, and arguably rigid, procedures, for example, relating to the payment of 'expenses' to participants or the completion of consent forms, which we will explore later in this chapter. He suggests that there is an alternative to the 'one size fits all model' which allows for greater recognition of disciplinary differences and places a greater emphasis on checking the ability and commitment of researchers to act ethically rather than requiring written 'proof' that they will do so.

It would be wrong to give the impression that research conducted prior to the introduction of research ethics committees was unethical but there was little in the way of formal procedures in place to ensure that research was conducted ethically and there was considerable variation in practice. As an illustrative example, if I contrast my own experiences of doctoral research in the mid-1990s (a qualitative study of hostel provision for women awaiting trial) with that of the students I now supervise, there was previously no obligation to submit a research proposal to an ethics committee for formal approval nor a requirement to produce what has now become standard documentation when negotiating access and conducting interviews (see Chapters 4 and 6) such as information sheets and consent forms. Whilst at first glance this might seem appealing to students faced with lengthy forms to complete, looking back it left me as a relatively novice researcher somewhat unprepared and vulnerable. I was handed down what Johnstone (2005: 61) refers to as 'commonsense' advice and was also able to draw upon relevant codes of ethics. Like many criminologists I drew upon my parent discipline (sociology) as at the time the British Society of Criminology did not have its own code.

CODES OF ETHICS

The rise of research governance has been accompanied by the publication of a series of ethical codes by a range of organisations. These include learned societies such as the British Society of Criminology; funders such as the Economic and Social Research Council (see Chapter 2); and universities. The status of ethical codes, as we will explore below, is the source of some debate, but generally they are understood as a set of guidelines and a voluntary code of conduct. They are designed to support professional researchers to make difficult decisions rather than prescribe how they should behave. In this way they serve as aspirational codes, aiming to spread good professional practice.

Codes of ethics typically describe the professional standards to which researchers should adhere to ensure they produce research which is high quality and methodologically sound whilst fulfilling their obligations to participants, colleagues and sponsors (referring to both funders and 'gatekeepers' – see Chapter 4 for a discussion of the latter term). Arguably they are focused on the first group and aim to safeguard their interests, sensitivities and privacy. They seek to strike a balance between providing sufficient guidance to assist researchers whilst avoiding rigid prescriptions of what researchers should do. Johnston (2005) argues that codes appear to have been produced in response to both public and political demands to exercise formal governance to ensure members are conducting research responsibly. Whilst undoubtedly true, this perhaps underplays the interest among researchers, and arguably particularly qualitative researchers, in ensuring research is conducted ethically.

Codes of ethics have a number of positive features. They can promote awareness of ethical issues within the research community and are particularly useful for research training purposes. They also help to 'professionalise' research by outlining expected ways in which researchers *should* behave. This might increase confidence among potential research participants making it more likely that researchers will be granted access. Despite these benefits, we do need to examine further the extent to which they promote ethical research. In this respect an important issue is their status. Codes of ethics outline what constitutes ethical research but often say little, if anything, about the consequences of conducting unethical research. Johnstone (2005: 62) suggests that the British Society of Criminology code reads as 'official rules of the game' but there appears to be little in the way of sanctions for those who do not play by the rules. Learned societies do not have the same powers as professional bodies such as the Law Society who can exclude those who do not act in accordance with its code of conduct, effectively barring them from practice. At best a learned society could remove the right to membership from the individual who has acted in an unethical manner but this would still allow him or her to conduct criminological research since membership of the British Society of Criminology is not a prerequisite for conducting criminological research.

The British Society of Criminology's *Code of Ethics* is a short yet wide-ranging document. It covers not only researchers' responsibilities towards the subjects, but also responsibilities towards other researchers, colleagues, sponsors, the discipline of criminology and their 'general responsibilities'. As Johnstone (2005) observes, the code veers between the highly general on some matters and the highly specific on others but given its wide coverage it inevitably provides cursory guidance and does not engage deeply with complex ethical issues. The purpose of Johnstone's critique is to highlight the limitations of the code rather than to denigrate the document. Nonetheless lack of detail does leave the novice researcher lacking a deep understanding of ethical issues which are undoubtedly complex. Those seeking more detailed guidance might look to alternative codes (see Box 3.3).

Box 3.3   Seeking ethical guidance: Alternative/complementary codes of ethics for criminologists

The British Society of Criminology *Code of Ethics* is likely to be the first port of call for criminologists but they may also wish to consult different codes. The main ones are listed below but given the interdisciplinary nature of criminology the list could be much longer. We draw attention to particular distinctive features of each code (known as various statements or guidelines). They can all be found on each organisation's website.

- British Sociological Association *Statement of Ethical Practice* (2002) Forming part of a set of guidelines on professional sociology, this wide-ranging code is accompanied by an extensive list of ethics websites and relevant academic literature (although now dated). It is particularly detailed on relationships with research participants and helpfully recognises how power shapes research relationships and the positive and negative aspects of participating in research studies.
- Socio-Legal Studies Association *Statement of Principles of Ethical Research Practice* (2009) An expansive code based upon ten principles. It is particularly detailed on the issue of consent covering issues such as the use of proxies for those with limited mental capacity, the renegotiation of consent for longitudinal research and the use of gatekeepers and covert research.
- Social Policy Association *Guidelines on Research Ethics* (2009) A relatively brief code organised around the obligation of researchers to society in general, research participants, research sponsors and funders, and colleagues and the profession. Of particular note are the references to data archiving (see Chapter 5), internet research and user involvement. It helpfully suggests establishing an advisory panel of experienced researchers for projects involving complex ethical issues.
- Social Research Association *Ethical Guidelines* (2003) A very detailed but more generic set of guidelines, again organised around obligations to different groups. It is accompanied by an extensive bibliography and links to other useful resources. The guidelines are particularly useful in relation to ensuring research is inclusive.

Increasingly researchers many find themselves needing to adhere to multiple codes of ethics. For example, one of my PhD students is expected to adhere to ethical guidelines provided by her institution (the University of Leeds) and funder (the Economic and Social Research Council) plus those related to her chosen professional body. Like many criminologists, she has chosen an interdisciplinary topic, reflecting her own academic background. For the most part codes of ethics are remarkably similar in terms of content, less so in terms of the level of detail or presentation. Nonetheless researchers will need to combine different forms of ethical guidance and manage potentially contradictory advice. The situation becomes more complex if we recognise that increasingly criminological research involves teams of scholars from different disciplines based in different countries.

In the remainder of this chapter we will focus on the key ethical principles which criminologists need to consider and how these are often accentuated when working with 'vulnerable' groups. These principles are covered in the various codes of ethics we referred to above and research ethics committees seek reassurance that they have been given adequate consideration in advance. Our focus is, of course, on how best to adhere to these ethical principles when conducting qualitative criminological research. For more general coverage of ethical issues, readers are directed to Israel (2014).

SECURING CONSENT

It is standard practice when conducting research to ensure that research participants give their consent. It is expected that the process of securing consent will have the following features in order for the research to be considered ethical: first, it should be informed; second, it should be freely given; and third, it should ongoing. These features are covered in the British Society of Criminology's *Code of Ethics* (2006). There may be very exceptional cases where consent is not secured and research is conducted covertly. These are considered in Chapter 4. Generally speaking, obtaining consent is fundamental and researchers need to be aware that research can constitute an invasion of privacy and can cause harm (Dixon, 1997).

In practice, informed consent is a thorny issue and can be difficult to obtain when conducting qualitative criminological research for a range of reasons. Taking each of the three features listed above in turn we explore the challenges some criminologists might face whilst attempting to secure informed consent. As illustrative examples we will focus primarily on conducting research in criminal justice institutions but reflect also on how the difficulties faced by researchers might be relevant when researching different criminological issues.

INFORMING PARTICIPANTS

It has become usual practice to provide participants with the information outlined in Box 3.4, usually in a written format. This is seen as good practice as it allows potential participants to make an informed decision about whether to participate, allowing them to assess the potential risks and benefits. It is also expected that participants should be given sufficient time to digest the information provided and ask any further questions.

Box 3.4   Informing research participants: What will participants need to know?

- What the research is about
- Who is undertaking it
- Who is financing it
- Why it is being undertaken
- Why they have been chosen
- What participants are asked to do and how long will it take
- How the data will be recorded and stored
- The extent to which the data will remain confidential
- The risks and benefits of participating
- The consequences of not agreeing to participate initially or withdrawing at a later stage
- How they can find out more about the study

There are two main ways in which informing participants might be complicated. The first relates to practical considerations. In Chapter 5, we explore this in relation to re-using data but it also arises when conducting different forms of qualitative research, for example, whilst carrying out observation in a particular setting (see Chapter 7). If we imagine conducting research in a courtroom, it would not be feasible to inform everyone present about the research given. Whilst for the most part courts are essentially public settings, formal access negotiations are still required to conduct research (see Baldwin, 2007 and Chapter 4). On the day, it would be possible to secure consent from the key players in the courtroom but difficult to do from all those present because courts are open to members of the public and journalists. These problems are likely to be exacerbated in a magistrates' court where there is a high turnover of cases, and consequently personnel. Whilst measures may be put in place to inform those present – for example, through posters and leaflets – it remains the case that not all might be aware of the research and they have to actively opt-out rather than the usual, and arguably more ethical, process of opting-in. Practical difficulties of securing consent from all those present are distinct from deliberately seeking to avoid obtaining consent which is rarely seen as ethically acceptable (see Chapter 3).

The second issue often requires practical solutions but relates more broadly to the challenges of communicating with a diverse range of participants. As noted earlier, there is an obligation placed upon researchers to provide full information to participants in terms meaningful to participants. On a general level, this involves providing an explanation appropriate for a lay audience; in other words, free from technical jargon and acronyms (although it may be appropriate to adopt terms used by the particular group you are seeking to recruit). More specifically, researchers need to reflect upon their target population and possible barriers to communication. These might relate to disability, levels of literacy and language ability. Sometimes these can be overcome with relative ease but sometimes they may require costly solutions, for example, the use of interpreters. Communication issues are often particularly pertinent when researching 'vulnerable' groups so we will return to these issues at the end of the chapter.

VOLUNTARY CONSENT

The notion of freely given consent is an important one but glosses over the power relations which operate in society. When conducting research in criminal justice institutions, there are a range of reasons why potential participants feel they *should* participate. First, as Johnstone (2005) argues researchers may be viewed as part of the criminal justice apparatus and consequently, participation may be viewed as advisable. Second, criminal justice institutions (for example, prisons, young offender institutions, approved premises) are essentially rule-governed institutions so those living within them may feel pressured to say yes, particularly if approached by a member of staff. This is particularly important as researchers often have to rely upon 'gatekeepers' to broker access (see Chapter 4) and therefore lose control not only over what information is being provided but also the way in which the invitation to participate is framed. As an illustrative example, I once overhead a manager of an approved premises where I was conducting qualitative interviews approach a resident with words to the effect of 'you can do this for me as I do so much for you'! Whilst far from ideal, it is possible to manage some of these ethical difficulties by viewing consent as a process rather than a one-off event.

THE PROCESS OF SECURING CONSENT

There are a number of ways in which it is helpful to view securing consent as a process rather than a one-off event which takes place at the beginning of the data collection process. In relation to the example referred to above, it was important for me – as the researcher – to ensure that the resident was happy to participate and provided with all the information necessary to make an informed decision to do so. For qualitative research, it is likely that the researcher will be able to do this face-to-face, picking up on non-verbal clues as an additional check of understanding and willingness to take part. In this instance, the resident had been approached by a member of staff immediately before the interview was due to take place. This is a pragmatic way of recruiting participants in institutions which have a transient population but departs from standard good practice of allowing time for individuals to choose whether to participate rather than having to make an immediate decision. Whilst approaching individuals in advance avoids putting them 'on the spot', there is a danger that they may forget important details about the research and informed consent would then need to be secured again.

It has now become the norm to ask participants to sign consent forms and this reinforces the view that consent is simply secured at the outset. However, forms usually emphasise that research participants have the right to withdraw from the research at any time and for any reason without adverse consequences. The latter is particularly important when conducting research in criminal justice institutions because participants might be fearful of the impact of withdrawing, or indeed not taking part at all. Similarly, those involved in ongoing criminal justice cases as defendants, victims or witnesses may also be wary about the impact of being unwilling to take part. This is captured in the British Society of Criminology's (2006) *Code of Ethics* which states that 'participants have the right to refuse permission or withdraw from involvement in research whenever and for whatever reason they wish'. The other side of this is agreeing to take part in the hope that it will lead to a positive outcome. This underlines the importance of providing clear information on the benefits to participants as outlined in Box 3.4.

VULNERABLE GROUPS

Concerns about the vulnerability of participants feature heavily in debates about the ethics of criminological research. We can locate this within a particular ethical orientation – what Reiman (1979) refers to as a Kantian orientation which starts from the premise that we need to respect the autonomy of individuals and rules out practices which do not do this. An obvious example in this respect is covert research (see Chapter 4) but more generally we might question whether 'vulnerable' individuals need additional protection from harm.

The notion of 'vulnerability' is a contested one and recently has been subject to scrutiny. For example, Brown's (2015) work on young people has explored how approaches founded upon protecting 'the vulnerable' can operate in ways contrary to the expectation that they will be caring and supportive. Often the term is too readily applied based upon stereotypical thinking about the needs of a particular group. Walklate (2007) makes this point with respect to victims and suggests that as research subjects they simply need to be treated with the same respect and sensitivity as other participants. Whilst appreciating the complex nature of the term, we use it here to refer to research participants who, for varying reasons, may not be in a position to make informed decisions about whether to take part. When conducting research with these groups, researchers need to adopt additional measures to 'protect' participants from harm.

Codes of ethics sometimes have their own definitions of who is termed 'vulnerable'. For example, the Social Policy Association guidelines state that vulnerability is linked to 'incapacity, social status or powerlessness' (Social Policy Association, 2009: 3). The British Society of Criminology's *Code of Ethics* makes links between 'vulnerability' and age, social status or powerlessness. Other codes (for example, the British Sociological Association) do not specify who is vulnerable but do recognise the power relationships which frame social science research and how these are often characterised by disparities of power and status. Qualitative criminological research tends to involve studying the powerless rather than the powerful, although there are of course counter examples, and there is a growing literature on the issues associated with researching this group (see Open University, 2016).

Two vulnerable groups have been selected for closer scrutiny here. The first group is offenders, a term used here to refer to individuals who have been convicted of a criminal offence and those who are judged to have committed a criminal offence (for example, arrestees, bailees, defendants). The issue here is less about whether consent is informed – although that is relevant particularly for ethnographic research – but more about whether consent is freely provided and whether the potential participant feels they have sufficient autonomy to decline to participate. The same issues might apply in other contexts, for example if police constables are requested to take part in a research project by those in a higher rank. The second group is children and young people who are often viewed as lacking the capacity to make informed decisions by virtue of their (young) age. The same concerns might apply to older participants, for example due to a learning disability or mental health issue. In these instances, consent may need to be sought from an additional person (for example, a parent or guardian). Codes of ethics are not always sufficiently detailed to cover the ethical challenges associated with obtaining consent in this way – the Socio-Legal Studies Association statement is a notable exception. Collectively, these two examples provide a further illustration of the problematic nature of informed consent.

'OFFENDERS'

'Offenders', particularly those who are currently incapacitated, are often perceived to be 'vulnerable' groups. The main concern here is because they are examples of what Trotter (2006) refers to as 'involuntary clients'; they may be under the impression that participating in research is something they are expected to do, indistinguishable from other requirements imposed upon them by the criminal justice system. Additionally, they may feel that there are negative consequences associated with refusing to participate or withdrawing at a later stage (for example, a prisoner may feel it will jeopardise their chance of being given parole) or may be under the impression that participating might be lead to some positive benefit (for example, an individual detained in police custody may perceive participating might secure them a lesser charge). Case studies in Chapters 9 and 11 provide further consideration of how to conduct ethical research with this particular 'vulnerable' group.

Before moving on to look specifically at children and young people, it is worth noting that 'offenders' may be deemed 'vulnerable' for a wide range of reasons other than being subject to the criminal justice process. For example, a significant proportion of 'offenders' experience poor mental health and/or have a learning disability (Loucks, 2006; Seymour, 2010), and they may also be young.

CHILDREN AND YOUNG PEOPLE

Criminologists sometimes wish to conduct research with children and young people (defined here as those under 18 although the term 'young' is open to interpretation).

Often this involves researching specific subgroups, for example young offenders (i.e. those aged 17 and under in England and Wales). The issues which arise when researching those aged under 18 are far more complex than it is possible to convey here but are discussed again in Chapter 11. Briefly, these issues centre around a desire to protect children from harm. Here there has been a shift of attitudes and as Williams (2006: 23) notes 'children are no longer viewed as inarticulate or as uniquely in need of protection from researchers' and this has influenced attitudes towards consent and risk. Traditionally, consent has been sought from an adult, typically the parent, who is deemed capable of making an informed decision about research participation, and so by implication, their 'dependants' are not. This, however, has been viewed as problematic because it appears to undermine a child's competence. One difficulty is the lack of agreement upon when a child is able to provide informed consent. Linking this to chronological age is unsatisfactory as there are a range of factors which can influence a child's ability to provide consent, for example whether a child has a specific learning disability. The legal position is far from clear and involves drawing inferences from parallel situations relating to parental consent, for example in relation to medical treatment (see Williams, 2006). Given this it is unsurprising that research ethics committees have erred on the side of caution and view seeking parental consent as non-negotiable. Whilst research involving children and young people does not require the application of different ethical principles to research with older participants, the vulnerable nature of the participants – and this is perhaps of greater significance when research involves young people as offenders or victims – does require close attention to whether those aged under 18 fully understand the implications of agreeing to take part in a research study. Williams (2006) provides an example when a research ethics committee required parental consent for a study of young prisoners (aged 14–17). This proposal was both unrealistic given that so many young prisoners do not have ongoing relationships with their parents and inappropriate since it overrides young people's ability to choose whether to participate.

So far we have focused on the process of obtaining what Williams (2006: 19) refers to as 'meaningful' consent but the issue of confidentiality is also of paramount importance. It is possible that researchers collect information during the data collection process which may need to be disclosed because of concerns for the welfare of the child or young person. There is likely to be a shared consensus that confidentiality should be broken if abuse is disclosed but it becomes more problematic if we reflect upon our stance if the disclosure relates to pregnancy, substance use or health problems. In this instance, we need to reflect upon our own personal ethics.

CONFIDENTIALITY

Like consent, confidentiality is a problematic concept. Whilst for the most part we can assume that data gathered as part of the research process will not be shared more widely, under certain circumstances this may not be the case. Rather than tackling this thorny issue retrospectively through 'breaking' confidentiality, it is far easier to address this issue at the outset so that participants can factor it into their decision about whether to participate, and if they choose to do so they can reflect upon what to disclose. This is particularly important for qualitative research when data are typically gathered through personal encounters in contrast to the anonymous data collection process characteristic of some forms of quantitative research (for example, use of questionnaires) which do not allow disclosure to be traced back to specific individuals. Moreover, qualitative research provides more scope for researchers to encounter information which may need to be shared, for example if there is a risk of harm to the research participant or to others. Consequently, researchers need to think through the limits to confidentiality in advance and advise participants accordingly when securing informed consent. As they do so they need to be mindful of their own moral and ethical stance, legal requirements, professional responsibilities (for example, included in ethical 'codes') and institutional obligations (for example, specified in access negotiations). In terms of legal requirements, the relevant legislation is the Data Protection Act 1998. A detailed examination of its coverage is beyond the scope of this chapter and interested readers are directed to Charlesworth (2015).

A particular concern of criminologists is becoming party to knowledge about criminal acts. Surprisingly, criminological researchers are provided with little guidance on how to handle disclosures of criminal acts. The British Society of Criminology's *Code of Ethics* simply states that offers of confidentiality may be overridden by law and that researchers should consider the circumstances in which they might be required to pass on information to legal or other authorities and make this clear to participants when seeking informed consent. Feenan (2002) helpfully sets out the legal position (although note that the article was published over a decade ago) in some detail. He suggests that whilst the legislation seems relatively clear in requiring citizens to report offences to police, there is no relevant UK case law, although Schneider (2006) outlines a 'close shave' which she experienced whilst conducting qualitative interviews with known offenders. Feenan is keen to emphasise that the risk of being required to disclose information collected for research purposes is real. He notes that journalists have been targeted frequently in the UK, and North American jurisdictions have subjected academic researchers to subpoenas (see Lowman and Palys, 2014).

There is a danger that criminologists – particularly now that their work is subject to a higher level of ethical policing – become over-cautious, informing participants about the limits to confidentiality in advance in the hope that they will avoid disclosing anything which may need to be shared further (but see Schneider, 2006 for a discussion of the limitations of this strategy). This approach is often adopted for qualitative studies using interviews as the main research method but cannot be universally adopted by qualitative researchers, especially those engaged in ethnographic research. To do so would mean that vital research into illegal behaviour could not be conducted. For example, criminology would be poorer without the theoretical insights which developed through Becker's (1963) ethnography of marijuana-smoking jazz musicians which was pivotal in recognising how being labelled 'deviant' can in itself encourage further 'deviance'. For Lowman and Palys (2014), whose recent discussion of the betrayal of confidentiality in British Sociology draws upon a number of criminological examples, subjugating research ethics to law undermines the academic freedom which sociologists have traditionally enjoyed.

PRIVACY AND ANONYMITY

Privacy is in some respects related to the concept of confidentiality. Usual practice, even when individuals have provided informed consent, is to take all reasonable steps to protect the anonymity of those who have participated in the research. This is typically achieved through the use of pseudonyms so that the identity of each participant is not revealed. Sometimes this is combined with using a pseudonym for the organisation which provided access. This avoids the scenario where it is possible to deduce who said what because they happen to be the only person occupying that role within an organisation. Qualitative researchers have to tread carefully between the lines providing sufficient contextual information and preserving anonymity. In some instances, researchers do disclose where their research took place but if this strategy is adopted it needs to be discussed in detail with participants and gatekeepers.

Respect for privacy is broader than this. It also refers to being aware of the intrusive nature of research which may be particularly relevant for qualitative criminological research exploring sensitive issues such as victimisation or drug dependency.

ADDITIONAL RESEARCHER RESPONSIBILITIES

So far in this chapter we have focused on responsibilities to participants but codes of ethics rightly draw attention to other responsibilities. These include colleagues, sponsors and more generally the discipline of criminology. Given the intended readership of this text – namely those at the beginning of their research careers – we will focus on the former but before doing so we will consider briefly the other responsibilities.

Sponsors in this context could include gatekeepers – both in an organisation and individuals – and funders. We explored obligations to gatekeepers in the previous chapter. The British Society of Criminology's *Code of Ethics* prioritises funders, although there is a fleeting reference to 'professional agencies'. The code states that researchers have responsibilities to maintain good relationships with funders, to ensure that there is sufficient clarity about the respective obligations of researchers and funders and for researchers to complete research as originally envisaged or update funders on points of departure. The latter caveat recognises the need for flexibility when conducting research.

Finally, members are advised to avoid committing to what is often colloquially termed 'quick and dirty' research which compromises quality, or to agree to restrictions on the dissemination of research findings. The latter issue was explored in

Chapter 2. All these requirements seek to protect the discipline of criminology. The relevant extract from the *Code of Ethics* is reproduced below.

> Responsibilities of Researchers Toward the Discipline of Criminology
>
> Researchers have a general duty to promote the advancement and dissemination of knowledge, to protect intellectual and professional freedom, and therefore to promote a working environment and professional relationships conducive to these. More specifically, researchers should promote free and independent inquiry into criminological matters and unrestricted dissemination of criminological knowledge. As part of this, researchers should endeavour to ensure that the methodology employed and the research findings are open for discussion and peer review. (British Society of Criminology, 2006: 2)

The section on responsibilities towards the discipline of criminology overlaps with the one outlining responsibilities toward colleagues. A recurring theme in both is that members should act professionally with honesty, integrity and respect for others. It seeks to protect those at the beginning of their academic careers from exploitation by senior colleagues by insisting that their full contribution to research projects and publications is acknowledged appropriately. It emphasises the importance of professional development so that those new to research receive adequate training to carry out the assigned task. Furthermore, it draws attention to the importance of providing support to researchers who might be carrying out research in environments which can jeopardise their physical and/or mental well-being. This is important as criminological research – and in particular qualitative research – can be both risky and/or emotionally exhausting (Wincup, 2001, 2013). Tagged on to this section in the *Code* is a commitment to promote equality and diversity. Whilst out of place it reminds members of a range of responsibilities to ensure criminological research engages with a wide range of groups and is both inclusive and anti-discriminatory.

CHAPTER SUMMARY AND CONCLUSION

In this chapter we have considered how conducting qualitative criminological research often presents a wide range of ethical challenges, some of which can be considered in advance and some of which need to be negotiated during the data collection, analysis and writing stages. Each research project is unique in this respect but we have identified some of the most important ethical considerations for qualitative criminological researchers. Additionally, we have drawn attention to the changing landscape of research governance and the various requirements now placed on researchers to demonstrate that their research will be conducted in an ethical manner. There is a professional obligation upon criminologists to conduct research which is ethically sound. This extends beyond the most obvious focus on protecting research participants and requires criminologists to reflect upon their broader responsibilities to colleagues and the discipline as a whole.

Exercises

1   You receive a phone call from a research funder (in this instance the Home Office) asking you to consider making incentive payments to your research participants (in this instance young homeless people aged 16–25). What ethical issues might this raise?

    [This relates to an actual research project (Wincup et al., 2003). The previous edition of this book (Noaks and Wincup, 2004) includes a discussion of the methodological and ethical issues related to the use of incentives associated with this project.]

2   You are interviewing a prisoner on remand and he confides in you that he has a very small blade which he has been using to self-harm. He shows you some superficial injuries. What would you do?

    [This is something I experienced when conducting a research project on remand prisoners' access to justice (Brookman et al., 2001).]

3   You are commissioned to conduct an evaluation of a school drug education pro-gramme run by a local police force. Part of the research will involve collecting data from primary-school aged children. Qualitative data will be gathered via focus groups and classroom observations. What measures will you put in place to ensure the research is conducted in an ethical manner?

    [This relates to an actual research project (Downey and Wincup, 2004).]

FURTHER READING

- Farrimond, H. (2012) *Doing Ethical Research*. Houndmills, Basingstoke: Macmillan.

  This 'hands on' book provides practical advice to support researchers to negotiate ethical considerations at each stage of the research process, from the approval application to the final 'write up'.

- Hammersley, M. and Trianou, A. (2012) *Ethics in Qualitative Research: Controversies and Contexts*. London: Sage.

  Focusing specifically on qualitative research, this book focuses on three values which are intrinsic to research, namely minimising harm, respecting autonomy and protecting privacy. It draws attention to the challenges of upholding them in practice.

- Israel, M. (2014) *Research Ethics and Integrity for Social Scientists*, 2nd edn. London: Sage.

  Recognising that research now involves addressing more complex problems in the face of expanding and sometimes unsympathetic regulation, this recent contribution to the literature includes a discussion of contemporary challenges relating to international, interdisciplinary and internet research.

- Johnstone, G. (2005) 'Research ethics in Criminology', *Research Ethics*, 1(2): 60–66.

  This succinct article, which has a particular focus on conducting research with 'deviant subjects', highlights the implications of the distinctive ethical and political terrain which criminologists occupy.

- Wiles, R. (2012) *What are Qualitative Research Ethics?* London: Bloomsbury Academic.

  A short volume which covers a lot of ground, balancing a discussion of debates surrounding research ethics (particularly in the context of the emergence of 'new' qualitative methods) with encouraging ethical literacy among researchers through practical guidance. It helpfully includes an annotated guide to resources.

PART II
THE RESEARCH PROCESS

NEGOTIATING AND SUSTAINING ACCESS

4

One of the key issues likely to confront qualitative researchers as soon as they begin to consider collecting data for their project is access, since all empirical social research involves gaining access to data. Depending on the topic they select, qualitative researchers may need to negotiate access to documents (which may or may not be in the public domain), individuals, social groups or institutions. Access issues are not just problems which need to be solved at the beginning of a project but are also a continuing concern throughout the process of data collection. For these reasons, good researchers should be alert to potential problems at the outset and should 'adopt a reasoned, planned and modest strategy' (Blaxter et al., 2010: 158) to increase the likelihood of securing the access they need.

The purpose of this chapter is to sensitise researchers to the wide range of issues they need to consider when embarking on a research project. In order to do this the discussion draws heavily on my own experiences and those of other criminological researchers. The available literature is largely concerned with ethnographic research but we attempt within this chapter to identify considerations for all qualitative researchers, regardless of the approach they have selected. Whilst access is in many ways a 'thoroughly practical matter' (Hammersley and Atkinson, 2007: 41), as we will explore in this chapter, researchers need to ensure that access negotiations follow appropriate ethical procedures. Hence this chapter should be read in conjunction with Chapter 3. Equally access negotiations do not take place within a political vacuum so the discussions in Chapter 2 are highly relevant too.

GETTING IN

We start with a discussion of physical access which refers to the process of securing agreement to begin to collect data. This might be formal, for example if requesting access to an organisation, or informal if negotiating access to social groups.

Crucially it is important to emphasise that being granted physical access does not necessarily mean that the data collection stage will be unproblematic. For instance, being granted permission to undertake research in a prison does not inevitably mean that prisoners will be willing to participate or that those who do will provide all the data a researcher might need.

Research settings vary considerably in the extent to which they are 'open' or 'closed' to public scrutiny. These differences, in turn, impact upon the nature and degree of negotiation necessary to secure access. To complicate matters further not all parts of the setting will be equally open. For example, as Baldwin (2007: 375) notes, 'conducting research within the criminal courts need involve no more than turning up with a notebook, finding a convenient vantage point, and watching whatever takes place'. Whilst this is true – with the exception of the youth courts – it only provides a partial insight into court process. Even with formal access in place researchers are often limited to the announcements of sentencing decisions on the 'front stage' rather than the decision-making process which takes place on the 'back stage', away from the open court. Should the researcher wish to look at court files or interview court staff, defendants, victims, witnesses, judges, magistrates or legal professionals they need to secure permission from HM Courts and Tribunals Service. Even if this access is agreed this precludes researchers having access to particular groups and to particular settings. Researchers are actually prohibited by law from speaking to people who sit on juries, during or after the trial. Judges, lawyers and other court personnel have proved in the past to be unenthusiastic about participating in research, sometimes being 'resistant, even downright hostile' (Baldwin, 2007).

For many researchers, whether they are investigating the workings of the criminal justice agencies or the activities of criminal groups, some aspects may be 'closed'. Sometimes they can be 'opened up' when relationships based upon trust have been established but as in the example above, there are occasions when researchers cannot go beyond a particular point. Negotiating access can be time-consuming and uncertain, not least because of the sensitivity of many criminological research projects. For researchers interested in the criminal justice process or seeking to secure access to offenders via a criminal justice agency, the political context can provide a further obstacle (see Chapter 2). Often a researcher finds themselves reliant upon a particular individual (a gatekeeper) as we will explore below.

ENABLING AND CONSTRAINING: THE ROLE OF GATEKEEPERS

In order to begin access negotiations, key individuals, often known as 'gatekeepers', need to be identified. Gatekeepers can be defined as 'those individuals ... that have the power to grant or withhold access to people or situations for the purpose of research' (Burgess, 1984: 48). Knowing who has the power to open up or block off access, or who consider themselves and are considered by others to have this authority, is an important aspect of academic knowledge about the setting (Hammersley and Atkinson, 2007). Burgess (1984) emphasises that the 'getting in' process can reveal to the researcher the configuration of social relationships at a research site.

At this stage, researchers need to present themselves and their projects to potential gatekeepers. This is a key research phase because the initial presentation will influence the ways in which potential research participants define the research. Useful advice is offered by Burgess (1984) in relation to accessing organisations, but it applies equally to research with individuals. He suggests that researchers should not offer a 'theoretical treatise or a research design' (1984: 50), but instead give a clear indication of those aspects of the setting which will be focused upon and the individuals that they would like to work closely with. The accounts given need to be plausible to those involved. In other words, researchers should be explicit about the implications of the research for the setting and those who work within it. In order to do this, researchers need to make an assessment of the demands their research requests will make on others so this can be conveyed to them. Research requirements need to be realistic because potential research participants will be doing the researcher a favour if they agree to help, and some particularly useful advice is offered by Bell (1999) in this respect. She puts forward these words of warning.

> If at some time in the future, colleagues or other research workers ask for your co-operation with a project, would you be willing to give the same amount of time and effort as you are asking for yourself? If not, perhaps you are asking too much. (Bell, 1999: 46)

However tempting it is to be economical with the truth in order to increase the chances of securing access, honesty is the best policy. Requests should be reasoned, planned and modest. As King (2000) notes in relation to studies of imprisonment, research inevitably disrupts normal prison activities and will require input from staff. These inputs always have costs attached because every activity involving the research is at the expense of something else.

For the reasons outlined above, researchers often promise to give something back to gatekeepers. The researcher may freely offer this, either at the outset of the project or in the later stages. Alternatively, the gatekeepers may make requests for reciprocal help. There might be a number of conditions of access. Below is an extract from a letter received in response to a letter requesting access to a bail hostel for my doctoral research (Wincup, 1997).

> Dear Emma,
>
> I am writing to inform you that 'Anyshire' Probation Service agrees to participate in your research project. This is on condition that the usual confidentiality of clients is ensured. We would also wish to receive copies of your research reports (including interim reports, journal articles and conference papers).

However, even if requests for assistance such as providing copies of reports are not a condition of access, researchers often feel a sense to duty to help so the relationship established is one of mutual support. I have often provided the following to gatekeepers: copies of reports or summaries, a workshop to disseminate the findings, a paper at a practitioner conference and participation in policy development meetings. Whatever research bargains are negotiated they need to be something the researcher and the gatekeeper are willing and able to live with. Such agreements are sometimes included in contractual arrangements for funded research.

Researchers need to draw upon resources available to them to identify people who can help with access. Existing social networks can be used based on acquaintanceship, kinship and occupational membership (Hammersley and Atkinson, 2007). For example, a number of researchers have commented upon the key role that can be played by colleagues who can act as academic gatekeepers to the organisational gatekeepers (Brookman, 1999). Below is an example of how gatekeepers can operate in a positive way, ensuring that the project gets off the ground. It is taken from Mary Eaton's research on women leaving prison which required her to gain access to 34 women who had previously served a custodial sentence.

> At this stage I was fortunate in receiving encouragement and help from Women in Prison, particularly from the director. She contacted a number of women on my behalf and asked if they would be willing to be interviewed. All agreed – I do not know whether this was as a result of the director's skill in choosing possible research subjects or her persuasive powers when explaining the project. (Eaton, 1993: 124)

Readers may want to reflect critically on the appropriateness of allowing gatekeepers to become so involved in the research project, and ask questions such as how far should the gatekeeper be responsible for selecting interviewees? Whatever the conclusions reached in this respect, the example does illustrate the centrality of gatekeepers to the research project. This is illustrated further below in the actions taken to negotiate access to women awaiting trial (Wincup, 1997).

1. Advice was sought from an experienced criminological researcher about suitable approaches to ensure access negotiations to bail hostels for women were successful because at the time there were only three hostels for women and access was required to two of them. This provided not only advice but also the name and contact details of a researcher working for the National Police Chiefs' Council, which at the time was the professional body representing those who managed the 54 probation areas in England and Wales.
2. An initial letter and summary of the research was sent to the named person, followed up with a telephone call. It was suggested that having the approval of ACOP would help to facilitate access by adding credibility to the project. An invitation to include a summary of the research in the ACOP fortnightly bulletin was accepted. This led to one unsolicited offer of help. Unfortunately, this offer could not be taken up because the hostel was some distance away from the university and repeated trips and overnight stays were not possible given the small travel budget.
3. Letters and summaries of the research were sent to the Chief Probation Officers in the areas selected and were followed up by phone calls.
4. Invariably these letters were passed on to hostel managers, sometimes via the Assistant Chief Officer of Probation with particular responsibility for hostels.

5. In the case of voluntary-managed hostels, the letters were then shared with the management committee. Typically hostels are managed by the probation board operating in the area and hence senior managers in the probation area can make decisions about access. Voluntary-managed hostels are run by management committees appointed by the charitable body who owns the hostel and hence access decisions need to go before this group.

Fortunately all three areas agreed to participate and the whole process was relatively smooth running, even though it lasted for several months. Waiting to hear if the research could go ahead as planned was frustrating and stressful.

According to Hammersley and Atkinson (2007), one of the most famous gatekeepers is undoubtedly 'Doc' who sponsored, in a non-financial sense, Whyte's (1943) study of 'corner boys'. Doc agreed to offer Whyte the protection of friendship, and coached him in appropriate conduct and demeanour. Doc had no formal authority to grant or deny access but used his status within the group to open up the possibility of Whyte making contact with the young men he wanted to study. In informal settings gatekeepers act as people who can vouch for the researcher. They use their status and relationships with potential research participants to facilitate contact and trust between them and the researcher.

There are undoubtedly plenty of examples in criminological research that illustrate the unwillingness of gatekeepers to help research, and how this can potentially threaten the viability of research studies. These examples rarely appear in the published literature and typically take the form of 'war stories' circulated at academic conferences or through other networks. One example here is King's (2000) study of the origins and operation of super-maximum security custody in the United States, which I worked on as a researcher from September 1996 to August 1997. Despite his experience of advising HM Prison Service on the feasibility of a supermax facility in England and Wales, which facilitated obtaining a letter of recommendation from the Director General for Prisons, he was twice refused access by the Federal Bureau for Prisons to their administrative maximum facility at Florence, Colorado. This was particularly puzzling because he had been previously granted access to a number of Federal penitentiaries, and no clear reason was given for the refusal to grant access. However, he was able to continue with his study by securing access to supermax facilities in other US states.

Between the extremes of gatekeepers excluding researchers or being willing to do everything possible to help are the typical responses faced by criminological researchers. They may be faced with a range of possibilities with gatekeepers being more or less willing to help, although often their ability to help may be compromised by other demands on their time. Gatekeepers cannot be disregarded once their initial approval has been obtained. They can continue to exercise influence over the research and hence the influence of gatekeepers goes beyond simply granting or denying access. As Denscombe (2014: 85) suggests, 'access, in the sense of permission from a gatekeeper, is necessarily renewable and renegotiable'. For these reasons he suggests gaining access should be perceived as a relationship rather than a one-off event.

Access negotiations in relation to specific projects are explored in Chapters 9, 10 and 11. Here we turn our attention to providing guidance on how to obtain access to criminal justice agencies, documents and criminal groups.

ACCESS PROCEDURES AND PROTOCOLS: SECURING ACCESS TO CRIMINAL JUSTICE AGENCIES

Access procedures vary considerably between criminal justice agencies but there is some common ground. For access to be granted, the research project needs to be at least acceptable to the agency, and preferably perceived as beneficial to them. Some institutions and organisations may insist that researchers complete an application form as part of their formal procedure for requesting permission, whilst others are happy for researchers to send a letter and short research proposal. It is also possible that some institutions and organisations may additionally request that the research has been approved by an ethics committee (see Chapter 3).

As Liebling (1992) notes in relation to her study of suicide and self-harm, formal access procedures can have hidden advantages. Working in prisons with the fewest operational problems cleared the way for the research. This was particularly important as the research was conducted at a turbulent time in prison history with widespread prison disturbances (Player and Jenkins, 1993). She also suggests that repeated contact with Home Office researchers and policy-makers facilitated intense scrutiny of the research design and provided expert advice and comment throughout the negotiation process. Her views may not be shared by all. Other researchers may view such guidance as intrusive and be alarmed at HM Prison Service steering her away from young offender institutions which accommodate remand prisoners, and as a consequence those prisoners most likely to commit suicide or self-harm (Howard League for Penal Reform, 2016). Researchers need to be aware that strings may be attached if access is agreed and they need to consider the implications of these. However, as Liebling points out, whilst this resulted 'in a possible bias towards the smooth end of the young offender spectrum' (1992: 123), it allowed her to question why suicide and self-harm are widespread even amongst sentenced young offenders in relatively smooth-running institutions? For Liebling, the bottom line was that not agreeing with the gatekeepers would necessitate abandoning the study. Her experience is encapsulated in the quotation below.

> Negotiating access is a balancing act. Gains and losses now and later ... must be traded off against one another in whatever manner is judged to be most appropriate, given the purposes of the research and the circumstances in which it is to be carried out. (Hammersley and Atkinson, 2007: 58)

For Liebling, the gatekeeper was HM Prison Service. Researchers need to identify influential gatekeepers at a national or local level (see Table 4.1). Gatekeepers may not necessarily be those with the power to grant access. For instance, securing the

Table 4.1 Gatekeepers in criminal justice settings in England

Aspect of criminal justice	Examples of national gatekeepers	Examples of local/regional gatekeepers
Police	National Police Chiefs' Council	Chief Constable, Police and Crime Commissioner
Courts	Chief Executive, HM Courts and Tribunal Service	Justices' Chief Executive (Magistrates); Manager court centre
Prisons	Director of Public Prisons, Her Majesty's Prison and Probation Service; Chief Executive of contracted provider of private prisons	Governor (public prison); Director (private prison)
Probation	Director of Probation, National Offender Management Service	Chief Executive (Community Rehabilitation Companies); Head of National Probation Service Regional Division
Youth justice	Chair, Youth Justice Board	Youth offending team manager
Victims	Chief Executive or Chair of the Board of Trustees, Victim Support	Manager of local Victim Support Service

support of a prisoner governor does not necessarily mean that permission has been granted to carry out a project. This is determined centrally by the National Offender Management Service, and this requires researchers to complete a lengthy application form (available from www.myresearchproject.org.uk) even if they only plan to conduct a small-scale qualitative study in one prison.

GETTING IN: ACCESSING DOCUMENTS

The use of documentary sources is attractive to many researchers because of their accessibility. Increasingly vast amounts of information are available to the public without requesting permission. Access may be immediate and free, particularly as documents are often available on the internet. Whilst documentary research may appear to pose fewer access problems than the use of other qualitative research methods, researchers need to remind themselves that not all forms of documents are freely available. Denscombe (2014: 229) distinguishes between three types of documents: 'public domain', 'restricted access' and 'secret'. Below are some examples of the types of documents which may be of interest to criminological researchers interested in qualitative research.

1. *Public domain*: newspapers, annual reports produced by criminal justice agencies, reports produced by the criminal justice inspectorates.
2. *Restricted access*: files belonging to criminal justice agencies, audio and video recordings of police interviews, court transcripts.
3. *Secret*: minutes of government meetings, e-mails produced by companies illegally trading.

As Denscombe (2014) notes the first two types are those most commonly used by academic researchers. The latter are typically used for fraud detection and under-cover work and investigative journalism (see Rawlinson, 2000 for a discussion of the blurred boundaries between investigative journalism and academic research). To access such documents sometimes requires insider knowledge, participation and deception which may only be possible through conducting covert research, which we will explore later. No access negotiations are needed to access those documents in the public domain (see Chapter 5 for a discussion of how they might be used in qualitative research projects). Box 4.1 provides an example of a criminological research project which required negotiating access to police murder files – restricted access documents. The Freedom of Information Act 2000 (which applied to England, Northern Ireland and Wales but equivalent legislation was introduced in Scotland in 2002) has blurred the boundaries between the three categories. This gives people a right of access to information held by or on behalf of public author-ities (see Chapter 3). Whilst most academic researchers favour the usual methods of negotiating access, one criminological example which has used this legislation to obtain (quantitative) data is Eastwood et al.'s (2013) study of racial disparities in the policing of drug offences.

Box 4.1   Investigating murder: Using police files as a research resource

Police murder files are a type of documentary source rarely used by researchers (Brookman, 1999) but were used by Brookman to obtain data for her study of patterns and scenarios of masculine homicide and violence across England and Wales. The data gathered supplemented the qualitative data obtained from in-depth interviews and quantitative data acquired from the 'Homicide Index', a large statistical database managed by the Home Office. Brookman explores the 'complex, dynamic and ongoing process' (1999: 48) in which she had to engage in order to secure access to the files she needed. As she remarks, the process required numerous forms of correspondence and contact, both formal and informal, with police officers of differing ranks in three police forces. This resulted in differing negotiations processes in the three force areas with differing outcomes. The most important variations included the length of time taken to locate (or more appropriately 'unearth') the relevant documents, the extent to which access was granted to the complete files and the extent to which poten-tially significant documents were missing. Two valuable lessons for researchers can be gleaned from Brookman's account: firstly, it is ill-advised to assume that documents, even highly sensitive and confidential ones, may be neatly filed away, and secondly, negotiating access to sensitive documents is highly dependent upon 'who you know'.

GETTING IN: ACCESSING CRIMINAL GROUPS

Negotiating access to criminal groups in their natural setting is fraught with difficul-ties, leading some researchers to focus their efforts on securing access to offenders via criminal justice agencies or to adopt covert techniques (explored later in this chapter). On the latter point, regardless of whether an overt or covert stance is adopted, researchers need to identify the group of interest and find some way of establishing a relationship with them. For Polsky (1971) this necessitates asking around to secure an introduction to a criminal or finding out where one or more can be met. This is easier for some researchers than others because of their networks. Most of the introduction to Winlow's (2001) book on violent men is dedicated to offering a reflexive account of the research process, and within this account the impact of his personal biography on the nature and quality of the research is discussed at length. Whilst critics might suggest it is at best self-indulgent and at worst irrelevant, Winlow argues that it was vital to successful commencement and completion of the study. His previous detailed knowledge of working-class North Eastern England 'subculture', his continued contact with it and his working-class accent are described by Winlow as 'tools' which helped him to negotiate access and conduct the research. In this way, he suggests that he was able to conduct a study that few educated, middle-class and middle-aged British researchers could have done because they would have so little in common with their research participants. The book is dedicated to his parents and he suggests that without their guidance he would have been the subject of the book rather than the author! This example illustrates the importance of what is sometimes referred as 'social access'; the process of 'getting along' after 'getting in'.

GETTING ALONG

Physical access is a prerequisite for social access but does not guarantee it. Social access describes the process of 'getting along' through establishing a research role, building up rapport with participants and securing their trust. Liebling (1992) argues that the researcher entering a prison for the first time appears naïve, green, uncomfortable and out of place. This could equally be applied to research in all criminal justice settings and to research with criminal groups. Particularly for ethnographic research, access needs to be sought to new people, places and events as further research questions begin to emerge. This happens as the data are analysed and the research design evolves. To become accepted, researchers need to be willing to fit into the timetables of institutional life. This applies also to research with criminal groups because researchers will soon become familiar, and need to fit in with, their routine activities. They also have to become acquainted with, and be seen to accept, the culture of the group they are investigating as the following case study illustrates vividly.

Sharpe's (1998) study of prostitution utilised first-hand lengthy observation and the methodological issues raised are explored in a chapter published separately (Sharpe, 2000). Her research had three central concerns: to analyse why women enter the world of prostitution, to examine the importance of prostitution in the individual's life and to observe how prostitution was policed. Inevitably these research concerns would require the police to have a major input in some form. The issue for Sharpe was that she had not only negotiated access to a police force in order to research their activities, but also to seek their co-operation to secure access to women working as prostitutes. Other agencies such as the Probation Service were not able to offer direct help. Motivated by 'practical expediency' rather than demonstrating 'political or ideological allegiance' (Sharpe, 1998: 18), conducting research on and with the police required her to manage diverse relationships in the field between potentially conflicting groups. The question – whose side are you on? – has been the source of considerable debate in the social sciences (see Box 4.2). It was difficult for her to assess the extent to which the study was compromised by her relationship with the police, although she does conclude that the 'research was completed largely *in spite* of the police, not because of them' (Sharpe, 1998: 21 emphasis in original). She also suggests that whilst the world of prostitutes is perceived as a hard world to enter, the same might be said about the police due to the collection of behaviours and attitudes typically described by police researchers as 'cop culture' (see Reiner, 2010 for a more detailed discussion). As a female researcher the masculinity of police culture came as a considerable shock. Female researchers conducting studies within other criminal justice agencies are also likely to encounter some form of masculine culture.

Box 4.2   Whose side are you on? Understanding the micro-politics of social research

Howard Becker's 1967 essay entitled 'Whose side are you on?' continues to offer a major contribution to the debate. Described by Delamont (2002: 149) as a 'manifesto on values and methods', his starting point is that neutrality is a myth shattered by the reality that personal and political sympathies inform research. This does not mean that the goal of research is the pursuit of political goals, although as we noted earlier in this chapter some researchers might argue that it is. Instead, it challenges the aim of positivists and naturalists to strive as far as possible to limit the influences of values on the research process. Qualitative research has little in common with positivist principles but qualitative researchers have been proponents of naturalism. This perspective attempts to study the social world in its 'natural state', undisturbed by the researcher, and offers a detailed description of some aspect of social life ('to tell it how it is'). This perspective has been subjected to criticism by qualitative researchers (see Chapter 7).

   The focus of Becker's essay was on research with deviant groups, chosen because researchers who focus on this group frequently have to answer to the charge that siding with deviant groups leads to distortion and bias. Becker suggests that a 'hierarchy of credibility' (1967: 241) operates in deviancy research (and in other areas such as education), and credibility and the right to be heard are distributed differentially throughout the hierarchy. Researchers interested in deviant groups concentrate on those who voices are normally unheard, and hence challenge what Becker (1967: 243) terms the 'established status order'. According to Becker, accusations of bias are levelled only at researchers who focus on deviants rather those concerned with criminal justice professionals. For Becker, researchers always have to take sides, and their challenge is to ensure that unavoidable sympathies with their research participants do not render their work invalid.

   Becker's essay received criticism shortly after it was published by Gouldner (1975) who insisted that value neutrality was possible and desirable. Remarkably, over 35 years after its publication, Becker's essay continues to be revisited by social researchers (see Atkinson et al., 2003; Delamont, 2002; Hammersley, 2001; and Liebling, 2001). In her article on prisons research, Liebling argues that 'it *is* possible to take more than one side seriously, to find merit in more than one perspective, and to do this without causing outrage on the side of officials or prisoners' (2001: 473; emphasis in original). She does note, however, that this is a precarious business and risks encountering the wrath of criminologists who are sceptical of any attempt to undermine officialdom. For Liebling, taking more than one side seriously does not lead to impartiality, and is therefore not a form of closet positivism. Instead, attempts to synthesise different or competing perspectives within the prison world at the analysis stage help to sharpen the focus, and consequently this is a valuable analytic task.

For many criminological researchers, regardless of whether they adopt Becker's position, they find themselves in the precarious position of trying to keep everyone happy. This is particularly true for those conducting research within criminal justice agencies who have to strive to avoid alienating groups who might be viewed in opposition to each other (for example, prisoners and prison officers or suspects and police officers) or who occupy different positions within an occupational hierarchy (for example, senior police managers and the 'rank-and-file').

Sharpe's (1998) research took place in an established red light district known as 'the patch'. This comprised three streets within an isolated non-residential area of a city (which remained anonymous in the published account) where the police tolerate prostitutes soliciting for business as part of a policing strategy for containing and controlling prostitution. In the course of one year, 29 patrols were accompanied, resulting in 120 hours of observation across all days of the week. These plain-clothed officers were part of a Divisional Enquiry Team, known to the prostitutes as 'the vice'. This is a misnomer because the remit of their work also included a wide range of other sexual offences, locating missing persons and drug offences. Interviews were also conducted with both prostitutes (40 in total and 95% of those working regularly in the area) and police officers (12 in total), taking an unstructured form with the former group and a semi-structured form with the latter.

Sharpe's honest account of the research process highlights some of the likely problems that researchers might encounter. These are detailed below.

- Access negotiations are often time-consuming and may lead to the project developing in a different way than originally anticipated.
- Access may have to be negotiated with different layers of the organisational hierarchy divided by authority and power. Additionally, members of each layer may not share the same interests.
- Researchers may not be trusted (at least not initially) and their trust may be continually tested.
- Potential participants may have good reasons for not wanting to take part in the study, especially if they are involved in criminal activities.

RESEARCH ROLES

An important dimension of 'getting along' is assuming a research role. There is a large amount of literature on research roles in relation to qualitative, particularly ethnographic, research. Space precludes a detailed discussion of this and instead we aim to highlight the most pertinent themes. A recurring theme in published accounts of the research process is that establishing a research role takes time, and researchers may need to adopt different roles throughout the research process (Hammersley and Atkinson, 2007). For these reasons, researchers need to engage in 'impression management', which may take different forms with different groups, in order for their research role to be accepted. For example, Adams (2000) explores how she engaged in 'dressing up' and 'dressing down' depending on whether she was interviewing suspects, solicitors or police officers. Impression management is only possible to a certain extent because aspects of a researcher's biography such as age, sex and 'race' influence the researcher's role. This has been particularly highlighted by feminist scholars (see Gelsthorpe, 1990; Rawlinson, 2000; Smith and Wincup, 2000).

The research role is not always fully understood and may be treated with suspicion. Hence alternative roles are assigned to researchers to make sense of their presence in the research setting. For example, throughout my career I have frequently experienced a case of mistaken identity, typically as a member of staff working at the setting I have been conducting research in. On a particularly memorable occasion, a female resident in an approved premise rolled up her jeans, showed me her 'tag' and asked if I was able to remove it! My response was to explain carefully my role as a researcher so that her decision to participate was not based upon the false understanding that I could assist with altering the conditions attached to her residence in an approved premise.

Researchers sometimes adopt 'cover' roles. McKeganey and Barnard (1996) in an ethnographic study of prostitutes and their clients assumed the role of a quasi-service provider by engaging in harm reduction work. Similarly, Wardhaugh (2000) describes how she became a volunteer in a day centre for homeless people when conducting research on crime and victimisation amongst this group. These researchers were not conducting covert research but felt the need to create an acceptable social role in order to be in the setting in the first place. In both cases the role adopted was limited but helped to overcome the awkwardness inherent in conducting research. There is an important distinction to be made between researchers assuming 'cover' roles and conducting covert research. All made their research role explicit when conducting interviews but such practices do blur the boundary between overt and covert research which we will explore in the section which follows.

CONDUCTING RESEARCH WITHOUT RESEARCH ACCESS

In this final part of the chapter we turn our attention to conducting research when a conscious decision is made not to negotiate access in the usual way by identifying yourself as a researcher (covert research) or when access is initially denied.

COVERT RESEARCH

Sometimes it may be judged that the relevant gatekeepers will almost certainly block entry altogether or that the very presence of a researcher will make it impossible to collect the types of data needed to answer the research questions posed. In these instances, if the research is to go ahead then one solution is to conduct it covertly. This involves the researcher adopting a plausible role so they can blend into the background. There are a number of classic criminological research studies which have been conducted in this vein including Holdaway's (1983) study of the British police, Ditton's (1977) analysis of 'fiddling' in a bakery, and Hobbs et al.'s (2003) research on door supervisors or 'bouncers' as they are more traditionally known. The difficulty faced by researchers is deciding whether to request access. Sometimes permission to conduct research can be given when it is not expected. One example of this is Fielding's (1982) study of the National Front, an extreme right-wing political organisation in the UK with explicitly racist views. These views are frequently condemned and therefore negotiating access to this group seemed unlikely.

The ethical dilemmas raised by covert research mean that it rarely used by researchers and it is actively discouraged in codes of ethics. The British Society of Criminology's (2006) code rather vaguely states that researchers should base their research on the freely given informed consent of participants in all but exceptional circumstances, with exceptional defined in terms of the importance of the topic rather than the difficulties of gaining access. Other codes are arguably more useful for those considering covert research. For example, The British Sociological Association's (2002) statement of ethical guidance included a section on covert research; advising when this type of research is appropriate, the legal risks involved (since participants have a right to privacy) and strategies for ensuring the research is as ethical in its approach as it can possibly be (for example, protecting the anonymity of participants). The Socio-Legal Studies Association (2009) covers similar ground and helpfully suggests that the overruling principle when considering covert research is whether it can be justified in the public interest. The Social Research Association's (2003) ethical guidelines incorporate a discussion of covert research exploring the danger of misleading subjects, raising an issue we will pick up again shortly about the need to locate studies on a continuum from overt through to covert.

In addition to the classic covert criminological studies we noted earlier in this chapter, there are some more recent criminological examples including Winlow's (2001) study of violent men, Calvey's (2000) research on bouncers and Treadwell and Garland's (2011) work on the English Defence League. In these instances, it can be argued that covert research was the only possible way to gain insights into these social worlds. In addition to ethical considerations, there is also the issue of risk. Conducting covert research places researchers in a position of danger. Polsky (1971: 122) famously urged researchers to steer clear of covert approaches.

> In doing field research on criminals you damned well better *not* (emphasis in original) pretend to be 'one of them', because they will test this claim and one of two things will happen: either you will ... get sucked into 'participant' observation of the sort you would rather not undertake, or you will be exposed, with still greater negative consequences.

Pretending to be 'one of them' is precisely what the covert researcher is expected to do. For Winlow (2001) this involved engaging in a type of masculine bravado with which he was not entirely comfortable but also skirting the boundaries of criminality on a number of occasions. His research therefore involved the risk of being arrested and violent attacks from drunken young people. Deciding to conduct covert research does not remove the need for access negotiations because researchers have to tread carefully to ensure their deception, and hence their true identity as a researcher, is not unveiled.

As Burgess (1984: 48) notes, covert research bypasses the negotiation of access with a gatekeeper but the trade-off is that limitations are placed on the research. One of the difficulties of assuming a covert role is that the researcher is unable to make field notes as incidents take place. Instead field notes have to be written up after leaving the setting. Winlow used the strategy of jotting down key words and phrases immediately after leaving the field and then used these as *aide-mémoires* to develop detailed field notes the next day. This can be time-consuming, and the ethnographer is reliant on reconstructing events based on what they can recollect some time after they took place. For covert research this is the only option but even if research is conducted overtly, taking field notes can still be problematic. It can be both intrusive and impractical to take notes in front of participants. Instead, the ethnographer has to try to write up their notes as soon as possible after a stint in the field and develop strategies to boost memory recall.

It might be argued that all research is more or less covert. As Hammersley and Atkinson (2007: 210) argue, 'even when operating in an overt manner, ethnographers rarely tell *all* the people they are studying *everything* about the research' (emphasis in original). Burgess (1984) makes similar arguments and remarks that the decision to do covert research is often posed as an alternative to overt research. However, he suggests that it is not as straightforward and simple as this. To support his argument, he outlines a number of points described below.

1. In some instances where access is openly negotiated not all individuals will know about a piece of research. For example, if a researcher has negotiated access to a local prison which accommodates unconvicted, unsentenced and short-sentence prisoners, the daily turnover of prisoners will make it difficult to ensure all prisoners are aware of the research.
2. Even if all individuals are aware of the research they are likely to hold differing interpretations about what is being done. For example, a study of equal opportunities and policing may be interpreted by male officers as a study of sexism and by white officers as a study of racism.
3. Some researchers may establish open access with some groups while closing off details of the research to other groups. For example, an observational study of shoplifting might involve negotiating access through store managers but details may not be given to all staff, and certainly not to customers within the store.

We have already noted the use of 'cover' roles and in Box 4.3 we describe a study which blurs the boundaries between covert and overt research.

Box 4.3   Policy-making in action: Understanding the ethics and value of (c)overt observation

Stevens (2011) describes how he used a six-month period on secondment to the UK civil service as an opportunity to observe crime policy-making in action. He also conducted interviews with five civil servants who had been his colleagues. He chose not to seek informed consent from everyone he observed for two reasons: first, it would have proved impractical to do so and second, it would have increased reactivity. He justifies this approach on the grounds that the participants were not vulnerable in any way and were engaged in work on behalf of, and funded by, the public. He took care to protect the anonymity of participants (for example, not disclosing where they worked or the policies they worked on) and ensured that he had informed consent from anyone quoted directly in subsequent publications.

This example illustrates that thinking about research as either covert or overt is unhelpful and misrepresents the complexity of researching the social world.

ALTERNATIVE STRATEGIES

We have already noted the uncertain nature of access negotiations. For this reason researchers need to be sufficiently adaptable to ensure the research continues wherever possible, even if it is not in the form that they originally envisaged because access negotiations do not work out as intended. There are constraints here – for example the funder might not be willing to allow alternative projects to take place – but many researchers do not end up studying precisely what they intended at the outset. In part this is because access negotiations can be unpredictable although there may be many other explanations. Qualitative research techniques are particularly suited to studies which are exploratory. For these reasons, researchers should not stick rigidly to the initial research design but allow the research to evolve in a controlled rather than an *ad hoc* way, particularly in response to initial analysis of research themes (see Chapter 8).

Blaxter et al. (2010) offer six strategies to consider if access is denied. These are listed below with some criminological examples.

1. *Approach other individuals*. This is frequently done in criminological studies involving interviews. For example, if one prisoner refuses to be interviewed then researchers simply approach others.
2. *Approach other institutions*. For instance, Punch's (1979) inability to gain access to police forces in Britain led him to eventually study the Dutch Police instead. This is an extreme example but it is not uncommon for one organisation to say no, so the researcher has to approach others.
3. *Approach another individual in the same institution*. For example, if a researcher is interested in neighbourhood policing and the head of a local division refuses to participate, then it may be possible to approach a colleague performing a similar role in another. This is unlikely to be possible if the chief constable has declined to participate.
4. *Try again later*. This is rarely an option for researchers because of time constraints but waiting until a resistant chief constable has moved on or a HM

Inspectorate of Constabulary visit has been completed can be fruitful. Securing access is, of course, never inevitable.

5. *Change your research strategy*. This might involve using different methods, modified research questions or studying alternative groups and organisations. For example, McEvoy (2001) explored informally the possibility of conducting interviews in Northern Ireland prisons for his study of paramilitary imprisonment. He was told frankly that this was 'not a mission' (2001: 371) and a formal approach via a letter was ignored. His solution was to secure access to prisoners after they were released or were on Christmas or summer leave programmes. The attendance of prison officers on university courses allowed him to identify those willing to participate.

6. *Focus your study on the research process*. This is rarely an option for researchers but students required to write a short dissertation could select this option, drawing on their own experiences and those of other researchers. The latter may be elicited by means of qualitative interviews with criminologists or by a virtual focus group using an electronic mailing list (see www.jiscmail.ac.uk for details of suitable lists). Do remember to ask permission from the list manager.

GETTING OUT

In 1980 Snow commented that the process of leaving the field was a neglected problem in qualitative research. A claim such as this is now no longer valid; however, it is fair to say that the researcher's departure from a particular setting has yet to receive the same systematic treatment as their entrance and presence. Much has been published since then on the process of leaving a diversity of research settings (see for example Shaffir and Stebbins, 1991 and Shaffir et al., 1980), although it is still difficult to find accounts by criminologists. Common themes within the published accounts are that the process of leaving involves reflecting on when to leave, managing the relationships formed and deciding whether to return. A further theme is that the researcher's departure, if misunderstood or viewed unfavourably by research participants, may strongly affect the efforts of future researchers in the same or similar settings. For these reasons, codes of ethics – as discussed in Chapter 3 – explore researchers' obligation to their discipline. As King (2000) argues, the reputation of all researchers can depend upon the legacy left behind by any one individual. For these reasons he recommends avoiding making promises that cannot be kept, taking time to discuss and explain the research throughout, being alert to rumours so they can be quashed as quickly as possible and tying up loose ends before leaving the field.

Box 4.4   Saying goodbye: Understanding the process of leaving the field

Wolf's (1991) discussion of leaving an 'outlaw' society is one of the few criminological accounts available on leaving the field. The group studied was a motorcycle club whose members were often involved in minor crimes and sometimes engaged in major organised crime. This group, one of approximately 900 in existence in the United States and Canada at the time of the research, was perceived as a deviant subculture. Wolf's account begins by acknowledging the relationship between the different progressive stages in his fieldwork career from entering the field, maintaining field relations, leaving the field through to writing up. All are interdependent and as he notes the difficulties he faced in leaving the field were because his initial access negotiations had gone *too* well, leading to the ironic situation that for a time he felt unable to leave and write up the study. The very purpose of the time he had spent with the group appeared to be under threat. He was experiencing over-rapport and appeared to be 'going native', abandoning the analytic role for full participation, thus rendering him incapable of making any kind of detached analysis.

Wolf's study was unusual in that it moved from being a covert to an overt participant observation study. This was largely the consequence of one member of the club inviting him to conduct research at a time when Wolf was struggling to broach the subject of how to reveal the genuine nature of his interest in the group; as he notes this was 'an incredible stroke of luck' (Wolf, 1991: 218). As he moved from group member to ethnographer, his role as biker became contrived and he became excluded from the group. In his words, he 'faded away' (1991: 222). Whilst he had initially planned to maintain ties of friendship this was not realised. The special world of the outlaw bikers necessitated intense comradeship and nothing less than this would suffice.

There is an important distinction to be made between getting out and getting away. Leaving the field physically can be relatively easy but getting away emotionally can prove more challenging, leading some researchers to describe the process as a 'psychological problem' (Shaffir, 1991: 210). As King (2000: 308) suggests, 'some researchers find it hard to leave the field, mostly because in the course of the research one inevitably makes rewarding relationships'. Some ethnographers (for example Shaffir, 1991) have suggested that research participants often expect researchers to continue on a permanent basis with the personal commitments they have established during the course of the research. However, when researchers physically leave the field they often find themselves consumed with analysis and writing, hence interest in their research participants diminishes, which can lead to feelings of betrayal and disloyalty. The analysis process serves as a constant reminder of who researchers have met, the stories they have told and the emotions they displayed when telling their stories.

Taylor (1991) suggests that there are three questions that researchers need to pose as they approach the final stages of the data collection process. The first concerns how and when to conclude a study by stopping collecting data and beginning the work of intensive analysis and writing. The second question is how to manage the personal relationships formed with research participants. Taylor suggests that this is a personal decision, and it depends upon how the researchers see the people and the nature of the relationship developed with them. Finally, researchers need to consider the social, political and ethical implications of the research. These issues have been discussed in earlier chapters.

There is no straightforward answer to the first question. Whilst researchers often set themselves goals to be achieved (or they are set for them by funders or academic supervisors) such as a certain number of interviews or fixed period of observation, the most straightforward answer to the question is that a study is complete when the researcher has gained an understanding of the setting or aspect of social life that they set out to examine. Nonetheless, this response is unsatisfactory because there is a sense in which studies of the social world are invariably incomplete and imperfect. Researchers need to strive for a 'good enough' understanding otherwise they run the risk of never completing the study. For these reasons, Taylor (1991) suggests that a more appropriate question to ask is 'when does fieldwork yield diminishing returns?'. Using a jigsaw puzzle as a metaphor, he suggests that the study nears completion when it becomes apparent how the pieces of the puzzle will come together and it becomes obvious what picture the whole puzzle portrays. At this stage, missing pieces can be identified but the search for them also generates pieces that the researcher is already aware of. What was once strange has become familiar and field notes and interview transcripts become repetitive. Leaving the metaphor aside, staying a while longer helps to confirm hunches and to find better examples of themes identified in the research. At this stage the data collection can become tedious. All experienced researchers can relate to the sense of research fatigue, which includes becoming bored by the data collection process, and physically and emotionally drained. The peculiarities of criminological research, which often expose researchers to situations of danger and distress and uncomfortable settings, can lead to this sense of fatigue taking hold at an early stage. Regular breaks can help to sustain the researcher to ensure that sufficient data are collected but as King (2000) proposes, research projects pursue a natural trajectory; hard work at the outset to win support followed by a core period of productive collaboration which fades towards the end of the study.

The reality is that researchers, whether they are postgraduate students or working on funded research projects, have to work with the constraints and pressures that flow from employers, institutions and/or funders. Deadlines for the submission of theses or reports are set and researchers sometimes have to stop collecting data before they have collected all the pieces of the jigsaw. Perhaps more commonly they are tempted to stay in the field longer than needed. Wax (1971: 104), in a text on fieldwork subtitled 'warnings and advice', confesses to being plagued by an impulse to stay longer than necessary and an irresistible urge to gather more data. The opportunity to conduct an additional interview or to observe a further court case is often seized, even if it is likely to produce data that are repetitious. Qualitative researchers sometimes work under the misapprehension that this adds weight to their conclusions in the same way that a large sample size does for quantitative research. This is, in some respects, ironic because it results in the qualitative researcher gathering more data than they can handle. Back (2002) warns of the dangers of becoming a 'fieldwork junkie' suffering from the 'one more interview syndrome' (paragraph 3.16) in an article focusing on doctoral research.

> Remember it is not the quantity but the quality of what you write about that matters. One of the frightening things about doing a PhD is that at the end of the day it's only possible to include a fraction of the empirical material you have recorded. So don't stay in the research phase longer than necessary.

Back's words of wisdom are also applicable to all forms of qualitative research.

Snow (1980: 101–2) suggests that one of the 'litmus tests' for indicators of what he terms a researcher's 'informational sufficiency' is heightened confidence about their knowledge of their area of study. For novice researchers, and indeed for many experienced ones, feelings of self-doubt can lead to delaying the decision to leave the field. Moreover, if researchers are honest, part of the temptation to stay in the field is because it delays the difficult process of analysing fully the data collected which is necessary to build up an understanding of the social world.

Related to the decision to stop collecting data is the decision of whether to return to the field. King (2000) advises prison researchers to leave one loose end hanging, explicitly or implicitly, to provide an opportunity for going back if need be. However, again, this should only be done if it will enhance the level of understanding, and often limited time and resources will preclude this. Researchers may also return to discuss their analysis of the research data with their research participants. This is explored further in Chapter 8.

CHAPTER SUMMARY AND CONCLUSION

Negotiating access is a continuous and frequently demanding process. Access is rarely negotiated on a single occasion but negotiated and renegotiated during different phases of the research process. As King (2000: 297) argues 'initial access is only the first hurdle. In fact negotiating and renegotiating access takes place on almost a daily basis once the research is underway'. Negotiating access, data collection and analysis are not distinct phases of the research process but significantly overlap (Hammersley and Atkinson, 2007). To this list we can also add the process of disengaging from the field.

Researchers need to be aware that access cannot be taken for granted and it is risky to assume it will be OK. Permission to carry out an investigation must always be sought at an early stage. One of the roles researchers must adopt is one of a salesperson, trying to convince those who are in a position to help of the importance of their research. Equally the researcher must adopt a diplomat role, engaging in explicit discussions or more subtle processes, to facilitate access to the data needed. Access negotiations often do not run smoothly but the good news is that some form of research is usually possible if researchers are willing to be flexible and think imaginatively about other possibilities.

Ultimately, therefore, research comes down to focusing on what is practically accessible. Research is the art of the feasible. (Blaxter et al., 1996: 160)

Exercises

1   Select a contemporary criminal justice issue, for example the use of restorative justice in prisons and occupational culture in community rehabilitation companies. Research what you might need to do to secure formal approval and reflect upon how you might convince gatekeepers to take part.

(Continued)

(Continued)

2   Select a criminal offence which appears to be increasing, for example hate crime or cybercrime. Imagine you are interested in talking to individuals who carry out these types of crime. How might you locate them and convince them to take part?

3   Repeat the exercise above but on this occasion turn your attention to victims of these crimes.

FURTHER READING

- Hammersley, M. and Atkinson, P. (2007) *Ethnography: Principles in Practice*, 3rd edn. London: Routledge.

  Written by two of the leading UK experts on ethnography, this textbook devotes an entire chapter to the issue of access and a further chapter to field relations.

- King, R. and Wincup, E. (eds) (2000) *Doing Research on Crime and Justice*. Oxford: Oxford University Press.

  This edited collection provides an honest account of the research process. The reflexive accounts in Part Four by criminologists at the beginning of their careers are particularly recommended.

- Lee, R. (1993) *Doing Research on Sensitive Topics*. London: Sage.

  Focusing specifically on topics which are politically or socially contentious, this useful guide reflects on the need for sensitivity during access negotiations.

- Shaffir, W. and Stebbins, R. (eds) (1991) *Experiencing Fieldwork: An Insider View of Qualitative Research*. Newbury Park, CA: Sage.

  This book is divided into four sections: getting in, learning the ropes, maintaining relations, and leaving and keeping in touch.

- Hobbs, D. and May, T. (1993) *Interpreting the Field: Accounts of Ethnography*. Oxford: Oxford University Press.

  The chapters by Armstrong, Norris and Fountain are particularly recommended as they explore their experiences of negotiating and sustaining access with football hooligans, police officers and drug dealers.

- In addition PhD theses are a useful source of information on access negotiations. These can be found online via the British Library's e-theses online service.

USING EXISTING QUALITATIVE DATA

In the previous chapter, we explored the challenges of negotiating access to settings – real and virtual – which would permit the generation of qualitative data. In this chapter, we take a different view and argue that there is an abundance of qualitative data which can be readily accessed by criminological researchers with only limited negotiation or none at all. Consequently, these data are ripe for analysis by taught undergraduate and postgraduate students that are often working to very tight timescales with limited resources.

Almost ten years ago, Rod Morgan and Mike Hough (2007: 70) commented that '[t]he great fortune of the British criminologist is that he or she inhabits a domain in which there is more than enough data available for secondary analysis'. This claim remains valid and applies to many other jurisdictions too. For a number of reasons which we will explore shortly, it is now possible to access with relative ease different types of qualitative data, and the variety of data available to researchers is expanding. It is our intention in this chapter to introduce the reader to these multiple forms, reflect upon their value as research data and identify the most pertinent considerations when using existing qualitative data. We hope that this will encourage novice researchers to think more broadly about how to conduct qualitative research whilst encouraging critical reflection about the data they are considering using.

The data which Morgan and Hough (2007) refer to comes in many forms and is produced for different purposes by a wide range of individuals and organisations across the public, private and 'third' (i.e. community and voluntary) sector. Categorising data is always an imperfect exercise but in general terms we can draw a distinction between data which were originally gathered as part of a research project and has been archived for use by qualitative researchers, and data (or more accurately what will become data) which was produced for different purposes in the first instance. The latter might include documents produced to support the administration of justice or to inform the public about crime. This is the focus of the next section. This is often referred to as documentary research but as we will explore shortly the term does not capture fully the plethora of resources which can be transformed into qualitative data. We will return to a discussion of archived data in the second part of the chapter.

USING DOCUMENTS IN CRIMINOLOGICAL RESEARCH

Before progressing further, we should pause for a moment and reflect briefly on what we mean by the term 'document'. Traditionally, documents have been viewed as 'written' texts (see Scott, 1990) which provide insights into both the past and present but given fast-paced technological change we should deploy a more catholic working definition of documents if we are to exploit fully the opportunities available to us as researchers and consider 'audio' and 'video' documents. Debates about what might be included within the category 'documents' are long-standing. For example, Scott (1990) raises the issue of whether printed ephemera such as travel tickets can be included, and similarly questions whether maps or photographs also 'count' as documents. Rather than become distracted, we concern ourselves below with the question 'what resources can be used to produce qualitative data for use in criminological research?'. At this point it is helpful to revisit the discussion of qualitative data in Chapter 1.

The discussion below is not intended to be an exhaustive list of all sources of data available to criminologists. Instead, it attempts to capture the range of possibilities which criminologists have already exploited or could do so with relative ease. It focuses on those which are publicly available, often electronically via the internet. At the same time, it is appreciated that access to many documents which may be of interest to criminologists requires negotiations which can sometimes be lengthy and complex requiring researchers to reassure 'owners' of the documents that they will fulfil the necessary ethical and legal obligations. There are numerous examples of criminological studies which have done this and an example is provided in Box 4.1 in the previous chapter to illustrate the challenges of gaining access to documents which can be used – with permission – for criminological research. It is also recognised that qualitative researchers may ask participants to generate documents (for example, diaries) alongside other methods of data collection or work with participants to produce documents whilst gathering data. For example, a research project on patterns of desistance may include interviewers working with interviewees to construct a timeline of their criminal career or studying experiences of imprisonment might involve asking prisoners to keep a diary.

ARCHIVAL RESEARCH AND HISTORICAL DOCUMENTS

Archives provide opportunities for researchers to make use of documents which Scott (1990: 10) refers to as a 'residue of the past'. These can include personal documents such as diaries or letters or institutional documents such as minutes of meetings or reports. Government documents are housed in the National Archives. Typically, these documents are at least 30 years old but increasingly more recent documents have been released as the UK government moves toward replacing the '30-year rule' (the informal name given to legislation that requires that government documents will be released 30 years after they were created) with a '20-year rule' and makes documents available under the Freedom of Information Act 2000 (discussed in Chapters 3 and 4). These developments form part of a broader global trend to promoting 'open' government with transparent decision-making in order to enhance accountability (see Mulgan, 2014). In addition to the National Archive, there are organisational archives (see for example, the Metropolitan Police Heritage Centre – www.metpolicehistory.co.uk/met-police-heritage-centre.html) or those which house a number of different collections, sometimes hosted by universities. The Archives Hub (www.archiveshub.ac.uk/) is a useful research resource because it provides a comprehensive, although not complete, gateway to thousands of UK archives.

Using archives to obtain secondary data is becoming common place among social scientists for a variety of reasons. Technological developments have made archives more accessible and archiving easier. Contrary to the image of the researcher hunting around dusty basements to find relevant material, many resources are now catalogued using a searchable database. Since documents are now created electronically or can be transformed without difficulty into an electronic format, they can be made easily available to researchers. The same capabilities allow organisations to archive documents in a systematic way routinely, avoiding attempts to create an archive retrospectively. A more challenging task is archiving the vast amount of material produced by organisations and individuals in the digital world on websites and across social media platforms. Described as 'the next generation of archiving' (Moore, 2013), generating a record of such material throws up a vast array of issues. For example, commercial interests may be involved as material can sometimes be hosted on private 'cyberspace', the content is dynamic in nature and subject to change, and ongoing technological developments can lead to earlier versions becoming obsolete.

Material included in archives has often been salvaged from the past but there are important exceptions, most obviously the Mass Observation archive. This contains material dating back to the 1930s which was collected specifically to document everyday life in Britain. The archive holds documents from the original Mass Observation project (from 1937 to the early 1950s) which attempted to create 'an anthropology of ourselves' (Mass Observation, 2016). In 1981, the Mass Observation work was revived as a unique national life writing project about everyday life in Britain, capturing the experiences, thoughts and opinions of everyday people in the twenty-first century. Hundreds of volunteer writers – known as observers – are asked to respond to three 'directives' each year which comprise of open-ended questions on a range of topics; personal, political and historical. As an illustration, the most recent directive (Autumn 2015) asked for observations on fraud and scams, bonfire night and the refugee crisis. In the past, directives have asked for contributions on a range of criminological issues including drugs, domestic violence and serial killers.

Crucially, it must be recognised that deposits within archives are not ordinarily produced for academic research purposes. Consequently, attempts must be made to understand the context in which they were produced, why they were produced and for whom. There are important questions to ask about what is made publicly available and what remains hidden from public view. Used judiciously archives provide fascinating opportunities for criminologists to explore the recent and distant past as described in Box 5.1.

Box 5.1 Using archives for research: Developing a historical criminological perspective on alcohol regulation

Yeomans' (2014) study of alcohol regulation made extensive use of archives to understand public discourse surrounding alcohol consumption and the need for regulation. His starting point is the beginning of the eighteenth century and he chose to capture public discourse in two ways. First, he used press sources which required him to make extensive use of the British Library archives, the archives of major newspapers (for example, *The Times*, *The Guardian/Observer*) and Lexis Nexus for material published since 1985 (an online archive, see Jewkes, 2011 for a discussion of its strengths and limitations). Second, he made use of non-press sources, ranging from material from campaigning and pressure groups connected with the Victorian Temperance Movement through to contemporary public health groups. Collectively, and in conjunction with a study of legal discourse, he argues that rather than understanding current calls to increase alcohol regulation as a response to increased consumption or awareness of harm, they can be viewed as 'hangovers', derived in particular from the Victorian period. This type of work is sometimes referred to as a 'history of the present', using the past to understand the present.

USING ADMINISTRATIVE SOURCES

The machinery of parliament and government produces a wide range of documents which criminologists can draw upon. For example, a criminologist interested in the development of the recently implemented Psychoactive Substance Act 2016 might decide to look at the multiple versions of the Bill which preceded the Act and accompanying explanatory notes, amendment papers, verbatim transcripts of parliamentary debates published in Hansard, briefing papers, committee reports, written evidence and advisory reports published by government-sponsored expert bodies. These, like all documents, might be treated as *resources* or as *topics* (see Scott, 1990). The former refers to using the documents to explore what insights they provide into a particular issue. Used in this way, they often form part of a first step in a qualitative research project. For instance, a researcher interested in courtroom decision-making might begin by looking at relevant documents produced by the Sentencing Council such as sentencing guidelines; information provided to victims; consultation documents and responses; equality impact assessment; minutes of meetings; research publications and corporate reports. These might present an insight into how sentencing should work in theory whilst flagging up concerns about how it might work in practice. This could usefully inform an interview schedule or guide observation. The latter refers to treating documents as social products, examining their form and content to gain an insight into the organisation which produced them. For example, examining a White Paper – which are used by the government to outline future legislative proposals – can be revealing in terms of how they identify the 'problem' which needs to be resolved through legislation and how they select the evidence to draw upon to justify the proposed changes.

Hakim (1983) usefully distinguishes between three types of document. These are routine, regular and special. The first refers to documents which are produced as part of the everyday operations of an organisation; the second describes those produced on an ongoing basis solely for external purposes; whilst the final category depicts those produced on a more *ad hoc* basis. As we have already noted, these documents are now more likely to be easily accessible as part of a commitment to make the work of government bodies more transparent. We illustrate this typology below with reference to one organisation of interest to criminologists: HM Inspectorate of Prisons (HMIP) (see Table 5.1). This is an independent inspectorate tasked with overall scrutiny of conditions for, and treatment of, prisoners and other detainees (for example, those in police custody).

Table 5.1   Types of document published by HM Inspectorate of Prisons

Type of document	Examples
Routine	Annual corporate plans
Regular	Annual reports, inspection reports of individual establishments
Special	Thematic inspection reports, research reports

MEDIA ANALYSIS

There is a long-established tradition of criminologists using media coverage of crime in their empirical work. Indeed, some important theoretical developments in criminology have emerged from this type of research. For example, in the 1970s a series of influential studies analysed news coverage of 'deviant' and 'criminal' acts, alongside other qualitative methods, to explore the social reaction to crime (Cohen, 1972; Hall et al., 1978). This allowed them to consider the role of the media in amplifying deviance and garnering public support for harsh crime control measures. In particular, they focused on the way in which the media created 'folk devils' – subcultural groups (Cohen, 1972) and young black men (Hall et al., 1978) who were defined as threatening and consequently, marginalised and vilified by the public. There is now a significant criminological literature on media and crime (see Jewkes, 2015 and Surette, 2014 for recent additions), and indeed a specialist journal – *Crime Media Culture* – was launched in 2005. We cannot do justice to this important aspect of contemporary criminology here through attempting to summarise the scope of criminological analyses of crime and its control. Instead, we will consider the diversity of media forms which can now be analysed and reflect on approaches that qualitative researchers might take.

In the past criminologists have made use of a range of media forms and most commonly have analysed news coverage of crime stories. A recent example is provided in

Box 5.2 below. In addition to embracing new and emerging social media technologies, which we will consider shortly, criminologists could take stock of long-established media forms and consider which ones have yet to be subject to academic analysis. Jewkes (2011) suggests that relatively little research has been devoted to crime fiction, despite it being one of the most popular literary genres, and ripe for analysis of fictional representations of serious crime in particular. In contrast, research on television representations of crime and criminal justice are plentiful. However, there may still be scope for original research projects. For instance, at the time of writing there are numerous programmes broadcast which attempt to portray the 'realities' of policing which could offer interesting insights into aspects of policing which might be difficult to research such as the operation of custody suites or traffic policing. There is, of course, a need for caution as we do not know the basis on which the material was selected. Nonetheless they can shed light on the image of police officers and policing that senior police managers are happy to convey to the public, for example in terms of integrity, justice and the role of discretion.

Box 5.2   Media constructions of masculinity: A case study of newspaper coverage of male violence

Ellis et al. (2012) chose to focus on media reporting of one high-profile case to shed light on how British newspapers account for male violence. In July 2010, Raoul Moat, a recently released prisoner, shot and seriously injured his former partner and murdered her boyfriend. A day later he shot and blinded a police officer before going on the run until he killed himself. Unsurprisingly this case dominated press coverage providing rich material for Ellis et al. to use. They selected three of the best-selling newspapers (*The Times*, *Daily Mail* and *The Sun*) and chose to focus on identifying narrative themes rather than conducting an in-depth discourse or content analysis (see Chapter 8). Using these three sources they focused on journalistic interpretation (through news articles and opinion pieces) and Moat's self-narrative in the form of his letters to the police (which were subsequently published). Ellis et al. (2012: 18) argue that journalists do not objectively report male violence; rather they utilise existing 'explanatory frameworks which reproduce conservative and traditional models of masculinity'. Moat was portrayed as an isolated man whose anger was directed at areas of his life (for example, the domestic sphere) where he did not live up to the normative expectation of how men should behave.

Media 'texts' can be approached quantitatively and qualitatively. The former involves content analysis, systematically counting and categorising the coverage to make observations such as the types of crime, offenders and victims covered in news stories. This can be compared with other sources of data, for example official crime statistics, to reflect upon the representativeness of media coverage of crime. The latter involves narrative or discourse analysis. This requires researchers to look in detail at the structure of a text and identify patterns within it, for example the repeated use of terms or metaphors. Media coverage is very powerful in shaping public attitudes by stereotyping particular groups of people as deviant or misrepresenting the delivery of criminal justice. Narrative analysis can expose these dominant narratives by deconstructing the text and revealing the underpinning social values and assumptions. This approach looks at the socio-political context in which the media 'text' was produced.

In our media-saturated society, researchers have ready access to a growing number of media forms via the internet. These include traditional forms which can now be accessed electronically, for example newspaper and TV news, as well as content specifically created for the internet. Internet usage is high. In 2014, 38 million adults (82 per cent) accessed the internet every day and 89 per cent of households have some form of internet access (ONS, 2016). As social scientists, we should also be concerned with those who do not use the internet. Data from the ONS surveys suggests this includes those who choose not to, alongside those who are excluded due to cost, disability and lack of skills, with higher levels of non-usage among older people. Individuals can be 'passive' recipients of internet content or actively create it through social media. In recent years, there has been a rapid expansion of social media platforms which provides us with access to a wide range of fascinating insights into both crime and its control, capturing public perceptions more generally but also more specifically the experiences of victims, former offenders and criminal justice professionals. Levels of social media usage are high, especially among young people who cannot recall anything other than living in a digital society but once again we also need to reflect upon the characteristics of those who do not use social media.

Social media has the potential to support research in a number of ways. This includes recruiting participants and disseminating findings, but beyond this, social media platforms can provide data, either making use of discussions which have naturally emerged or through initiating them. Here we focus on the former, and limit our discussion to two forms of social media: blogs and Twitter.

BLOGS

Blogs are effectively a form of self-publishing which emerged in the 1990s. Blogging allows authors to create content without the need for any specialist internet skills. Blogs tend to be relatively short and offer an opportunity for other internet users to add comments. Potentially they can be used to solicit responses by creating a blog specifically for research purposes but here we will focus on the use of existing blogs. Blogs take different forms: they can be used almost as a diary to share experiences publicly or as a vehicle to debate current issues. The writing is often candid, especially if the identity of the blogger is not revealed, although this raises issues about authenticity which we will return to later. Using blogs for research purposes provides ready access to data from across the globe about people's experiences, perceptions and feelings. There are, of course, many limitations to consider and in particular to think about the function of the blog – which may or may not be explicit – and its intended audience. If used as a resource, there are challenges in terms of sampling. For a qualitative research study, the sample need not be representative of a wider population in a statistical sense but it is still important to articulate the reasons for selecting a participant. Consequently, it might be preferable to use blogs alongside other data collection methods. If used as a topic, they can be valid in their own right. For example, there are now a significant number of blogs authored by police officers and it could be revealing to explore the types of issues which police officers focus on, ranging from macro-level concerns about resources and recruitment through to micro-level concerns about uniform and equipment.

TWITTER

Twitter is an online social networking site which describes itself as 'your window to the world'. Established in 2006, its reach is vast. By April 2016, it had reached 313 million active users worldwide (Statista, 2016). Users can choose to simply receive content by following individuals or organisations and/or repeat content produced by others ('retweeting') and/or engage in 'microblogging', i.e. composing 'tweets' with a 140-character limit. Material includes written text but also visual images, polls and hyperlinks. Content is generally public, although individuals can choose to protect their 'tweets' so they can only be seen by those they have granted permission to network with. The most commonly used topics are identified as 'trending'.

Criminologists have begun to experiment with using this form of social media as a research tool. For example, Williams and Burnap (2016) used Twitter as a source of data on cyberhate in the aftermath of a terrorist attack in London in 2013 which involved the attempted beheading of Lee Rigby, a British soldier. Their approach was quantitative, using advanced computational criminology techniques to identify, monitor and trace social reactions to this event in real time. There remains considerable scope to use Twitter as a source of qualitative data. For example, many police forces now have their own accounts which are used for different purposes: to deter potential offenders often in relation to motoring offences; to catch offenders through sharing information about crimes and links to CCTV images; to inform the public about crimes which have been detected; and to issue crime prevention advice, often in relation to burglary. Using these documents as a resource, a researcher could gain interesting insights into the use of social media as a tool of community policing.

THINKING CREATIVELY

We have outlined above the most obvious sources of data but there is scope for thinking creatively about what might potentially constitute research data. Criminologists have not been particularly imaginative in this regard but there are seemingly endless possibilities. For example, as a PhD student volunteering in HMP Pucklechurch (now closed), I was struck by the poetry produced by the female prisoners and the way in which they used it as a vehicle to explore deeply personal issues, including experiences of abuse. With their consent, these poems could have provided rich data on the particular vulnerabilities of women in the criminal justice system either in isolation, or combined with other forms of qualitative data from interviews or with quantitative data gathered via prisoner surveys or routine risk assessments. Chapter 1 includes an example of using creative methods to research desistance from crime.

The example below (Box 5.3) describes one approach to thinking creatively, using autobiographical accounts as the basis of a pilot study for a doctoral research project which also included qualitative interviews. Here they are used to explore individual experiences of establishing a life in a different country following horrific experiences of torture and abuse but we can think of a number of other contexts where autobiographies might be useful to support criminological research. For example, in recent years a number of prisoners have published autobiographies which could provide insights into pathways into and out of offending. Similarly, autobiographies published by women working in the criminal justice or legal system might allow researchers to appreciate the nature and extent of sexism within these organisational structures.

Box 5.3   Using autobiographies: A case study of researching life after genocide

Asquith (2015) chose to use published autobiographies as an initial stage in a study of life after genocide. Using these survivor accounts as a data source, she was able to identify the kinds of narrative constructed by those who had experienced such atrocities. She reflects critically on such sources, recognising that they tell the stories that people want to tell and that others want to hear. In many respects this is no different to other contexts in which life stories are collected (see Plummer, 2001). Linked to this is a recognition of the need to look at what is hidden as much as what is told. For Asquith (2015), what was rarely told was precisely what she was interested in, namely, post-genocide life in the UK. Consequently, this preliminary research served not only to provide an insight into themes relevant for exploring this dimension of the process of surviving but to reaffirm the importance of researching this neglected area.

EVALUATING DOCUMENTS

When discussing the different types of documents available to criminologists we have alluded to some of the methodological issues which surround their use. Crucially documents should not be taken at face value and researchers need to be clear about the purpose(s) for which they are collecting documents. Scott's (1990) four-fold criteria for assessing documentary sources provide a useful framework. These are outlined below. Before exploring them in a little detail it is worth emphasising that they are not distinct stages in assessing the quality of documentary sources, rather, they are interdependent.

1. *Authenticity*: Is the evidence genuine and of unquestionable origin?
2. *Credibility*: Is the evidence free from error and distortion?
3. *Representativeness*: Is the evidence typical of its kind, and, if not, is the extent of its untypicality known?
4. *Meaning*: Is the evidence clear and comprehensible? (reproduced from Scott, 1990: 6)

Scott's criteria are broad and designed to apply to all documents. Consequently, it is worth reflecting upon their particular meaning when documents are used for qualitative research. To illustrate, I will use one example of a collection of documents I stumbled across when completing fieldwork for my PhD on women's experiences of awaiting trial.

Part of the fieldwork for my PhD involved observing everyday life in three bail and probation hostels. Near the beginning of the fieldwork stage I was offered the opportunity to sleep over as staff did to allow me to observe what happened at curfew time (11pm) and early morning. Having retired to bed and unable to sleep, I found myself reading a collection of 'day books' which were stored in the room I had been allocated. They were from decades earlier when the hostel had been run by a warden and his wife who lived on the premises in their own private quarters. They offered an institutional record into the most significant events on the day as noted by staff, a practice which was still continuing in the hostel. I briefly contemplated using them as part of my PhD but the data they could provide – however fascinating – did not help me to answer my research questions so I quickly abandoned the idea. They could, of course, have been used to develop an alternative project as it is not unusual for documentary research to formulate a research question around the available data. Had I pursued this option, applying Scott's (1990) criteria would have been an essential first stage of the research process. I had no reason to think that the 'day books' were anything other than authentic, particularly as they were found in the hostel itself. Examining the credibility of the 'day books' involves asking questions about their construction, for example why were particular events recorded and not others? The 'day books' were clearly not representative: they covered a particular time period, possibly with some gaps, which may have been unique in some way. Finally, as institutional records they used terms which may be unfamiliar to 'lay' readers and also shorthand forms as they were not expected to function as a detailed log of daily life in a hostel. This has implications for extracting their meaning. Taken together – and with careful consideration of the context in which the documents were produced and their intended function – they could form the basis of a fascinating study of the social control of women who appear before the courts. Coincidentally at the time another PhD student who was also conducting research in a bail and probation hostel for women was able to locate a range of historical documents in the hostel's attic and used them alongside interview and observational data to write up her thesis on the disciplining of 'wayward' women in semi-penal institutions from the nineteenth century to the present day (Barton, 2004).

For pedagogical purposes, we have examined each of the criterion in turn but Scott (1990) argues that they should not be applied in a rigid and formalistic way and evaluating sources should become intuitive for the experienced research professional as they become experts in documentary research. An evaluative approach needs to be a feature of the entire research process as familiarity with the documents develops rather than a one-off check at the outset. Similarly, skills are needed when researchers make use of archived research data.

ARCHIVED QUALITATIVE DATA

In 1994, Qualidata was established by the Economic and Social Research Council (ESRC) as a resource centre to encourage secondary qualitative data analysis. Whilst there is no agreed upon definition of this form of analysis, a useful working version is reproduced below.

> Secondary analysis involves the use of existing data, collected for the purposes of a prior study, in order to pursue a research interest which is distinct from that of the original work. (Heaton, 1998: 1)

In practice this might mean posing a new research question or looking again at the original research question through a new theoretical lens. Secondary analysis can be undertaken by researchers who originally collected the data, thus blurring the boundary between 'primary' and 'secondary' research, or it may be carried out by independent researchers. Depositing data in an archive makes the latter possible.

Archiving has produced a cultural shift within the research community, particularly among those wishing to secure research council funding. Those wishing to collect new data must consider whether appropriate secondary data exists to justify the resource implications of additional data collection. If successful, research grant holders are expected to handover 'their' data for preservation in a data archive rather than the previous recommended practice of destroying data. The default position of sharing data – with few exceptions – is justified on economic and moral grounds: data gathered via publicly funded research is a *public* rather than *private* good and maximising its full use increases its benefit to society (Morrow et al., 2014).

Since 2003 qualitative datasets have been stored at the UK Data Archive, a government funded digital repository hosted at the University of Essex for both quantitative and qualitative data. It is an expansive resource with almost 7000 datasets deposited by researchers working in a range of social science disciplines. Datasets are divided into broad categories, including 'qualitative/mixed methods' datasets. Qualitative data includes that gathered via 'in-depth interviews, diaries, anthropological field notes and the complete answers to survey questions' (UK Data Archive, 2016). Some indication of its coverage of criminological issues is given below in Table 5.2 which includes the 'results' of searches of the 915 'qualitative/mixed methods' datasets in the archive using key criminological terms.

Table 5.2 Archived criminological research data

Key word(s)	Number of relevant datasets
Crime	84
Police	42
Violence	34
Criminal justice	18
Victim	17
Prisons	15
Offending	13
Probation	11
Criminal court	10

Source: UK Data Archive, 21 August 2016

A number of pragmatic considerations underpinned the development of the qualitative data archive. The first relates to the costs of conducting primary research. When the full costs of gathering qualitative data are considered, it becomes apparent that even small-scale qualitative studies can be expensive. Re-using data can offer a cheaper alternative but it is important not to gloss over the financial costs of archiving data. The second refers to the challenges of conducting qualitative research. As we discussed in Chapter 4, negotiating access to research sites and research participants can be difficult, time-consuming and with no guarantee of success. The final consideration relates to its potential to enhance research training. Whilst primarily a research resource, the archive also makes available datasets which can be used for student education purposes (see Corti and Bishop, 2005). This circumvents the ethical dilemma of collecting data which is used solely for skills development and/or to obtain a qualification, and is not designed to have 'impact' (see Chapter 2 for a discussion of this concept). A series of technological developments have supported the setting up and expansion of the qualitative data archive, particularly rapid developments within digital technology to facilitate archiving and sharing large amounts of research data. Researchers are now likely to work with data in an electronic form, even if it was originally gathered 'by hand' (for example, notes of observations in the 'field' as discussed in Chapter 7). The data analysis process is explored in more detail in Chapter 8 but a key development here is the growth of dedicated software packages to assist with data management.

As we will explore shortly, there has been little enthusiasm for secondary qualitative data analysis within the academic community, and there are only isolated examples of criminologists conducting this type of research (one is included in Box 5.4). The expansion of the qualitative data archive appears to be a consequence of ESRC requirements to deposit data rather than a function of demand although there is limited information available on data usage to support this view (see Parry and Mauthner, 2005). Whilst secondary analysis is common place and accepted practice for quantitative data, it is rarely used for qualitative data. The typical response has been one of ambivalence, but others have argued vehemently against this practice.

Box 5.4   Revisiting a classic criminological study: *Psychological Survival* (Cohen and Taylor, 1972) three decades on

Cohen and Taylor's (1972) study is well-known amongst criminologists, both for its contribution to the sociology of imprisonment and the battles faced by the authors when seeking to publish their findings (see Chapter 2). The two authors were invited to teach long-term prisoners at HMP Durham which housed some of the most notorious and violent prisoners. Despite its title, the work is a critique of the psychological understanding of crime and its control which dominated criminology at the time and privileged the collection of quantitative data. Cohen and Taylor (1972: 201) are keen advocates of qualitative approaches, stating that their book is 'not primarily addressed to those interested in the niceties of the social scientific method', and arguing that attempts to gather data via questionnaire would have been futile. Instead they chose to conduct unstructured group interviews (sometimes sharing feedback with prisoners), analyse examples of the prisoners' writings and gather data through discussion of literature on subjects relating to imprisonment and the men's offending. They also viewed 'writing up' as a research method, allowing prisoners to comment on drafts.

Fielding and Fielding (2000) chose to revisit this classic study. Their article suggests that using the secondary qualitative data can tell us a great deal about the messy realities of conducting criminological research but are keen to emphasise that there is an opportunity for more than methodological reflection. Fielding and Fielding (2000: 680) suggest that the richness of the original data could support 'further analytic burdens' despite acknowledging some of the limitations of the data, particularly since it was archived retrospectively. They argue that the role of secondary data analysis is not to check the analysis of the original researchers but to focus on the under-explored aspects of the data, thus offering a way to exploit more fully research on sensitive topics and hard-to-reach populations (see the discussion of ethical dilemmas later in the chapter).

Since the later 1990s, there has been a steady stream of articles published which have raised awareness of the numerous issues – methodological, ethical, professional, practical and legal – which arise from secondary qualitative data analysis. Space precludes a detailed examination of all these issues so instead we will focus on those which have been the source of most debate, namely ethical and epistemological considerations. Whilst professional issues have received rather less attention, we will explore them briefly as they are particularly pertinent to readers of this book; namely those at the beginning of their researcher careers.

ETHICAL DILEMMAS

The expansion of qualitative data archives has taken place alongside greater scrutiny of the ethics of social science research (see Chapter 3). Unsurprisingly this has provoked a series of discussions about the particular issues which are raised when re-using qualitative data, challenging the assumption that few ethical issues confront those who use existing research data, and raising questions over whether the ethical complexities are downplayed by current regulatory frameworks (Morrow et al., 2014). Ethical considerations concern both responsibilities to research participants and the original researcher(s), although the focus of attention has been largely on the former. In some respects, re-using data fulfils the ethical obligation to participants to ensure their data are used fully. This is not simply about ensuring value for money given the costs associated with conducting qualitative research but also relates to the emotional investment made by participants when telling their stories during interviews or when researchers are granted the privilege of being able to observe the personal lives of research participants. Re-visiting existing data also protects individuals and organisations from repeated requests for research access. On the other hand, secondary qualitative data analysis brings to the fore the issues of anonymity (and the related issues of confidentiality) and informed consent. The former relates to whether sufficient contextual information can be given about the research project without exposing the identities of the research participants. This could be a particular issue if the research participants are distinctive in some way, for example by virtue of their professional role. The latter refers to whether research participants are fully aware when they agree to participate in a study that their data may be used again without them knowing by who and for what purpose (see Grinyer, 2009; Parry and Mauthner, 2004).

The methodological literature also raises the issue of misinterpretation. This is problematic in a number of respects as it implies there is a 'correct' interpretation of the data. There is a risk that not being 'there' compromises analysis of the data leading supporters of re-using qualitative data to argue for the archiving of contextual material to facilitate meaningful data analysis, 'not to recreate the context of the original project, but rather to recontextualise the production of new data' (Bishop, 2007). Equally it can be argued that 'distance', and consequently the lack of immoveable ideas about the data, can be advantageous. The debate usefully raises the possibility of tensions and conflict between the original researcher(s) and those re-using the data, and the importance of establishing a relationship based upon mutual respect and collaboration between parties where feasible (see Morrow et al., 2014).

We can therefore conclude that re-using qualitative data accentuates some of the ethical issues which are already present when conducting qualitative research. Consequently, proposals to re-use such data need to be subject to close ethical scrutiny and those depositing data need to be alert to future ethical issues when seeking initial ethical approval – via research of ethical approval processes and 'in the field' – and also when depositing their research data.

EPISTEMOLOGICAL AND PROFESSIONAL ISSUES

A discussion of epistemological issues has also been prominent in the debates. Mauthner et al. (1998) argue that the lack of a relationship between the original dataset and the secondary analyst is incompatible with the interpretive and reflexive epistemological approach which underpins qualitative research. Whilst this is undoubtedly problematic, others have treated this as a practical issue and have argued that taking steps such as archiving supporting material to provide context to the data (for example, the original research proposal or minutes of research meetings) and contacting the original researcher(s) can bridge the gap between data and analyst. Whether this can be fully realised in practice remains a moot point and in this respect it is worth noting that once qualitative research moves beyond the 'one researcher' model, researchers will often find themselves working with data that they have not collected.

In many respects, re-using data collected by others sits awkwardly with the prevailing culture in academia. Academic careers are established by becoming an 'expert' on a particular subject and conducting original research on it. Originality is a contested concept but a requirement to produce 'original' research is typically included in the learning outcomes for a PhD. When students have worked in collaboration with others (for example, when a PhD is linked to a research project they have worked on as a paid researcher) they need to demonstrate clearly what is their 'own' work. These problems are not insurmountable, and there is an established tradition of conducting doctoral studies using secondary analysis of quantitative data (for example, Lightowlers' (2011) exploration of the links between alcohol and crime using the Offending, Crime and Justice Survey).

There are important differences between secondary quantitative and qualitative data analysis. First, it is likely that quantitative data have not been gathered by other academics, thus avoiding the potential for professional overlap, and that akin to the oral history archive it has been collected with a key objective to facilitate secondary analysis. Second, it is not feasible for a sole researcher to produce from scratch with minimal resources a large dataset. Finally, arguably a key motivation for conducting qualitative research is the opportunity to gather data 'from the horse's mouth' so re-using data might appear as a poor substitute, not least because it does not permit novice researchers the opportunity to develop their qualitative data collection skills.

The debate between proponents of archiving qualitative data and those who question whether secondary analysis of qualitative data is tenable has become polarised (see Parry and Mauthner, 2005), which has detracted from informed debate about the advantages and disadvantages of secondary qualitative data analysis, and deterred researchers from seizing the opportunities offered by archived qualitative data. Like all research methodologies, secondary qualitative data analysis has to be used judiciously, with researchers carefully reflecting upon the quality of the available data and metadata and the degree of fit between the available data and the research question(s) posed. In time, it may become more common place. The latest ESRC strategic plan (2015) does not make explicit reference to archived qualitative data but includes '[c]reating and maximising data infrastructure for research' (ESRC, 2015) as one of its four priorities. A focus on quantitative data is implicit in the discussion, for example exploiting opportunities to create 'big data' through linking datasets at a national and international level but the ESRC's call for projects under its 'Secondary Data Analysis Initiative' includes qualitative datasets among the list of data it wishes to encourage re-use of.

CHAPTER SUMMARY AND CONCLUSION

In this chapter we have encouraged critical reflection on the wide range of resources already open to criminologists which in some instances require little more than opening up a laptop and connecting to the internet. We have explored how to use existing sources as data to help us understand both the past and the present and elucidate on a range of topics from criminal justice policy-making to public understanding of crime. This needs to be coupled with a deliberation of the strengths and weaknesses of these sources, and whether they can be used alongside or in conjunction with other methods. We have also considered how increasingly we have access to data collected by others and whether this under-used research can play a role in criminological research at a time when funding is limited. This form of research is more controversial and there appears to be little appetite among criminologists to use it.

Exercises

1   Select ONE of the following topics. Reflect upon what existing data might be useful
    to enable you to research ONE aspect of it. Is there data of sufficient quantity and
    quality to enable you to answer your research question?

    • Drug use in prisons
    • Public attitudes to sentencing
    • The changing nature of policing

2   Go to the UK Data Archive (www.data-archive.ac.uk/). Select a QUALITATIVE
    study of interest to criminologists. You can do this by searching for key terms
    and then refining your search further by selecting from the different types of data
    available. What do you think the main challenges would be if you decided to
    re-analyse the data? How might you overcome them?

3   Consider the advantages and disadvantages of collecting new data if you wished
    to repeat a similar study to that selected for Exercise 2.

FURTHER READING

• Corti, L., Van den Eynden, V., Bishop, L. and Woollard, M. (2014) *Managing
  and Sharing Research Data: A Guide to Good Practice*. London: Sage.

  This book, written by experts from the UK Data Archive, provides practical advice for
  researchers on how to develop the essential data management skills for a changing
  research environment.

• Fielding, N. and Fielding, J. (2000) 'Resistance and adaptation to criminal identity:
  Using secondary analysis to evaluate classic studies of crime and deviance', *Sociology*,
  34(4): 671–689.

  This article reflects upon the author's experience of re-using data from a classic
  criminological study of long-term imprisonment. It considers both alternative conceptualisations of the data gathered and methodological issues.

• Hammersley, M. and Atkinson, P. (2007) *Ethnography: Principles in Practice*,
  3rd edn. London: Routledge.

  Hammersley and Atkinson devote a chapter to using documents and other artefacts,
  real and virtual within ethnographic research projects.

• Prior, L. (2003) *Using Documents in Social Research*. London: Sage.

  This offers a concise and theoretically informed introduction to how to use a wide range
  of documents in social science research.

• Scott, J. (1990) *A Matter of Record: Using Documents in Social Research*.
  Cambridge: Polity.

  This is the most authoritative text on documentary research. It elaborates in some detail
  on Scott's criteria for evaluating documents and explores the range of documents available to social scientists.

INTERVIEWS AND FOCUS GROUPS

This chapter explores the use of interviews which are arguably the method of choice of many qualitative researchers researching criminological topics. Whilst referred to as a method, Arksey and Knight (1999: 3) propose it is more helpful to view interviews as 'a family of research approaches that have only one thing in common – a conversation between two people in which one person has the role of researcher'. At the same time, we will reflect upon different types of qualitative interviews and their fit with particular theoretical traditions. Much of this chapter has a practical focus since novice researchers are drawn to this method, often because they appear to be deceptively simple to conduct, drawing on the skills that people already have as conversations form part of everyday life. Despite their apparent simplicity, the use of interviews within social science research has sparked considerable debate, and we consider these in the context of criminological research. The chapter also considers the distinct role of focus groups in criminological research.

THEORISING THE QUALITATIVE INTERVIEW

Using interviews is not peculiar to the qualitative tradition. There are multiple criminological examples which have used interviews to generate quantitative data. The most obvious example is the Crime Survey for England and Wales (see Chapter 1). We note here two important features of interviews when used in quantitative research. The first is that the interview schedule used has a rigid structure. Each question needs to be asked in exactly the same way and in the same order. No additional questions are permitted. The second is that the data gathered should be easily quantified, typically using closed questions or open questions, which produces data which can then be assigned to particular categories and quantified. Box 6.1 provides an illustration of both types of questions and illustrates how using both open and closed questions to gather data on the same issue leads to different responses.

Box 6.1   Asking questions: Open and closed variants

In a neighbourhood study of fear of crime, Noaks (1988) asked residents during a door step interview about their image of crime in their community. This was achieved by asking an open-ended question: what kinds of crime are committed around here? The framing of the question allowed them to volunteer responses without prompting from the interviewer. They were then read a list of questions and asked if this category of crime was a problem in their area. The list consisted of burglary, vandalism, car theft, assault, robbery, sex crimes, drug use, teenage nuisance and rowdiness. The subsequent analysis was able to distinguish those crimes that were volunteered and those that were prompted. Vandalism was the most commonly cited crime (60% volunteered and 29% prompted). Burglary ranked second with 56% volunteered and 26% prompted. Certain crimes were mainly mentioned once the probing question was used. This applied to drug use (2% volunteered and 14% prompted) and robbery (3% volunteered and 14% prompted). These crimes could not be said to be in the forefront of residents' minds as contributing to the crime problem in their area.

From the perspective of qualitative researchers, the structured interview stifles the interaction and this compromises the quality of the data generated. In contrast to structured interviews, qualitative interviews have a more fluid structure, ranging from little more than an opening question (unstructured interviews) through to those which have either a series of questions or topics to cover (semi-structured interviews). There is no requirement to ask each question in the same way or in the same order, or even ask the same set of questions. Qualitative interviews allow for a different form of input from the person being interviewed, actively encouraging participants to share their experiences on issues which are important to them which may not have been on the radar of the interviewers. These types of interviews generate different types of data in contrast to structured interviews; that which is arguably richer but which can be challenging to analyse (see Chapter 8). The choice of interview method also has implications for the types of conclusions which can be reached given that qualitative interviews are not normally conducted with representative samples. Instead non-probability sampling techniques are often used to select informants of interest, for example based upon their position, expertise or views.

We will shortly examine different types of qualitative interview but first need to reflect upon the apparent strengths of qualitative interviews and the contexts in which they might be used appropriately. In so doing we will hint at some of the potential weaknesses and these are emphasised in Box 6.2 as a checklist of considerations. Qualitative interviews are best suited to projects which aim to understand the perspectives of interviewees and what is important to them (Arksey and Knight, 1999: 34) rather than focus on the collection of factual information. They tend to be informal in style, creating a suitable environment to co-produce knowledge (Mason, 2002) through reflexive rather than standardised interviewing (Hammersley and Atkinson, 2007). Qualitative interviews allow a dialogue to be established between the interviewer and the interviewee so the latter can tell their story in a way which allows nuances to be captured (Arksey and Knight, 1999: 34). Their emphasis is on flexibility of approach rather than rigidly adhering to an interview schedule which cannot be altered. Qualitative interviews are particularly appropriate when covering sensitive or personal issues or wishing to elicit privileged information from interviewees. However, they are not the only means of conducting these types of research projects. For example, there are many examples of conducting structured interviews on sensitive topics such as offending, drug use or victimisation (for example, the Crime Survey for England and Wales adopts this approach). What qualitative interviews offer is an opportunity to explore these issues in-depth, capturing opinions, feelings, emotions and experiences.

Box 6.2   Appraising the qualitative interview: Key considerations

- Is breadth needed or depth? Qualitative interview studies are better suited to the latter
- How much time and budget is available? Qualitative interviewing is expensive, particularly if the interviewer has to travel some distance to conduct interviews and/or if interviews are recorded and need to be transcribed
- How important is it to ask the same questions in the same way in the same order? Qualitative researchers tend not to do this and instead use a range of strategies to elicit more data (see Box 6.6) and follow the natural course of the 'conversation'
- What skills and qualities do you have? Qualitative interviewing requires excellent communication skills, sensitivity, a non-judgemental approach, flexibility and confidence
- What skills and abilities do your interviewees have? Interviewees do not need to be highly articulate, although it is easier to conduct interviews if they are

---

Feminists have made important contributions to theorising the qualitative interview. As the feminist movement began to re-emerge in the 1960s those scholars involved with empirical research sought to question accepted wisdom on the research relationship. Feminists have sought alternatives to the objectification of the subject as represented in positivist approaches thereby opening the way for greater use of qualitative methods (Oakley, 1981). In terms of the interview, the influence of feminism has seen a preference for semi- and unstructured approaches which allow the interviewee greater scope in making an input. They argue that an interview based on closed questions with a rigid structure overwhelmingly serves the interests of the interviewer. The qualitative approach gives more scope for the interviewee to set their own agenda and typically provides a more in-depth response to questions posed. This is not to naively suggest that feminists reject quantitative methods. Some important work has been done on how feminist ideologies can be brought to bear on quantitative approaches. Kelly et al. (1991) emphasise that quantitative methods can be important in identifying the nature and extent of social problems (for example, violence against women and children).

We have noted already that the main purpose of qualitative interviewing is not to elicit 'facts' but to construct knowledge about the social world interviewees inhabit with an emphasis on interpretive understanding (see Mason, 2002). Those who use qualitative interviewing techniques will need to use their subjective judgement about the data they subsequently produce. Since the researcher is integral to helping the interviewee tell their story, it is vital to reflect upon how their individual characteristics may have influenced the encounter. For example, Belur (2014) reflects upon using interviews to research policing in conflict zones and concludes that her role as an outside-insider (a former high-ranking police officer) was more influential than her gender, age and ethnicity. Similarly deciding whether an interviewee is providing a full and accurate account is a subjective judgement on the part of the interviewer (O'Connell Davidson and Layder, 1993). For qualitative researchers, the notion of accuracy is complex because the focus is on individual experiences and understandings rather than verifiable facts. Consequently, the question 'is the interviewee telling the "truth"?' has become the 'elephant in the room'. It is an important consideration because very occasionally an interviewee might decide to deliberately mislead an interviewer. Denscombe (2014) outlines a number of strategies to ensure the validity of interview data, both quantitative and qualitative. He suggests checking the data with another source, checking the transcript with the informant, checking the plausibility of the data and looking for themes across a range of transcripts. Whilst this is sensible advice in some respect, there is a danger that it misrepresents the nature of qualitative data (see Chapter 1).

TYPES OF QUALITATIVE INTERVIEW

Within the broad category of qualitative interviews are a number of different approaches to generating qualitative data, and we consider both semi-structured and unstructured approaches below. Structured interviews comprising of open-ended questions are sometimes inappropriately described as qualitative interviews because they produce qualitative data (Mason, 2002). Semi-structured and unstructured interviews are not mutually exclusive categories and different approaches can be deployed within the context of one interview. For example, a researcher interviewing a criminal justice professional might provide them with the opportunity to talk at some length about their career to provide context for the more specific questions which follow later. They may also ask a series of closed questions to elicit demographic information and background detail about their educational and professional qualifications. It has been suggested that conceptualising interview types on a continuum is more helpful (Mason, 2002) although we use the categories here for pedagogical purposes. We begin with semi-structured interviews which are the favoured method among qualitative criminological researchers.

SEMI-STRUCTURED INTERVIEWS

Semi-structured interviews offer an opportunity for dialogue and exchange between the interviewer and interviewee. They are based around a topic guide or interview schedule. The former is a list of issues which need to be covered in the interview whilst the latter is a list of questions which the interviewer expects to cover. The semi-structured interview provides opportunities to probe using follow-up questions and other strategies and therefore elicits more in-depth data. There is flexibility in the order in which the questions are asked and the interviewer is free to deviate from the initial structure, following the natural progression of the conversation if, for example, the interviewee begins to talk about an issue which is covered towards the end of the topic guide or interview schedule. Active listening is at the core of this approach; thinking about what the interviewer has said in order to respond appropriately, for example by asking a follow-up question to elicit more detail or selecting another question from the interview schedule (see Box 6.6).

UNSTRUCTURED INTERVIEWS

The term 'unstructured' interview is used here because it has currency in the methodological literature but it is important to be aware of its limitations. For Mason (2002: 62), the term is a misnomer because no interview can be completely lacking in any form of structure. As Denscombe (2010: 175) describes, the role of the researcher in unstructured interviews 'is to be as unobtrusive as possible', introducing a theme or topic to encourage the interviewee to begin talking and then encouraging them to continue doing so. The interviewer has a particular aim in mind but does not seek to constrain the 'conversation' by imposing a structure on it; instead preferring to give the interviewee the freedom to talk and set the agenda. Advocates of this approach would see this as contributing to the richness of the data gathered. The data will be even richer if interviews are conducted over several sessions. Establishing rapport (an issue we will return to later in the chapter) is essential to encourage the interviewee to 'open up', particularly if they are being asked to recount personal experiences.

Whether unstructured interviews can yield useful data is a source of debate among social science researchers. Advocates of this approach (see for example, Hollway and Jefferson, 2008 whose work is described in Box 1.2) recognise the additional value to be gained from allowing individuals to structure their own narratives. In contrast, sceptics raise concerns about unstructured interviews. In their textbook on interviewing, Arksey and Knight (1999: 82) suggest that these types of interview result in 'a mass of incompatible data ... which can leave the researcher wondering whether other informants would have endorsed or rejected points that some made but which [they] themselves did not spontaneously volunteer'. They can certainly be challenging to analyse but that can be mitigated by close attention to analytic strategy (see Chapter 8). The second point made by Arksey and Knight (1999) applies in some respects to semi-structured interviews since interviewers are encouraged to ask additional questions. If universal responses to particular questions are required then qualitative interviewing is not the best approach.

So far we have categorised interviews in terms of structure but more descriptive terms are sometimes used which characterise the type of approach. We turn our attention to these in the remainder of this section of the chapter.

RETROSPECTIVE INTERVIEWS

The term retrospective is used here to refer to those interviews which focus on the past. It includes those which centre on the life of the individual, often referred to as biographical or life history interviews, but also those which aim to construct the past through the accounts of individuals who, for example, lived in a community or worked in an organisation. Box 6.3 provides a criminological example of the latter.

Box 6.3   Researching police culture: Using oral history to document change

Cockcroft (1999, 2012) adopted an oral history approach in his work with former Metropolitan police officers. The research sought to explore their experiences of how the police culture had shifted over time. The sample consisted of 26 officers who had joined the force between 1930 and 1960. In eliciting oral histories from such individuals he sought to go beyond the official accounts represented in force documentation. He hoped that as former officers they would be more prepared to be open and revealing in their accounts. He used semi-structured face-to-face interviews, gathering the sample through snowballing techniques (i.e. asking participants to recommend others who might be prepared to be interviewed). Using this approach, Cockcroft (1999: 133) was able to collect detailed and revealing accounts as illustrated below.

> You knew full well ... you had to stretch the evidence a bit. To get a conviction you could rely a hundred percent on whatever you said would be backed up by your fellow officer. It didn't matter who it was. You sort of had a ... you could rely on one another but the thing was you never, ever got an innocent man down. If you knew that person was guilty you did anything you could to make sure that he was convicted ... but you never, ever stretched it a bit to get an innocent man in the dock.

> I think anyone who's a decent person and has worked in the CID ... especially at that time ... can't look back without regretting a lot of the stuff they've done ... a lot of it was wrong but we were young and we thought what we were doing was right.

Goodey (2000) highlights the potential value of the biographical method for qualitative studies in criminology and criminal justice. She acknowledges that historically the method has been relatively under used by criminologists, even though Clifford Shaw, one of the founders of the Chicago school, incorporated accounts written by boys on parole into his 1920s study of juvenile delinquency (Shaw, 1930). She recognises the scepticism which surrounds an individualised focus to criminological research yet makes a convincing case for the manner in which life story accounts of criminal acts can be informative. Carlen's (1985) book entitled *Criminal Women* and Campbell's (1984) *Girls in the Gang* both provide important examples of the biographical approach being deployed by criminologists. Carlen's text incorporates detailed accounts of four female offenders and their related experiences with the criminal justice process. Campbell's work also reflects on the female experience focusing on young female members of New York gangs in the early 1980s.

It is important to reflect carefully on the data retrospective interviews will yield. When individuals are being asked to give retrospective accounts of events which occurred some time ago the passage of time means different accounts of events will be produced to those which would have been provided in a series of contemporary interviews. Memories can be unreliable and hindsight influences people's construction of the past.

EMBRACING TECHNOLOGY: TELEPHONE AND ONLINE INTERVIEWS

Another way of categorising interviews is to refer to the means by which the interaction will be facilitated. In the past most interviews have been conducted face-to-face and this approach has come to be understood as the 'gold standard', relegating other forms of interviewing to second best and only to be used when face-to-face interviews are not possible (Deakin and Wakefield, 2014). This glosses over the unique strengths of alternative forms of interviewing, which we will explore here, noting that there may be valid methodological reasons for choosing them rather than doing so solely for practical reasons, for example to save time and money. The majority of interviews are still conducted face-to-face but technology – new and not-so-new – provides scope to carry out interviews by telephone (see Box 6.4) or through differing means of internet communication. We focus on the latter below as the most recent offering.

Box 6.4   Interviewing by telephone: An acceptable method for gathering qualitative data?

Historically telephone interviews were used to conduct structured interviews, although there was some initial scepticism because telephone ownership was confined to the most affluent members of society. This is now less of an issue since the vast majority of people have access to a phone (93 per cent according to Ofcom [2016] data for January to March 2016). Alongside wide ownership, advances in technology now allow calls to be recorded, should the interviewer agree, so that transcripts can be produced as for recorded face-to-face interviews.

The relative cost-effectiveness of such methods has been highlighted as a distinct advantage. It reduces the amount of time spent travelling to conduct interviews and the associated costs. It opens up the possibility of interviewing individuals based some distance away from the interviewer, perhaps in another country (although there are time differences to consider here and the cost of international calls). It is possible that some people might be more willing to agree to a telephone interview, for example because they perceive it to take less time, it is more convenient for them or appears less intimidating than meeting with a stranger face-to-face.

These advantages need to be weighed against possible disadvantages. A key one here relates to encouraging full responses. Arksey and Knight (1999) draw attention to

(Continued)

(Continued)

the challenges of eliciting full responses, noting that individuals may be distracted and will tend to offer less in-depth answers. Conversely proponents of telephone interviews have argued that there may be a positive advantage in having a lack of visual contact when asking about sensitive issues. Interviewees may feel able to answer more honestly because they feel less exposed.

The literature on telephone interviewing (see for example, Bourque and Fielder, 2002; Lavrakas, 1993) focuses on their role in survey research, where they might be best suited. Nonetheless telephone interviews can play a role within qualitative criminological research projects.

The internet has opened up new modes of communication, facilitated by widespread internet access (see Chapter 5). It opens up an inexpensive way of interviewing individuals, across the globe if necessary. Accompanying such innovations is a growing body of literature on email interviews (see for example, Burns, 2010) and online audio and video interviews (see for example, O'Connor et al., 2008 on the latter) but to date there has been limited empirical testing of the impact of using different techniques within the same research project or reflexive accounts of using internet-based interviewing (Deakin and Wakefield, 2014). Nonetheless the discussions which have taken place have usefully drawn attention to the main differences between online and face-to-face interviewing, which we will now explore. This will highlight the relative strengths and weaknesses of online interviewing. It is worth emphasising that these approaches to conducting qualitative research remain 'work in progress'.

Online interviewing can be both asynchronous and synchronous (Deakin and Wakefield, 2014). The first form, sometimes referred to as e-interviews, facilitates interaction but is punctuated by delays whilst an individual types their response. This can be advantageous. It naturally creates space for both parties to reflect upon what has been said without the sense of awkwardness which might be felt if there was a long pause in a face-to-face interaction. It automatically produces a transcript so that there is no delay in commencing analysis. It allows interviews to take place over a protracted period of time although this can be problematic too, for example should the interviewee decide not to continue. A key concern is that the interview is a disembodied one. There is no context as the interviewer and interviewee cannot see each other or where they are and it is not possible to pick up on the non-verbal cues which help to facilitate discussion. Consequently, the richness of the data might be compromised, although the points made in Box 6.4 about the potential advantages of using telephone interviewing to research sensitive topics apply here. Accessibility is an important consideration too. This form of interview might exclude those who lack the appropriate level of written skills but conversely might include those with a disability which precludes them participating in a face-to-face interview.

Some of the disadvantages identified above can be overcome through synchronous online interviewing. This allows individuals to 'meet' in virtual space using software packages such as Skype. The use of video – which may be off-putting to some interviewees – recreates an interaction which is more akin to the face-to-face interview. Those considering this form of online interviewing are strongly advised to read Deakin and Wakefield (2014) who reflect carefully on their experiences of conducting Skype interviews for their doctoral research projects. They discuss the more obvious issues, for example logistical considerations, but crucially they identify the need for qualitative researchers to reflect upon how technological developments might encourage researchers to change our assumptions about interviewing and the value attached to face-to-face encounters.

JOINT OR GROUP INTERVIEWS

For the most part qualitative interviews are conducted on a one-to-one basis but there are exceptions. For example, if I reflect on my own experiences of interviewing I can recall interviews at which two people have been present. The first time was when I was researching women awaiting trial for my doctoral research. Two women agreed to be interviewed but only with the proviso that they could do it as a pair. One was due to leave later that day and they were keen to spend the last few hours together. They also implied that they would find being interviewed on their own quite daunting and preferred to have 'safety in numbers'. On other occasions, I have had to interview pairs of practitioners because the person being interviewed thought it would be a good idea to invite another person along.

In many respects interviewing more than one person at once is far from ideal. Arksey and Knight (1999) explore this neglected research issue in some depth. They recognise both the practical and methodological benefits of joint interviews if planned (the examples provided above refer to unplanned interviews). On a practical level, they suggest it can be easier to foster the atmosphere needed to make interviewees feel at ease but there is a risk that one interviewee may dominate and it might be difficult for the interviewer to listen attentively to two interviewees. They express particular caution about the use of joint interviews for sensitive topics or where there is a risk of provoking friction. Despite these potential problems, joint interviews have the potential to produce rich data by offering two accounts (which may or may not produce a coherent joint account) and can offer an insight into a relationship through observation of verbal and non-verbal forms of communication.

There are some occasions when it might be particularly appropriate to conduct joint or group interviews. For example, if a criminological researcher was interested in traffic policing it would be apposite to interview together police officers who usually went 'on patrol' together. Similarly, interviewing a number of family members together might be apt for study of the wider impact of imprisonment. Interviews involving more than one person are sometimes incorrectly referred to as focus groups which are considered in the next section. The main distinction between the group interview and the focus group is the explicit encouragement of a social dynamic between participants so that they talk to each other rather than simply answer questions posed by the researcher.

FOCUS GROUPS

Focus groups are an increasingly popular way to gather data and a recent criminological example is included in Box 6.5 (see also Chapter 10). Their origins lie in market research where they were deployed as a mechanism for gathering customer feedback. As they developed as a social research strategy it was recognised that they can offer 'more than, say, the generation of information on collective views' (Bloor et al., 2001: 4). They can facilitate opportunities to yield data on meanings and group processes which underlie group assessments and the normative understandings which groups draw upon to arrive at collective judgements (Bloor et al., 2001: 4). They can be deployed in social research as a standalone method but as Bloor et al. (2001) describe they can also be used prior to the main data collection stage to generate insights to help design instruments or towards the end of a project to help interpret findings. This might be where they have the greatest potential.

Box 6.5   Using focus groups to understand the problematic usage of gang terminology

Smithson et al. (2013) conducted eleven focus groups with 68 young people who were predominantly Asian males aged 16 to 20. These were carried out alongside semi-structured interviews with community members, practitioners and young people (50 in total) and informal observation in their three research areas. The starting point for the research was a concern about the uncritical use of the term 'gang' (broadly defined to include agencies other than the police) in UK policing policies and practice and the potential for this to further marginalise and isolate some ethnic minority communities. The use of qualitative methods allowed the young people who participated (mostly via focus groups) to suggest that contrary to the use of 'risk talk' by control agencies, the area was not marked by the presence of distinct gangs and instead they focused on other social problems in the area, for example drug dealing.

Focus groups typically have between six and eight participants, a sufficiently high number to generate lively discussion but not so many that individuals might find it difficult to participate. Often more participants will be invited as drop-outs are inevitable, for example people may have to prioritise urgent work commitments, decide they no longer wish to participate or simply forget. On average focus groups last between 60 and 90 minutes. They may include an opportunity at the outset for members to talk informally over refreshments, particularly if they do not already know each other. This might serve as an incentive for participating. Focus groups can also be undertaken in the virtual arena (see Bloor et al., 2001 for a detailed discussion of their strengths and weaknesses alongside practical and ethical considerations).

Focus groups, like interviews, can appear deceptively simple but can be difficult to arrange and conduct. They require extensive planning and skills to generate and manage group discussion and dynamics. The researcher takes on the role of facilitator or moderator with responsibility for initiating and managing the discussion. They are likely to have an agenda which they would like to follow but this method takes advantage of the dynamic interaction of groups, allowing members to respond to each other's input. This might involve asking questions or generating data through another activity (which we consider in 'focusing exercises' later in the chapter). The researcher will need to be alert to group dynamics and sometimes manage those, for example by drawing in silent group members, steering the discussion back if it is going too far off topic and intervening if it becomes heated. Since this can be a challenging task it helps to be accompanied by another researcher who can take responsibility for recording data.

The composition of groups merits further reflection (Bloor et al., 2001 dedicate an entire chapter to this issue) since the success of the focus group depends upon the dynamic created. On some occasions, it might be possible to use pre-existing groups. Others groups need to be constructed for the purpose of the research. I have used both strategies. As part of an evaluation of a police-led crime reduction and drug education programme, we used focus groups with primary-school aged children. The children were all classmates and knew each other well. I have also led focus groups with drug treatment professionals and 'customers' (as the organisation referred to them) of an assertive outreach programme for homeless people. In these latter two examples, the groups were a mixture of people who knew each other and those who did not. On all three occasions, the focus groups worked well because the participants had something in common. It is usual practice for the researcher to construct focus groups in such a way that individuals have a shared characteristic. Loader et al. (1998) used focus groups with various groupings of citizens (young, older people and upwardly mobile 'twenty-somethings') to construct an 'ethnography of anxiety' in a suburban English community. Their rationale for undertaking focus groups consisting of separate categories of people was that complex inter-relationships existed between the individual citizen, their assessment of crime-related risk and their connection with their locality. The focus group provided the opportunity to explore the extent to which fear of crime reflected personal biography and affiliations with the community. Morgan (1997) argues that homogeneity of participants is especially important when researching sensitive topics.

In the remainder of the chapter we will consider some of the issues associated with conducting interviews and focus groups. Some are practical, others methodological or ethical. Often they incorporate a number of these dimensions. This should convey the importance of planning carefully prior to using these methods of data collection. Readers are also directed to the discussion in Chapter 8 about recording interviews and preparing transcripts. The coverage is far from exhaustive. There are many more relevant considerations than we have been able to explore here. To find out more readers are directed to the further reading section at the end of the chapter but also to the reflexive accounts of conducting interviews and focus groups that criminologists sometimes publish. A useful starting point is to read those contained in Chapters 9, 10 and 11.

LOCATION, LOCATION, LOCATION

We focus in this section on the choice of location for face-to-face interviews. We have already noted that interviews can take place without the interviewer and interviewee being in the same physical space. If this approach is adopted the main consideration is for the interviewer to find a quiet space free from interruptions and background noise. The chosen location of an interview is of primary importance. It needs to be accessible to both the interviewer and interviewee and given that the main aim of qualitative interviewing is to create a space for the interviewee to 'open up' and provide the interviewer with full and frank answers to the questions posed, it follows that the most desirable location will be a private space in which the interviewee and interviewer feel comfortable. Finding a space free of interruptions to conduct interviews can be challenging. Private space can be in short supply in many organisational settings. During my research career this has been a particular issue when interviewing in prisons (see Wincup and Hucklesby, 2007). Often there is limited space available except in areas reserved for visits. The main visit room is communal and far from ideal. Towards the end of one interview in a young offender institution I found myself joined by other prisoners who were either waiting to be interviewed by me or who had completed their interviews with other members of the research team. The 'legal' visits (a term which in practice is used for professional visits generally) offer private space but can lead to incorrect assumptions being made by other prisoners, for example that they are 'grassing' to the police. This area has the advantage of being supervised which might be preferable to interviews taking place out of sight, for example on offices on wings. In the first edition (Noaks and Wincup, 2004) we described our experiences of interviewing remand prisoners in a local prison. While a room was set aside on the remand wing for interviewing, some prison officers insisted on leaving the door of the room open and entering at uninvited moments. Their rationale for such actions was the security of the researchers (all female). However, the risk of being overheard can be inhibiting for some respondents and may impact on the material they are prepared to share.

As the above discussion implies the interviewer often has little control over where an interview takes place. They will have to use whatever space is available or allow the interviewee to decide. The choice of location is often a compromise, although this should not be at the expense of putting either the interviewee or interviewer at risk. The location can have implications on the quality of the data collected and requires flexibility of approach. For example, it may be convenient for an interview to take place in a coffee shop near to the interviewee's workplace but this is likely to be busy so they run the risk of being overheard which may make the interviewee reticent about answering questions. It is also likely to be noisy making it difficult to record without picking up background noise. Location is similarly important for focus groups. Ideally it needs to be familiar territory so the participants feel at ease and with sufficient space to accommodate the maximum number of people who might attend. It also needs to be easily accessible, even if travel expenses are being covered, to ensure as many participants as possible attend.

STRATEGIES FOR GENERATING DATA

At its simplest qualitative interviews involve little formal preparation, although it would be wrong to give the impression that the absence of a detailed interview schedule implies a lack of planning. Arksey and Knight (1999) emphasise the importance of 'doing your homework'. For example, should you be fortunate enough to secure an interview with a chief constable, you should dedicate some time to making use of publicly available sources to find out more about the individual and their police force. Whilst there is less emphasis on 'piloting' in qualitative research (in contrast to quantitative research), it is an important stage in the research process. My advice to new researchers (who typically opt for semi-structured interviews) is to find a willing volunteer to role play a member of your chosen interview group. Whilst this inevitably creates an artificial environment, it provides space to reflect upon the appropriateness of the questions posed and the order in which they are posed. Whilst qualitative researchers do deviate from the original structure, it needs to have been designed with a logical running order. Following this, it is wise to schedule a small number of interviews and then allow space for reflection both about the interview process and the quality of the data gathered. Seeking advice from an experienced researcher – for example an academic supervisor – can be useful here. In my experience, those new to interviewing sometimes miss opportunities to elicit more data. Exploiting these opportunities lies at the core of qualitative research but is represented as a distraction when collecting quantitative data and frowned upon due to its emphasis on a consistent approach.

Box 6.6 outlines strategies for generating data with respect to qualitative interviews. In focus groups, 'focusing exercises' should be used to concentrate the group's efforts on the research issues. Examples are provided by Bloor et al. (2001). These include *ranking exercises* (for instance, place in order the crime and anti-social behaviours which you think are most prevalent in your neighbourhood); *using vignettes* (for instance, asking police officers how they might respond to hypothetical incidents); *using news bulletins* (for instance, asking young people how they might present a story about cyberbullying); and *photo interpretations* (for instance, showing photos of a neighbourhood and asking whether they might feel safe if walking around there in different contexts – with others or alone, at different times of the day). These strategies could also be used in qualitative interviews. In focus groups it is important to avoid 'the deadly hush' (Bloor et al., 2001: 50). Whilst for qualitative interviews silences can be useful (see Box 6.6), it is typically counterproductive for focus groups.

Box 6.6   Generating richer data: Strategies for qualitative interviewers (drawing upon Denscombe, 2014: 191–2 and Arksey and Knight, 1999: 84)

- Follow up what has already been said with a further question asking for more detail, an explanation, clarification or an example
- Remain silent when needed: the interviewee might continue if there is a pause but silences can be uncomfortable or they may have nothing more to say at that point so be prepared to interject

(Continued)

(Continued)

- Summarise what has already been said ('if I have understood you correctly ...') allowing the interviewee the opportunity to clarify your understanding or expand on what has been said
- Offer an alternative view, drawing upon other interviewees' accounts
- Make it explicit that you are listening, for example you could repeat back what they have said ('so you were telling me ...') or use non-verbal cues (for example, a nod of the head)

Beyond this, what social scientists refer to as 'impression management' is important. This refers to the conscious management of the self in order to gain and maintain research access (see Coffey, 2006). This manifests itself in different ways ranging from how an individual might dress through to how they behave and act. It is always a judgement call but in general terms you need to minimise the distance between yourself and your interviewee, although this is more problematic than implied here. This might involve dressing up or dressing down and using appropriate language. A poor impression can make relationships difficult to forge or sustain and can jeopardise the establishment of trust and rapport. Imagine for the moment the impact of turning up late and unprepared in jeans for a meeting with a legal professional or arriving to interview a prisoner wearing a suit and using overly formal language.

Establishing trust and rapport are viewed by qualitative researchers as essential to the research process. Without these interviewees may be reluctant to open up, especially if they are being asked about sensitive issues, which is frequently the case for qualitative criminological research. In the context of an interview, there is often little time to establish trust and build rapport. This focuses attention on the importance of reflecting upon how to start the interview, particularly as the need to conduct 'ethical housekeeping' (for example, ensure consent forms are signed) at the outset can make the initial interaction seem rather formal. The literature offers practical tips (see for example, Arksey and Knight, 1999) but there have also been important methodological discussions. For example, feminist researchers have acknowledged the hierarchical power relations embedded in the traditional dichotomy between researcher and researched. They have proposed that interviewers should strive towards partnership in the researcher/researched relationship in the hope that this will lead to greater levels of trust and rapport. In practical terms, this means interviews might be mutually self-revealing, rather than disclosure only being forthcoming from the interviewee (Finch, 1984; Oakley, 1981). This is not universally supported and the debates which have followed have been useful in drawing attention to the complex nature of power in research relationships (see Smith and Wincup [2002] who explore these issues with reference to research with female offenders).

CHAPTER SUMMARY AND CONCLUSION

This chapter has emphasised the range of interviewing techniques that are available to criminologists and identified the key features of qualitative interviewing. We have problematised the notion that these interactions are 'conversations'. Whilst there are obvious parallels, thinking about interviews in this way runs the risk of under-estimating the skills needed for qualitative interviews and underplays the impor-tance of planning and the range of issues to be considered in advance. For instance, we explored at length the issue of where to conduct interviews since what appears to be a highly practical issue has wider methodological implications. We have also drawn attention to the use of focus groups, a method which criminologists have yet to exploit fully but which may be particularly useful as part of a multi-method research design.

Exercises

1   Select ONE of the research questions below and decide whether to collect data via qualitative interviews (if so, what type?) or focus groups. Reflect both on the data you would like to collect and the processes of gathering and analysing the data.

- Public perceptions of sentencing
- Desistance and female offenders
- Special constables' experiences of policing

2   Criminological research often involves interviewing 'vulnerable' groups (see Chapter 3 for a discussion of this term). In the context of criminological research this might include victims of hate crime, young offenders or prisoners with learn-ing difficulties. You can assume you have secured access to these groups and the appropriate ethical clearance has been granted.

- What are the specific issues you may need to consider when conducting interviews with these groups?
- Are there any situations in which you might decide not to interview them or end the interview?

3   What skills do you need to be an effective interviewer? Are different skills needed for different types of interview?

FURTHER READING

- Arksey, H. and Knight, P. (1999) *Interviewing for Social Scientists*. London: Sage.

  This book – described as a 'no-nonsense, comprehensive and authoritative introduction to interviewing' and an 'interviewer's bible' (back cover) – explores the principles and practices of all types of interviewing.

- Bloor, M., Frankland, J., Thomas, M. and Robson, K. (2000) *Focus Groups in Social Research*. London: Sage.

  This concise text offers a critical appreciation of the role of focus groups in social research, coupled with practical guidance.

- Brinkmann, S. and Kvale, S. (2014) *InterViews: Learning the Craft of Qualitative Research Interviewing*, 3rd edn. London: Sage.

  Brinkmann and Kvale take readers on a journey through the landscape of interview research, addressing the 'hows' and 'whys' of using interviews for social science projects.

- King, N. and Horrocks, C. (2010) *Interviews in Qualitative Research*. London: Sage.

  Focused specifically on qualitative interviewing, this book recognises that the method is forever changing in response to both theoretical and technological advances and offers a guide to using interviews in contemporary qualitative research.

- Soothill, K. (1999) *Criminal Conversations: An Anthology of the Work of Tony Parker*. London: Routledge.

  This collection brings together interviews by Tony Parker, an oral historian, who skilfully conducted interviews with 'criminals'. These are published alongside his notes on the principles and practice of interviewing and reflection on his methodology.

ETHNOGRAPHY

Within criminology the ethnographic tradition is long established. Indeed, some researchers have gone so far as to suggest that ethnography has been especially reliant on studies of deviance (Adler and Adler, 1995; Lofland, 1987; Manning, 1987), leading to studies of youth subcultures, gangs, prostitution, professional and organised crime and illicit drug use (see Hobbs, 2007 for an overview). This is a contentious view but it can be argued that some of the most important contributions to the sociology of crime and deviance have developed out of ethnographic work. Coupled with the use of ethnographic approaches to explore the workings of the criminal justice system, ethnography has proved its value as a way of conducting criminological research. As we shall explore in this chapter, there is no universal definition of ethnography but broadly speaking it involves a researcher participating, overtly or covertly, in people's daily lives for an extended period of time and collecting whatever data (typically but not exclusively qualitative) are available to throw light on the issues that are the focus of the research (Hammersley and Atkinson, 2007: 3). This leads to the creation of 'long-term and multi-stranded research relationships that provide the detailed contextualisation characteristic of good ethnographic research' (Davies, C., 2002: 419). The extended tradition of adopting ethnographic techniques within criminological research studies implies the appropriateness of this approach to researching issues of crime and justice.

The basic shape of the chapter is as follows. It begins with an attempt to define ethnography and to dispel some of the myths which surround this approach to social science research. This is followed by a chronological account of the rise and, some might argue, fall of ethnography in criminology. In so doing it considers the relationship between ethnography and a variety of theoretical perspectives. Two case studies are used to illustrate some of the practical, ethical and methodological issues connected with ethnographic research on criminological topics.

WHAT IS ETHNOGRAPHY?

A close examination of the methodological literature reveals a lack of clarity about what ethnography actually is. Hammersley and Atkinson (2007: 1) note 'the label is not used in an entirely standard fashion' and 'its meaning can vary'. The term ethnography is often misunderstood and oversimplified. A number of myths surround ethnography and these will be dispelled below.

1. *Ethnography is synonymous with participant observation.* Whilst ethnography is typically associated with participant observation it can involve the use of different research methods, either on their own or together. Whilst sometimes referred to as a 'method' it is best described as a 'family of methods' (O'Reilly, 2011: 3). However, Pearson (1993: ix) suggests that for some ethnographers the 'participant observer' method 'is the key-stone of the claim to authenticity'. Frequently ethnographic work involves mixing methods and contemporary ethnography tends to be multi-method research combining participant observation, in-depth interviews and documentary analysis. By utilising different approaches ethnographers are not naïvely suggesting that this will increase the validity of their data or that data gathered from different sources can be used to produce a single unitary picture of the 'truth' (see the discussion of triangulation in Chapter 1); instead it helps to uncover multiple versions of reality. For instance, an ethnography of drug recovery wings within a prison has the potential to reveal the conflicting perspectives of prisoners, prison-based staff and contracted drug treatment providers about the most appropriate method to 'treat' problem drug users.

2. *Ethnography is 'telling it like it is'.* Naturalistic realism is built into ethnographic methodology. Naturalism is a methodological approach which proposes that as far as possible the social world should be studied in its 'natural state', undisturbed by the researcher. Thus ethnographers need to adopt an appreciative stance and describe cultures though obtaining direct access to 'objective' knowledge about them. This latter principle is also true of realism, a methodological position which also advocates that there is an external world independent of people's perceptions of it. The naturalist realist notion that researchers can 'tell it how it is' and write ethnographic accounts which present social reality in an unproblematic way has come under attack as postmodern critiques have been developed (see for example, Denzin, 1997). The inherently political nature of the research process (as discussed in Chapter 2) and the construction of ethnographic texts has been brought to the fore (Atkinson; 1992; Fetterman, 2010; Van Maanen, 2011). 'Telling it like it is' implies presenting an account of the social world from the perspective of those being researched; telling the story as they would tell it (based on the unlikely assumption that all would tell the same story). This is an overly simplistic view because if an ethnographer was able to do this she or he would have 'gone native', in other words become so immersed in the culture they were studying that they had left their academic culture behind. Ethnographers are required to be in two places at the same time as they assume the role of storyteller and scientist (Fetterman, 2010) in order to

bridge the gap between the research participants and research audiences. These ethnographic descriptions are 'partial, selective, even autobiographical in that they are tied to the particular ethnographer and the contingencies under which the data were collected' (Brewer, 2000: 24–5). This debate is explored in more detail in Brewer (2000) and Hammersley and Atkinson (2007).

3. *Ethnography is simple to do.* It is often assumed that ethnography is unproblematic, and requires little preparation and no special expertise. Novice researchers are sometimes misled that they can head off armed only with pen and paper (or more technologically sophisticated methods of collecting data) to find a suitable group to study. Ethnographic techniques resemble to the routine ways in which people make sense of the world in everyday life through watching what happens, listening to what is said and asking questions helps to fuel this myth. The difficulties of negotiating access to social groups aside (discussed in Chapter 4), conducting ethnographic research requires some degree of training and preparation. As Delamont et al. (2001) argue the former is sometimes rejected and ethnographic techniques are perceived as an innate quality rather than a masterable skill. Similarly, the need for preparation is refuted because the course of ethnography cannot be predetermined. Whilst this is true would-be ethnographers can be instructed to expect the unexpected, to develop a research design, to reflect on how they might gain access to the setting and manage field relations within it, to consider strategies for recording data and to learn about techniques for analysing it, and finally to select the most appropriate way of presenting their findings.

4. *Ethnographic research lacks rigour.* As LeCompte (2002) notes, since ethnographic research lacks experimental controls and fails to generate the reliable and replicable results widely perceived as the only hallmarks of legitimacy, critics may suggest ethnographic research is not rigorous. For these reasons, she suggests that ethnographers need to be active lobbyists of their work to convince suspicious academic audiences and policy-makers.

There is also considerable confusion surrounding whether ethnography can be appropriately described as a research method or whether it might be more accurately described as a methodology. The former describes a data collection technique and the latter a theoretical and philosophical framework. This debate is explored in detail elsewhere (see for example, Brewer, 2000). Suffice to say here that it is helpful to see ethnography as a research strategy rather than a method and one which is linked especially with two data collection techniques: participant observation and in-depth interviews.

Given our starting point in this section, developing a definition of ethnography is in many respects a dangerous pastime which risks glossing over the contested nature of the concept. Nonetheless, a working definition is offered below to give the reader a personal interpretation of ethnography.

> Ethnography is the study of groups of people in their natural setting, typically involving the researcher being present for extended periods of time in order to collect data systematically about their daily activities and the meanings they attach to them. These data are used to construct a theoretically informed ethnographic account of everyday life.

THE ORIGINS OF ETHNOGRAPHY

Brewer (2000) argues that the roots of ethnography are ancient, noting that travellers and outsiders of different kinds have for centuries lived among strangers and recorded their way of life. Similarly, in a brief historical sketch of ethnography, Wax (1971: 21) suggests that 'descriptive reporting of the customs, inclinations, accomplishment and accomplishments of foreign people is almost as old as writing itself'. It is, however, difficult to be precise about the origins of ethnography, not least because, as we have already noted, it relies upon the same ways in which people make sense of the world in their everyday lives. Despite this the turn of the twentieth century is usually perceived as the point at which conducting ethnography emerged as a specialist skill.

Ethnography, as described above, has its origins in anthropology. The work of Malinowski (see for example his work on crime and custom in a 'savage' society – Malinowski, 1926) is significant because as well as claiming to be the first British social anthropologist to pitch his tent in a village and observe and record what was actually going on, he was also the first professional anthropologist to give his readers a relatively detailed account of his experience of conducting fieldwork (see Wax, 1971 for a discussion of his influence). Traditionally anthropologists like Malinowski attempted to immerse themselves in the particular culture of the society under study in order to develop 'thick description' (Geertz, 1973); in other words, rich and detailed description of the accomplishment of everyday life. Typically this involved studying pre-industrial cultures radically different from those of Western (mainly British) anthropologists. This work has been described as the product of an undesirable colonial legacy of exploitation and domination, and contemporary anthropologists – and increasingly researchers more closely aligned with other disciplines such as criminology – have explored issues closer to 'home'.

THE CHICAGO SCHOOL AND ITS LEGACY

The development of ethnographic fieldwork in criminology is inextricably linked to the development of the Chicago School. As Deegan (2007) describes the Chicago School was particularly influential in sociology between 1892 and 1942. A powerful and prolific subgroup of these sociologists created the Chicago School of Ethnography. They produced analyses of the everyday life, communities and symbolic interactions characteristic of specific groups, particularly in the period from 1917 to 1942. Robert Park was particularly influential and his contribution is described in Box 7.1.

Box 7.1   Establishing the ethnographic tradition
in criminology: The influence of Robert Park

In a lecture to undergraduate students at the University of Chicago in the 1920s, Robert Park urged his students to conduct their own fieldwork by advocating 'Gentlemen go get the seat of your pants dirty in real research' (see Bulmer, 1984). The gendered language should be noted here, and feminists have been influential in unearthing women's involvement in the Chicago School (see for example, Delamont, 2003). Park hoped to inspire students (and he succeeded in doing so) to study deviant groups within their natural setting and to make connections between their lifestyles and the social turbulence of Chicago at that time. Park had studied psychology and philosophy but it was his background as a journalist which encouraged him, and others, to go out on the streets to collect information by whatever means they could. Park's own work is testimony to the view that ethnographic studies can consist of multiple research methods, including those leading to the generation of quantitative data.

As detailed in Chapter 1, the Chicago School made important theoretical and methodological contributions and launched a tradition of conducting ethnographic research on aspects of crime and deviance. The second Chicago School (Fine, 1995), developed in the post-World War Two period, continued to be dominated by ethnographies of deviance. Undoubtedly the most well-known of these is Becker's study of marijuana users (Becker, 1963). His ethnographic work explored the social processing involved in becoming deviant by examining the process by which a particular behaviour is labelled deviant and the impact this labelling process has on the individual who has been labelled deviant. In this way he highlighted the socially constructed nature of crime and deviance. Hobbs (2007) goes as far as to suggest that Becker's work has assumed iconic status with successive generations of scholars. There is some evidence to support this. In a chapter describing the social organisation of British criminology, Rock (1994) reports on a survey of criminologists (106 in total). Becker's *Outsiders*, described by Rock (1994: 141) as an 'interactionist manifesto' was named most frequently as the publication which had had the greatest influence on those surveyed.

Brewer (2000: 13) suggests that by focusing on deviant subcultures, the Chicago School helped to create a commonsense view that ethnography 'offers mere description of things foreign, exotic and peculiar'. This is ironic given that conducting ethnographic fieldwork with these deviant groups can be a prosaic business. Even in the supposedly action-packed lives of youth gangs or drug users, there is a measure of repetition. The same is true of ethnographic research within criminal justice agencies. The criticism Brewer describes probably relates more to the type of theoretical work with which ethnography has been associated rather than being a direct criticism of ethnography itself. In the post-war period ethnography was the main tool used to develop a sociology of the underdog and to develop the labelling perspective, typified in the work of Becker. This was crudely characterised as the sociology of 'nuts, sluts and perverts' (Liazos, 1972) by critics who went on to develop more radical approaches for explaining crime and deviance.

A NEW TWIST: THE DEVIANCY SCHOOL AND ETHNOGRAPHY IN THE UK

The ethnographic tradition came alive in the UK in the mid-1960s when the hegemony of positivist criminology was threatened (Bottoms, 2008). Positivism has at its heart a belief that criminality is a characteristic of individuals. Hence the challenge for criminology is to identify the causes of crime by emulating the methods used by natural scientists. Ethnography has different emphases – rejecting the idea that social phenomena can be studied in the same way as natural phenomena, stressing the importance of deep involvement in the everyday lives of research participants and offering a commitment to understanding the meanings human beings attribute to their actions.

The National Deviancy Conference of 1968, with the benefit of hindsight, marks a watershed in British criminology. Dissatisfaction with positivism coupled with a lack of faith in interactionism created the intellectual space for alternative theoretical frameworks to develop. Sumner (1994) notes that the National Deviancy Conference had no collective position, hardly surprising because it consisted of interactionists, anarchists, phenomenologists and Marxists, and it made few theoretical advances other than developing deviancy amplification 'theory'. This involved consideration of the role of the mass media in highlighting and developing further what it perceived to be 'deviant' threats to social order. The New Deviancy theorists adopted a more politicised approach than earlier sociologists of deviance such as Becker. For example, the work of Stuart Hall and his colleagues analysed conflict between 'deviant' groups or subcultures and disapproving establishment forces including the media and the State (see for example Hall et al., 1978). Ethnography was championed in rhetoric but the reality was that few papers based on ethnographic research were presented at subsequent colloquia (Hobbs, 2007). Stan Cohen's (1972) study of mods and rockers is one of the most well-known examples of ethnographic research by an author involved in the National Deviancy Conference and this is described in Box 7.2.

Box 7.2   Observing youth subculture: Generating theory through ethnography

Cohen's (1972) study involved a number of methods including participant observation, interviews and documentary analysis of media reports. He examined the battles between two opposing working-class youth subcultures (mods and rockers) on public holidays in British seaside towns in the mid-1960s. His research led to the development of the concept of 'moral panic' to describe the media and political over-reaction to the perceived threat these groups (cast as 'folk devils') posed to societal values. The data which informed his study have now been archived and can be found at the Radzinowicz Library at the Institute of Criminology at Cambridge University.

FEMINIST CRIMINOLOGIES AND ETHNOGRAPHY

Despite the radicalism of the New Deviancy Conference there was little acknowledgement of the emerging feminist critique of criminology. The second wave of feminism, which began in the late 1960s, inspired a number of female criminologists (Heidensohn, 1968; Smart, 1976) to develop a critique of the different explanations of crime and noted that women who offend are typically neglected or misrepresented. Feminist critiques of criminology almost always explore the shortcomings of ethnographies conducted by men on men (see for example Millman, 1975). As feminist criminologists have argued, ethnographies of crime and deviance tend to be conducted by men on men (Hobbs, 2007). There are, however, a number of examples of ethnographic studies carried out by women on women. A recent example is described in Box 7.3.

Box 7.3   Making women visible: ethnographic work with female 'drug mules'

Jennifer Fleetwood's (2014) research focused on female 'drug mules'. Drawing upon ethnographic data gathered in prisons in Ecuador over a period of five years, she sought to make women's involvement in the international cocaine trade visible and represent them in a way which recognised the structural constraints they faced as women, often living in poverty, but did not deny them a sense of agency. Her ethnographic work initially involved 'hanging out', getting to know people and immersing herself in the daily life of three prisons (one for women, two for men). Over time she was able to establish trust and conduct a series of formal interviews with 31 people imprisoned for drug trafficking offences and informal interviews with many more. The rich data gathered – which was subject to narrative analysis (see Chapter 8) – allowed Fleetwood to argue that women's involvement in the international cocaine trade cannot be adequately understood through the lens of either victimhood or volition.

The relationship between feminism and ethnography has been explored by a number of feminist researchers (see Wincup, 1999 and Skeggs, 2001 for an overview). Of particular concern is Judith Stacey's (1988) claim that feminist ethnography is fundamentally contradictory. She suggests that feminist scholars have identified ethnographic methods as ideally suited to feminist research because of their contextual, experiential approach to knowledge, emphasising empathy and human concern, and because they facilitate equal and reciprocal relationships between the researcher and research participants. However, Stacey argues that paradoxically such methods subject research participants to a greater risk of exploitation, betrayal and abandonment than positivist research (see Chapter 1 for a discussion of this term). Her concerns lie with the research process and its product. Fieldwork, she points out, inevitably represents an intrusion because it intervenes with a system of relationships that the researcher can leave more freely. Moreover, there are difficult compromises to be made between respect for participants and producing authentic accounts when research participants are promised control over the final product. Despite this she believes the potential benefits of a 'partially' feminist ethnography seem worth the serious moral costs involved.

This view is not shared by all. Indeed, many feminist researchers have drawn our attention to the dilemmas of feminist ethnography, yet at the same time do not regard feminist ethnography as a contradiction in terms. For example, whilst acknowledging the potential of feminist ethnography to make women's lives visible,

Reinharz (1992: 65) notes that 'feminist ethnography is burdened with many controversies and dilemmas'. She labels these the problem of trust, the closeness/ distance dilemma and the dilemma of complete participation/observation. The problem of trust refers to the realisation that rapport and trust are not immediately established on the basis of shared sisterhood. Instead this needs to be worked at. A further dilemma is that the development of closeness to further understanding may be seen as 'going native' or 'over-rapport'. This is problematic in two ways. First, it might be seen to compromise the very academic understanding that feminist ethnographers set out to achieve, but can also be seen as exploitative in the sense that superficial friendships are created for the purpose of data collection. Total immersion in the social world in which they are studying through complete participation in it is viewed positively by some feminist researchers as a means of integrating their selves into their work and eliminating the distinction between subject and object (Roseneil, 1993; Stanley and Wise, 1993). These dilemmas cannot be easily resolved and they shatter any images of ethnography as simple to do. What the critiques elude to, a point that Hammersley and Atkinson (2007) make explicitly, is the need for reflexivity.

Reinharz (1992) suggests that feminist ethnographers typically make double contributions when they conduct their research. They contribute to our understanding of feminist ethnography as a research strategy and they contribute to our understanding of the subject matter they choose to study. Every feminist ethnographic project generates its own new set of concerns, in addition to touching on existing ones. Despite the controversies within feminist ethnography, ethnographic research has enormous potential to make visible the lives of women in general, and the lives of women in contact with the criminal justice system as victims, offenders or professionals in particular.

REFLECTIONS ON THE STATE OF ETHNOGRAPHY

In the conclusion (subtitled 'whither ethnography?') to his text on ethnography, Brewer (2000) suggested that the future of ethnography is uncertain. In addition to facing the challenges to its underlying basis, namely naturalism, ethnography has had to defend itself from the march of globalisation. People are now often described as living in a 'global village' in which people live their lives on a larger scale. They are exposed almost immediately to events happening elsewhere in the world as they watch or read global media products and travel more extensively. Moreover, the growth of cultural homogeneity and recognition that people's lives are shaped by events outside the control of the nation state and its economy is a major threat to ethnography. Ethnography thrives upon researching difference through attempting 'to bridge between the experiences of actors and audiences' (Pearson, 1993: xviii). Ethnographers assume that they are researching a social group with clear boundaries and distinct social meanings. As LeCompte (2002) notes, ethnography has traditionally been thought of as the investigation of the culture of small, relatively homogeneous, naturally or artificially bounded groups. Brewer (2000) recognises that globalisation potentially robs ethnography of the specificity of the local, yet notes that global processes are always mediated locally. Ethnography can elucidate these processes.

As a means of conducting criminological research, ethnography faces further challenges in recent years. Around the time the first edition of this book was published there was a sense of pessimism surrounding ethnography. For example, Maguire (2000: 121) noted that 'criminologists nowadays spend surprisingly little of their time talking to "criminals"', and a few years prior to that, Parker (1996: 282) pointed out that British criminology has 'largely retreated from qualitative, ethnographic community-based studies of subculture and deviant lifestyles'. It would be wrong to give the impression that criminologists had stopped talking to offenders. They continued to do so, but in many respects their research projects did not resemble the ethnographic studies of previous decades. Instead of talking to offenders in their natural settings, criminologists typically access offenders through criminal justice agencies, particularly through police forces, prisons and young offender institutions, probation areas or youth offending teams. These constitute artificial settings and institutional timetables and resources influence the type of research methods which can be utilised. Characteristically these are formal interviews. More often than not, these interviews are likely to focus not on offending behaviour but offenders' experiences of being arrested, remanded in custody, undertaking a community punishment order or other aspects of the criminal justice process. In the first edition, we noted the temptation to end the chapter with the phrase 'criminologists don't do ethnographies like they used to' (Noaks and Wincup, 2004: 103) but recognised that this implied that there was a golden age of ethnography. Certainly ethnographic research, particularly on criminal behaviour, was more frequent in the past and researchers got closer to offenders but studies often lacked methodological sophistication and there was too little attention paid to ethical considerations or fieldwork safety.

It is not difficult to imagine why criminologists had retreated from conducting ethnographic work, and especially what might be described as 'street' ethnography. It presents a range of practical, ethical and personal safety dilemmas and these are explored in the final part of the chapter through discussion of two ethnographies. In order to complete such a study, researchers need to be both highly skilled and receive appropriate training. They also need to be sufficiently convinced of the appropriateness of their approach to defend it when faced with criticism that it is unscientific. This is especially important given the politics which surround criminological research which tends to favour particular forms of research (see Chapter 2). Most of all they need to be passionate about their research topic so they enjoy all stages of their work and can produce a well-crafted ethnographic account in spite of the problems they are likely to encounter along the way. In addition, a willingness to talk openly, and at length, about the process of conducting research is also one of the characteristics of a first-rate ethnographer.

In the decade since the first edition was published, there are some indications of a healthier future for criminological ethnography, as demonstrated by the publication of edited collections or special issues of criminological journals dedicated to crime ethnography (Bartels and Richards, 2011; Earle et al., 2015; Travers et al., 2013) and a book series edited by two criminologists and dominated by criminological studies (Routledge Advances in Ethnography).

It still largely remains the case that ethnography has become an approach adopted by researchers studying for a PhD and this approach is abandoned through personal choice or more likely necessity once they embark on an academic career. Hobbs (2007) also makes this observation suggesting that his review of ethnographies of deviance indicates that the ethnographer's craft is practised for the most part by younger academics just launching a career. There are, of course exceptions, including one of the examples (Fassin, 2013) we will explore in the final section of the chapter. Before we consider them, we should acknowledge, first, the contribution that cultural criminology has played to the future of ethnography as an approach for understanding crime, and, second, the emergence of virtual ethnography.

CULTURAL CRIMINOLOGY AND ETHNOGRAPHY

Cultural criminology – which at its simplest aims to 'bring back sociological theory to criminology' (Hayward and Young, 2012: 113) can be identified as a significant new development in criminology in recent years, evidenced by its inclusion in a range of leading textbooks (Hale et al., 2013; Maguire et al., 2012). In many respects the term 'new' is misleading as its origins date back to the 1960s. Challenging the positivist tendency to regard crime as the 'result of a lack of culture' (Hayward and Young, 2012: 113), cultural criminology seeks to develop a theoretical approach which incorporates a notion of culture, albeit one in flux and with the potential for creativity and transcendence. Whilst cultural criminologists now utilise a range of methodological approaches, ethnography was fundamental to its early work (Ferrell, 1999), utilised to study homelessness, sex work and drug culture (Ferrell and Hamm, 1998). It remains a key method, contributing to a broader project to free human actors from 'the condescension both of inappropriate quantification and of deterministic methods which diminish and obfuscate the underlying creativity of social action' (Hayward and Young, 2012: 133). In 2008, Maguire qualified his earlier pessimism about the decline of ethnography (referred to above) and suggested that the growth of theoretical interest in cultural criminology was likely to produce more ethnographic studies to aid understanding of the lived realities of those who engage in crime.

Box 7.4   Researching gambling online: A virtual ethnography of a subculture

Banks (2013) conducted a virtual ethnography (defined in the section below) of online gambling which was influenced by cultural criminological perspectives. Data from observing online gambling subcultures was analysed alongside data (both qualitative and quantitative) from textual and visual analyses of e-gambling advertising and the records of player-protection and standards organisations. Recognising the intricate links between online gambling and crime, he argues that online gambling provides an opportunity for individuals to engage in 'edgework', taking what are perceived to be 'safe risks' in order to secure reward. His experiences of conducting a virtual ethnography are described in Banks (2014).

VIRTUAL ETHNOGRAPHY

With only rare exceptions (for example, Williams' (2007) study of deviance in a cyberworld – see Box 1.2 and Box 7.4) criminologists have yet to transfer ethnographic approaches to the study of computer-mediated social interaction. Yet virtual ethnography or 'netnography' (see Hine, 2015; Kozinets, 2015; Pink et al., 2015) provides opportunities as well as challenges for criminologists. Increasingly we are aware of cybercrime, a term used to refer to existing crimes committed in cyberspace (for example, related to pornography or drug dealing) through to new crimes (for example, automated hacking) (see Williams and Wall, 2013 for an overview). Conducting ethnographic research on such crimes is fraught with difficulties as they may take place on the 'dark' or 'deep' net, thus hidden from view. A more fruitful avenue for criminologists to explore is ethnographic studies of online communities (for example, of victims with criminal justice professionals). This requires some degree of participation to be described as ethnographic so that the researcher is not simply a 'lurker' collecting data. Crucially the same ethical principles apply to the virtual world as other settings in terms of securing informed consent (see Chapter 3).

CONTEMPORARY ETHNOGRAPHIES OF CRIME AND CRIMINAL JUSTICE

In this final section, we will consider two examples of recent ethnographic work on crime and criminal justice which will be used to illustrate some of the themes introduced earlier in the chapter. The first, a study of crack cocaine users (Briggs, 2013), documents users' day-to-day struggles to survive in a violent and intimidating street drug scene in South London whilst attempting to turn their lives around.

DANIEL BRIGGS (2013) *CRACK COCAINE USERS: HIGH SOCIETY AND LOW LIFE IN SOUTH LONDON.* LONDON: ROUTLEDGE

This research monograph – a contribution to the Routledge Advances in Ethnography series – is based upon nine months of fieldwork (comprising of both formal and informal interviews and participant observation) in 'Rivertown' (a deprived south London borough). Focusing specifically on crack cocaine users, Briggs set out to explore how macro-level political and economic forces shape the daily lives of arguably the most stigmatised group of problem drug users. In this way he illustrates the potential of ethnography to bridge the gap between structure (at a macro level) and agency (at a micro level) to understand how the day-to-day lives of individuals are influenced but not determined by factors outside their control.

His starting point is that crack cocaine users place a significant burden on health and social services, the criminal justice system and drug treatment agencies.

Noting that they are heavily stigmatised, Briggs aims to unpack the myths surrounding their drug use and highlight their fragile position as they attempt to free themselves from a violent and intimidating street drug scene and make changes to their lives. Through his research findings, Briggs attempts to make policy-makers and practitioners aware of the realities of crack cocaine users. Ultimately this culminates in the inclusion of recommendations for policy in the final chapter. In many respects, this is unusual for an ethnographic study, contributing to the impression that ethnographic research on crime fails to take it seriously. Similar criticisms are levelled at cultural criminology and in challenging them Hayward and Young (2012) argue that an 'appreciative' approach (referring to the work of Matza's [1969] research on the process of becoming deviant) does not inevitably mean romanticising or valorising research 'subjects' or resisting state intervention. Instead, they suggest that successful policies and practices require 'verstehen'; in other words, putting oneself in the place of others to see what meanings they attribute to their actions.

Perhaps what is more unusual is that the study was funded by a drug action team (locally based multi-agency partnerships responsible for the co-ordination of drug services) and conducted whilst Briggs was employed with a private drug and alcohol research company. This situation was a response to his inability to secure ethical approval for the research from two university ethics committees on the grounds that it was 'too risky'. The book gives some insight into the reasons why: he spent time in a number of high-risk locations such as crack houses and open drug markets and was exposed to threats of, and actual, violence. Nonetheless, it is regrettable that researchers now struggle to gain approval to conduct important criminological studies, although the reasons why are valid.

Conducting research with the drug action team provided some degree of access, particularly to services and professionals but also to crack cocaine users through being able to accompany outreach workers. His work vividly illustrates the importance of developing relationships with individuals who served as gatekeepers. In his acknowledgements he singles out four crack cocaine users and categorically states the book was only possible because of their assistance. They helped to secure his access to crack houses and were pivotal in ensuring his (relative) safety. His honest account reveals the challenges of working with a number of gatekeepers (the metaphor of spinning plates comes to mind) and the fragility of those relationships, particularly given that instability and insecurity characterised their lives.

The final chapter of the book is in the form of an epilogue, which makes a contribution to the small literature on ending ethnographic research. In this short chapter, Briggs recalls some of the interactions he had with research participants after the study had officially ended. The justification for including them is not wholly clear but crucially they illustrate that relationships do not end once the data collection phase is over and, as discussed in Chapter 4, it can be difficult for ethnographers to leave the 'field' fully.

DIDIER FASSIN (2013) *ENFORCING ORDER: AN ETHNOGRAPHY OF URBAN POLICING.* CAMBRIDGE: POLITY PRESS

The second example – an ethnography of urban policing in Paris (Fassin, 2013) – provides a very different ethnographic account which is focused on the workings of criminal justice rather than engagement in criminal behaviour. Fassin's (2013) ethnography of urban policing is based upon 15 months of fieldwork carried out in the Parisian suburbs between May 2005 and June 2007. During that period he spent time both in the police station and on patrol, in particular with 'anticrime' squads during the evening and at night. The fieldwork commenced shortly before the 2005 riots. His research is focused on France but he notes that almost all major disturbances since the mid-twentieth century have resulted from a violent interaction between law enforcement officers and residents of disadvantaged communities, particularly those who are young and/or from minority ethnic groups. Whilst acknowledging the specificities of policing in France, he suggests that through studying the singular (in this instance one policing area) we can reveal the general through accessing 'processes and logics that have a wider meaning' (2013: xvii). In this way, he refutes the commonly held view that ethnographic research is not generalisable and suggests that his argument that the police are engaged in the task of enforcing an unequal order in the name of public security, rather than enforcing the law, might have greater applicability.

Fassin's work illustrates how personal and professional lives can become intertwined for ethnographers. First, he notes that his own son and his friends were arrested during the fieldwork period and in the acknowledgements describes how his son had encouraged him to make public what he had seen and heard. Second, he includes an epilogue entitled 'Time' and describes his own experiences of growing up in the greater Paris region in a neighbourhood which resembled those where he conducted his fieldwork.

A useful feature of the book is Fassin's exploration of his interpretation of the term ethnography and how he distinguishes it from other attempts to share the experiences of policing and being policed, for example the memoirs of former officers or investigative journalism. This is buried in the preface; note our advice in the further reading section to read all parts of ethnographic texts. In so doing, he is keen to dispel the myth that ethnography 'is not about producing otherness' (2013: x). He avoids this by focusing on the mundane rather than the spectacular, distinguishing ethnographic research from other attempts (for example, by the media) to render visible social worlds which are typically hidden from view.

Finally, it is worth noting the length of time taken to produce an ethnographic account. The book was published a number of years after the fieldwork was conducted. Academics rarely get to devote all their time to research so part of the explanation for the time lag might be other work pressures on the author. However, it is also likely to reflect the considerable amount of time needed to make sense of ethnographic data, starting with collating the different sources of data (for example, field notes, interview transcripts and documents collected) through to analysing the abundance of data gathered or the process of producing an ethnographic account. For Fassin, ethnography is about 'entering and communicating the experience of others: both verbs are crucial' (2013: x) so the production of the ethnographic account is as important as the conduct of the fieldwork. He describes his own approach to writing as 'the tentative application of the art of storytelling to the monotony of routine', highlighting that ethnographers make choices about the data they collect and how they present it. The end result is a narrative account of events which are used to develop theoretical arguments around issues such as morality, discrimination, violence and politics.

CONCLUDING COMMENTS

We began this chapter by dispelling some of the myths surrounding ethnography. Through exploring the varying ways in which criminologists have employed ethnographic approaches we have reflected upon some of the key characteristics of ethnography, and these are listed below.

1. Ethnography involves studying people in their natural setting and revealing the complexity of their social world, their experiences and their subjective attitudes.
2. Ethnography is flexible and can be used to study a wide variety of social groups and settings using a range of theoretical frameworks. Indeed, a recent special issue of *Current Issues in Criminal Justice* (Travers et al., 2013) demonstrates that ethnographic approaches can be used to explore innovations in criminal justice such as restorative justice conferences (Bruce, 2013), and also continue to offer insight into the lives of indigenous populations, marginalised young people and drug users (Putt, 2013). The use of ethnographic techniques to understand social worlds in cyberspace is further testimony to its flexibility.
3. Ethnography contributes to the development of theoretical knowledge. It offers much more than amassing detailed information about aspects of social life. An ethnography which only did this would be indistinguishable from the reality TV programmes which have come to dominate schedules.
4. Conducting ethnography is a 'messy business' (Pearson, 1993: vii). This is reflected in the confessional tales of ethnographers which stand in stark contrast to the sanitised accounts in many 'research methods' texts.

We have also considered that whilst ethnographic research appears deceptively simple it is challenging yet rewarding. This is vividly described by Sharpe below in a chapter reflecting on her experiences of ethnographic research on prostitution.

The research was not a dull experience. It ranged from being extremely interesting, hilariously funny and enjoyable to being conversely tense, frustrating and totally exhausting. Providing you are not of a nervous disposition and do not mind getting freezing cold, mercilessly teased, tried out and 'tested', sworn at, laughed at, generally abused and half frightened to death, it is a research strategy that makes library based research seem a trifle dull in comparison. (Sharpe, 1998: 12)

Exercises

1   What are the main risks associated with ethnographic research? You might find it helpful to think about these in terms of (a) legal, (b) ethical and (c) personal risks. Imagining conducting research with different groups should assist with this task.

2   Select a criminological topic which you feel is suitable for study using an ethnographical approach and imagine you are attempting to seek funding for this work. How would you justify your approach? Try to anticipate the comments you might receive from peer reviewers (those tasked with scrutinising your proposal).

3   What do you think are the essential skills ethnographers need to possess? How might these skills be developed?

FURTHER READING

- Atkinson, P. (2015) *For Ethnography*. London: Sage.

  Described as part manifesto and part guidance on the appropriate focus of the ethnographic gaze, this text makes a strong case for this distinctive way of knowing about the social world. The author encourages researchers to think about what to look at and what to look for when conducting fieldwork.

- Brewer, J. (2000) *Ethnography*. Buckingham: Open University Press.

  Written at a time when the future of ethnography was uncertain, the author offers a robust defence of this methodological approach and argues for its continued relevance in the social sciences. The book contains a number of examples of criminological research studies, including references to the author's own fieldwork on the Royal Ulster Constabulary.

- Ferrell, J. and Hamm, M. (eds) (1998) *Ethnography at the Edge*. Boston, MA: Northeastern University Press.

  This book focuses specifically on crime, deviance and field research. It covers a range of topics including sex work, drug taking and drug dealing and terrorism, alongside methodological and ethical issues associated with researching 'risky' populations. Refreshingly honest, the contributors offer many 'true confessions'.

- Hammersley, M. and Atkinson, P. (2007) *Ethnography: Principles in Practice*, 3rd edn. London: Routledge.

This is the classic text on ethnography in which the authors explore different dimensions of conducting ethnographic work from research design through to writing ethnography. The discussion is littered with references to ethnographic studies from a wide range of disciplines, including criminology.

- Travers, M., Putt, J. and Howard-Wagner, D. (2013) 'Ethnography, crime and criminal justice', *Special issue of Current Issues in Criminal Justice*, 25(1).

This special issue includes a number of articles which illustrate the ways in which ethnography can be used to research social groups, communities and criminal justice processes. It also provides contemporary reflections on long-standing debates, for example the use of covert techniques.

In addition to the methodological literature on ethnography, reading ethnographic accounts are highly recommended. There are numerous examples referred to in this chapter spanning a wide range of criminological topics. In selecting texts to read, ignore the typical advice you have been given as a criminology student and read some of the 'classic' ethnographies – even if they are over 50 years old – as well as some of the more recent contributions. Do take care to read all sections of the book. Some of the most revealing insights about ethnographic research are too frequently hidden in the preliminary pages or at the end of the book.

WORKING WITH QUALITATIVE DATA: ANALYSIS, WRITING AND DISSEMINATION

8

Blaxter et al. (2010: 224) note that 'analysis can be a fearful word for the novice researcher'. In recognition of this the main aim of this chapter is to demystify qualitative data analysis, although we will also reflect upon writing as a stage in the research process indistinguishable from analysis. By their very nature qualitative methods can generate a vast amount of rich and detailed data. The challenge for the researcher is to make sense of that data and provide an illuminating analysis. As others have warned, it is inappropriate to outline a recipe (see Hammersley and Atkinson, 2007) or set of rule-bound prescriptions (see Tesch, 1990) for qualitative researchers to follow. Instead we will consider the main approaches to managing, analysing and presenting the main types of qualitative data collected by criminological researchers, combining a discussion of the principle of qualitative data analysis with helpful pointers and practical advice.

WHAT IS QUALITATIVE DATA ANALYSIS?

We start by unpacking what is meant by the term 'qualitative data analysis' and being explicit about the stance adopted in this chapter. As Coffey and Atkinson (1996: 6) explain below there is some disagreement over which stage in the research process can be described as analysis.

> For some authors, analysis refers primarily to the tasks of coding, indexing, sorting, retrieving, or otherwise manipulating data ... From such a perspective, the task of analysis can be conceived primarily in terms of data handling. Whether it is done by hand or by computer software, data analysis at this level is relatively independent of speculation and interpretation ... For others in the field, analysis refers primarily to the imaginative work of interpretation, and the more procedural, categorizing tasks are relegated to the preliminary work of ordering and sorting the data.

The approach we will take here is that analysis encapsulates both the technical and creative processes referred to above. Blaxter et al. (2010) helpfully suggest that the analytic stage of the research process includes managing your data *and* analysing the managed set of data. The former aims to reduce the size and scope of the data whilst the latter is focused on abstraction, drawing attention to what might be of particular importance or significance. Crucially it is important not to see analysis as a discrete stage in the research process which takes place once data have been collected, and it is misleading to view analysis as merely managing and manipulating data. As Hammersley and Atkinson (2007: 158) argue 'data are materials to think with'. These data are, or at least should be, rich and detailed and capture the complexities of social life with its uncertainties, ambiguities and contradictions (Denscombe, 2014: 302). The process of analysis needs to respect the nature of the data and resist the temptation to oversimplify. Doing so undermines the decision to adopt a qualitative approach through failing to appreciate its strengths.

TYPES OF DATA ANALYSIS

A broad variety of analytic strategies are available to qualitative criminological researchers and it is beyond the scope of this chapter to review all of them. Entire books have been dedicated to the subject, some of which are listed in the further reading section at the end of the chapter. We focus on techniques for analysing the written word, although acknowledge that researchers often have different forms of qualitative data (see Chapter 1).

Each one is based upon a particular understanding of the data and the purpose of analysis, which influences how the data are managed and interpreted. The choice of approach should fit with the theoretical approach adopted. For example, Aiello (2014) chose qualitative content analysis to analyse six of the highest-grossing American police movies. Since qualitative content analysis is focused on looking for meaning it is an appropriate fit with the selected cultural criminological perspective which aims, amongst other things, to uncover the role of meaning within mediated constructions of crime (see Ferrell, 2013). He combined this with criminological work on masculinities, again apposite given this involves an attempt to understand representations of hegemonic masculinity in a particular historical moment (see Jefferson, 2013). The importance of fit between theory and analytic method is also illustrated in Box 8.3.

Qualitative researchers commonly favour a combination of analytic strategies, and an example of this is provided in Box 8.1. While Coffey and Atkinson (1996) acknowledge the value of this approach they press for avoidance of an over-simplified understanding of the process. They suggest:

> We can use different analytic strategies in order to explore different facets of our data, explore different kinds of order in them, and construct different versions of the social world. That kind of variety does not imply that one can simply take the results from different analyses and stick them together like children's building blocks in order to create a single edifice. (Coffey and Atkinson, 1996: 14)

Table 8.1   Approaches to qualitative data analysis

Type of analysis	Definition	Typical uses	Criminological example
Qualitative content analysis	A term used to describe a range of approaches which interpret meaning from the context of textual data (Hsieh and Shannon, 2005)	Analysis of documents	Phillips and Strobl (2006): analysis of how American comic books construct crime and justice, revealing a focus on organised crime and support for vigilantism
Conversational analysis	Like content analysis, there are different variants (which may be combined) but generally the term refers to the analysis of the structure and sequencing of talk and the underlying rules	Analysis of interviews	Stokoe (2010): analysis of the ways male suspects deny accusations of assaulting women in interrogations with police officers (see Box 8.3)
Discourse analysis	Focused on the exercise of power through language, sharing some common features with conversational analysis	Analysis of documents and interviews	Worrall (1990): analysis of the discourses used by criminal justice professionals to categorise (inadequately) female lawbreakers
Grounded theory	A methodology which aims to generate theory built upon theoretical concepts and/or categories which emerge from the data (De Bie and De Poot, 2016)	Suitable for all forms of qualitative data but particularly exploratory studies	Tong and Du (2014): analysis of public service announcements and print newspaper articles to argue that the media place a key role in constructing risk and fear in Hong Kong by enabling consumers to imagine that they might become victims
Narrative analysis	Focused on the story in its entirety and the implicit meanings as individuals present their own identity and social domain	Analysis of interviews and personal documents (for example, diaries)	Maruna (2007): analysis of interviews with repeat offenders to argue that those who are able to 'make good' have developed personal narratives which enable them to explain the past, lead a 'good' life and feel in control of their future

In other words, while different strategies can provide varying perspectives on the data, researchers need to think carefully about how to connect the different interpretations they are likely to produce and make principled decisions to justify particular combinations of analytic strategy. Once choices have been made it is important that the researcher continues to reflect critically on the appropriateness of the analytic strategy for the task in hand.

Box 8.1   Combining approaches: Analysing interaction in criminal justice groupwork

In a blogpost, Kirkwood (2014) describes his decision to combine discourse and conversation analysis to explore interaction during the delivery of groupwork programmes for offenders. The research used video recordings. Whilst acknowledging the limitations of analysing interactions out of context, he argues that it encourages reflection on how participants embrace, resist or show ambivalence to the processes of desistance. He argues that this can enhance practice by reflecting upon how social workers (the programme is delivered in Scotland where criminal justice social workers have responsibility for supervising offenders in the community) can work with those who are undecided, creating opportunities for positive change or identifying existing successes. The research findings were shared with stakeholders at a knowledge exchange seminar which provided an opportunity to consider how the research can enhance reflective practice.

Given its centrality in qualitative research we will now focus on grounded theory.

GROUNDED THEORY

Some qualitative researchers favour a grounded theory approach whereby analytic themes emerge from the data collected. This was originally developed by Glaser and Strauss (1967) but as De Bie and De Poot (2016: 583) observe there is no longer one form of grounded theory. Broadly speaking, rather than the researcher entering the field with preconceived ideas, the expectation is that analytic themes will emerge from the data. This approach bridges the gap between theoretically uninformed empirical research and empirically uninformed theory by grounding theory in data. It is based on the premise that theory at various levels of generality is indispensable for deeper knowledge of social phenomena but theory ought to be developed in close relationship with data. The principle is that detailed analysis of data helps to produce an emergent theory to guide data collection focused on making comparisons. In due course theoretical saturation is reached where additional analysis no longer contributes to discovering anything new. The results are then written up with 'thick description' (Geertz, 1973), with the presentation of specific incidents from field notes and interviews organised around analytic themes and discussion of an empirically grounded theory. This inductive method is particularly useful for those undertaking ethnographic research. In the case of those conducting interviews, particularly those which are semi-structured in format, there is likely to have been more advanced planning in relation to identifying key themes. Box 8.2 describes the use of grounded theory in a criminological research project.

Box 8.2   Grounded theory in action: Analysing police files to understand Jihadist networks

De Bie and De Poot (2016) dedicate an entire article to explaining their choice of analytic approach. They analysed confidential police files over a 13-year period combined with interviews with police investigators, public prosecutors and defence lawyers, and observations of criminal court hearings and trials in order to develop and test new theories to explain Jihadist networks and make a contribution to the literature on terrorism and radicalisation. They used Charmaz's (2014) constructivist approach to grounded theory and argue that it added value to their study by focusing data collection, encouraging them to collect different types of data from that originally anticipated to 'sharpen and enhance ... understanding of a particular phenomenon' (De Bie and De Poot, 2016: 594). They describe how they were able to 'test' emerging ideas and develop greater theoretical insights. From their perspective these advantages outweighed the investment of resources needed to conduct analysis in this way.

Grounded theory has been subject to a great deal of critique, in part due to a misunderstanding of the approach which has been misrepresented as a set of rules and procedures rather than broad principles (see Atkinson et al., 2003). Reflecting upon her use of a grounded theory approach, Asquith (2015) suggests that it is useful to view grounded theory as providing a set of tools which provide a flexible way of exploring the data. Debates about the value of grounded theory are beyond the scope of this chapter (see Bryant and Charmaz, 2010; Charmaz, 2014). Perhaps the best advice is to recognise that there is something of a continuum in the extent to which qualitative researchers follow a grounded approach. Advocates of grounded theory are marked by the openness of their approach and a lack of rigidity in the planning stages of their research. Consequently, they are receptive to the themes that emerge from the fieldwork and may not have been anticipated by the researcher. It does not necessarily preclude drawing upon the extensive work that might have been done in the past on the topic of interest. For example, in describing his approach to observing crime policy-making Stevens (2011: 239) argues that 'it would have been wasteful to ignore all the previous attempts to explain the evidence-policy link by limiting myself to the development of theory from the data alone'. His approach was to follow Layder (1998) and use 'adaptive coding' which begins with generating a list of provisional codes from previous work, which we explore in the next section.

THEORY AND DATA ANALYSIS

Above we began above to explore the role of theory in qualitative criminological research. Through our discussion of critiques of grounded theory, we thought about how the conceptual understanding researchers have acquired from conducting the initial literature review or their previous work might inform the research process. Advocates of grounded theory adopt an inductivist approach and view research as a means of generating (micro-level) theory but given that many criminologists view research as a cumulative process, adding to a body of existing theoretical and empirical research, it is problematic to suggest that research projects can start with a 'blank canvas'. It is not necessary to adopt a deductivist approach instead which perceives the role of research as testing a theoretically informed hypothesis, not least because this is more closely aligned to quantitative criminological research (see Wincup, 2013). Neither of these positions are wholly adequate for many forms of qualitative research.

Using theory does not mean that researchers have to force interpretations of data in their mould, rather it acts as a resource for making sense of the data (see Hammersley and Atkinson, 2007). It may be that the literature review suggests useful theoretical concepts or exposes the researcher to work of a particular theory or theoretical orientation. Layder's (1998: 150) 'adaptive theory' approach is helpful here which encourages researchers to construct a 'theoretical scaffold' which for qualitative research can be modified through inductive processes (see Bottoms, 2008). This is difficult to realise in practice. As Coffey and Atkinson (1996: 2) describe, it is not uncommon for the qualitative researcher who has gathered a vast amount of data to be without any clear plan in how they might use that data to construct explanations and develop theoretical concepts.

So far we have talked about theory in a general sense and it is worth reflecting further on the term. It can range from macro-level which 'are those which apply to large-scale systems of social relations' (Hammersley and Atkinson, 2007: 188) through to micro-level which are theories that focus on 'more local forms of social encounter' (Hammersley and Atkinson, 2007: 188) within institutions or social interactions. Bottoms (2008: 79) warns against some of the barriers within criminology which discourage 'creative theorisation'. He encourages empirical researchers to exploit (macro-level) general social theory and to be open about the types of theoretical work they can draw upon.

WHEN DOES ANALYSIS START?

Hammersley and Atkinson (2007) argue that the analysis of data is not a distinct stage within the research process. Their focus is on ethnographic data but can equally be applied to different forms of qualitative data. They suggest it begins at the earliest stage of research when formulating the research problem. At this point it is essential that researchers think ahead and reflect upon the nature of the data that their chosen research design and methods might generate and how the data gathered might be analysed in order to address the research questions. They might go further – 'pure' grounded theorists excepted – and consider the possible themes which might emerge. This early planning should be flexible. Researchers need to remain open to emerging themes but being prepared facilitates subsequent analytic focus.

For Hammersley and Atkinson (2007: 158) analysis starts to take place formally once the researcher starts to make analytic notes and informally once they begin to have 'ideas and hunches' about their data. The expectation is that the researcher will spend time away from the field engaging in preliminary analysis before returning with a clear focus of the type of data they need to collect. For example, during fieldwork on bail hostel provision for women awaiting trial I became aware of the importance of the period immediately before and after curfew (11pm for most residents) and asked to spend some time observing this period. The iterative process is particularly relevant when researchers are engaged in 'grounded theorising' but applies to other forms of analysis too. Hammersley and Atkinson's (2007: 160) 'funnel' metaphor is useful here; it describes the 'progressive focusing' which characterises qualitative research, which allows the researcher to move from 'thick description' to developing and testing explanations or theories. In practice this can be difficult to realise as the researcher may not have sufficient control over when the data collection takes place. They are likely to be working to a particular deadline and are dependent on others for access (see Chapter 4).

Whilst one of the most important rules is that the researcher should never see the completion of the data collection stage as the point at which they begin to think about and plan for analysis, researchers commonly visit issues of analysis once the data are collected (Coffey and Atkinson, 1996). Some of this is likely to be attributable to the relative lack of attention in many articles, books and reports on the chosen analytic strategy. Including this can help to enhance the validity of the data, an issue we explore in more detail in the final chapter by making it explicit that the researcher has not simply 'cherry-picked' data or offered the 'headlines' with little understanding of the complexities within the data. Whilst it is difficult to describe the complicated and messy processes of qualitative data analysis, qualitative researchers need to demonstrate that it has been conducted with attention to detail and rigour and convey how raw data have been transformed into the eventual findings.

As we are representing appropriate analysis of data as a journey rather than a single event we will now take the reader through the research process highlighting the analytic issues that need to be considered at each stage. We start by thinking about managing qualitative data.

MANAGING QUALITATIVE DATA

Effective data handling needs to begin with careful attention to how the data will be collected. Typically, this is through the use of a digital recorder allowing data to be transferred with ease to a secure location where it can be stored in an electronic format in compliance with the requirements of the Data Protection Act 1998 (see Chapter 3). Most qualitative researchers have stories about equipment failure so it should become custom and practice to make sure recorders are working effectively before the interview and store the recordings in multiple locations afterwards. There can be few worse scenarios for the social researcher than to have achieved access for a particularly valuable interview only to be let down by non-functioning equipment. This is especially important when recording focus groups and so it is advisable to have two facilitators, one of whom takes responsibility for monitoring that the tape is working as required, leaving the other to focus on facilitation of the discussion. Focus groups also require some attention to sound levels and background noise to ensure all voices are heard.

Another option for recording data is the use of video equipment. The same rules need to apply regarding participant consent with particular attention to questions of confidentiality. Effective means are also available for the recording of telephone interviews although it is important to stress the importance of informing the interviewee that a recording is being made and gaining their consent. During a telephone interview it will not be evident to the respondent that a recording is being made and it is therefore especially important that the researcher is explicit that they intend to record the interview. The respondent's wishes should be checked carefully.

Recording does raise ethical issues. Participants need to give permission for recording to take place (via a consent form, see Chapter 3) and should be provided with a clear and accurate account of how the recordings will be used. Researchers need to be willing to turn off any recording equipment if instructed to do so. Recording also raises methodological issues since the interviewee might be reluctant to open up if they are being recorded. It is not uncommon for the most interesting data to be collected after recording has ceased. In this situation, it is difficult to know whether these data can be used and it is good practice to clarify this with the interviewee.

While the use of recording equipment is increasingly common, scenarios are encountered in criminological research where their use is not allowed or they are not deemed appropriate. For example, they may not be allowed during prison-based interviews and the researcher will commonly have to rely on the more traditional method of note taking. Devoting attention to writing down what is said can detract from achieving a rapport with the interviewee and the researcher's observation of non-verbal cues. Key elements should be noted during the interview and a full account written up immediately after the interview is completed. This forms part of the process of organising data, which we consider in the next section.

ORGANISING QUALITATIVE DATA

The type of qualitative data collected depends upon the method chosen. Documents, for instance, come in all shapes and sizes ranging from those which are in an electronic format ready for analysis though to handwritten historical documents which may need to be turned into a more useable form. As noted above, interview data are typically turned into transcripts, a process which we will consider shortly. Ethnographic data is likely to be in multiple forms (see Hammersley and Atkinson, 2007) including copies of documents, field notes, entries in a fieldwork journal and notes from informal interviews. To greater or lesser extents, qualitative data are 'unstructured' and not organised into analytic categories in the way that quantitative data already are. The task of the researcher is to organise the data in this way, typically through coding, sometimes facilitated by the use of specialist computer software. Prior to that the data need to be organised into a form which facilitates this process. Denscombe (2014: 276) makes the important point that qualitative data need to be prepared and organised before they can be analysed and in its 'raw' state data can be difficult to interrogate in any systematic and meaningful way. He provides practical strategies which are highly recommended – keeping back-up copies of the original data and creating a referencing system for the data.

TRANSCRIPTION

Recordings of interviews and focus groups are usually transcribed. Researchers need to be aware that this is a labor intensive task and, where professional support is used, expensive process. A one-hour recording can take anything between six and ten hours to transcribe, depending on factors such as audibility, the level of detail needed and whether there are multiple participants. This can be balanced against the fact that researchers transcribing their own work will have the opportunity to become steeped in the nuances of the interview data. The transcription process offers the opportunity for reflection on the data and attention to emerging themes and should be seen as an integral part of the analytic process. Such opportunities for familiarisation need to be set against the speed and efficiency of a professional typist for those research projects where funds exist for transcription. In such cases proof reading of data can facilitate reflection and help develop an analytic focus. Proof reading should not be done too meticulously. Once transcribed the messiness of talk is revealed with incomplete sentences and misused words. Whichever strategy is adopted the time spent on familiarising oneself through close reading and re-reading of transcripts is invaluable.

Students, particularly those producing dissertations for undergraduate or taught postgraduate courses, will need to think about the scope of their project and in some cases transcribe and analyse only the most relevant parts of an interview rather than the full piece. As others have acknowledged (Arksey and Knight, 1999: 141), transcripts vary in the level of detail that they include. There are issues, for example, about the extent to which the transcript should include grunts, groans, chuckles, 'um's, 'ah's and pauses. Such elements in the delivery of speech can be highly telling and their inclusion will communicate more to the reader about the attitude and state of mind of the interviewee. While resources may not run to extending this type of transcription to the full dataset such an in-depth approach might be deployed with the more significant segments of an interview. Again it is important that the researcher consider carefully the reasons for their style of transcription and be explicit about their rationale for the format adopted. The decision is likely to be influenced by the choice of analytic approach. Box 8.3 describes the transcription needed for a criminological research study which used conversational analysis.

Box 8.3   Analysing talk: Conversations between police and arrestees

Stokoe (2010: 59) drew upon what she describes as 'a large corpus of British police interrogation materials' and used conversation analysis to understand how men (arrested for assaulting women) denied being 'the kind of men who hit women'. Her dataset comprised of 120 tape-recorded interviews which were originally made under the terms of the Police and Criminal Evidence Act 1984 and subsequently digitised, anonymised and transcribed. The transcriptions – extracts of which are reproduced in the article – were incredibly detailed (following guidance from Jefferson [2004]. For example, the length of pauses is noted and where emphasis is placed on a particular letter in a word. Producing this level of detail required high-quality recordings and skilled transcribers. It would be unnecessary for the majority of qualitative research projects but it was essential here to understand how men deny their violence both in response to questions posed by police officers and more generally in their own accounts.

CODING DATA

Many qualitative criminological researchers use coding as a means of bringing a measure of organisation to the data and identifying conceptual categories. It is particularly associated with grounded theory but it is fundamental to other analytic approaches too. For some researchers, the coding process decontextualises the meaning of the data (see Denscombe, 2014: 303) since it requires the researcher to deconstruct and then reassemble the data. This danger is a real one but coding does allow the researcher to get to *know* their data and give a familiarity which must underpin the analytic process (Hammersley and Atkinson, 2007: 172). At the coding stage the researcher works *with* the data to produce categories in line with areas of thematic interest. Such activity is achieved by reviewing the data and attaching what have variously been referred to as tags, labels or memos. Such activity should not be viewed as a mechanical process but as an opportunity for further reflection and thought on the part of the researcher regarding the messages that are emerging from the data.

Below is an extract from two interviews with staff working in bail hostels for women awaiting trial. It illustrates how coding can be applied to data. Some of the codes can be descriptive (for example, rules and regulations) whilst others are more abstract (for example, the concept of a 'haven').

Emma Wincup	What are your thoughts on mixed hostels?	
Residential worker 1	I guess I'm not opposed to them but I would say there has to be hostels for women only. I think one of the things we offer the women is that they come here and they've been given a breathing space. They know that this hostel is women only and you can have male visitors between 1pm and 6pm.	*Need for a range of provision* *Haven* *Rules & regulations*
Emma Wincup	What are your thoughts on mixed hostels?	
Residential worker 2	I think I have reservations about the mixed hostels where there are a small number of women. I think that creates pressures. I can't see how the women who are in mixed hostels are going to be less vulnerable than the ones in here. In which case they can't offer the same kind of respite, which can be beneficial, from men who have been abusive. I think that sometimes we have women who haven't done well in a mixed hostel who come here and do much better and that says something.	*Needs of female offenders* *Haven* *Evidence of success*

If we adopt the approach of Coffey and Atkinson (1996: 10) and view data analysis as 'artful and playful' it is important to encourage experimenting with the data. Not all initial codes will be used; some will be combined as the data analysis process moves on and some may become redundant. Box 8.4 considers strategies for generating codes.

Box 8.4 Coding qualitative data: Suggested strategies

- *Look at the language used by the participants*, what Strauss (1987) refers to as *in vivo* codes, for example interviews with newly recruited police officers might include references to 'learning the ropes' or 'being thrown in at the deep end'
- *Draw inspiration from the academic literature*, what Strauss (1987) refers to as sociologically constructed codes (but we can interpret them as criminologically constructed too), for example we might look at the same interviews described above through the lens of 'occupational socialisation' (from sociology) or 'cop culture' (from criminology) and use concepts from these bodies of literature to code the data
- *Use typologies*: it might be possible to distinguish between different types of research participant (see Box 1.3)
- *Use metaphor*: for example, the code 'haven' referred to in the earlier discussion of interview data on mixed hostels

---

Coffey and Atkinson (1996: 30) make a powerful argument that coding should be seen initially as a reductive process which facilitates manipulation of the data as a preamble to 'going beyond the data, thinking creatively with the data, asking the data questions, and generating theories and frameworks'. For Coffey and Atkinson (1996: 27) 'the important analytic work lies in establishing and thinking about such linkages [between codes], not in the mundane process of coding'. So while coding of qualitative data must allow for reflection and thoughtfulness it is an incremental stage in the interpretative process facilitating the final goal of considering the relationships between the conceptual categories, an issue we will return to once we have considered the role of specialist software packages in facilitating qualitative data analysis.

COMPUTER ASSISTED QUALITATIVE DATA ANALYSIS SOFTWARE (CAQDAS)

Increasingly qualitative criminological researchers make use of CAQDAS and it has become almost an expectation that this approach will be adopted for doctoral research projects, forming part of the research apprenticeship. The most commonly used package is NVIVO but there are a number of options available (see the list and associated reviews provided by the CAQDAS Networking Project at the University of Surrey – www.surrey.ac.uk/sociology/research/researchcentres/caqdas/about/) and a body of literature to support those who wish to use them (see for example, Silver and Lewins, 2014).

The introduction of CAQDAS has in many respects transformed qualitative data analysis. Researchers – like myself – had already begun to use word processing software as an alternative to the physical sorting of data used in the past (imagine lots of photocopies of the data, scissors and a collection of folders or shoe boxes!) in order to make their data malleable and open to systematic examination. Developments in CAQDAS were a step-change providing the researcher with 'the ability to interrogate data and revise conceptualisations through searching and retrieving categorised data [and it] promises to introduce a new flexibility and rigour into qualitative analysis' (Dey, 1993: 59).

Such optimism was not universal and many qualitative researchers were unconvinced about the value of CAQDAS suggesting it detracts from building up familiarity with the data and requires the investment of a disproportionate amount of time. Packages are now far more sophisticated than in the past and as use of CAQDAS has come common place such scepticism has fallen away. They now offer more than support for data storage, coding and retrieval and can assist with theory-building (Hammersley and Atkinson, 2007). Like any decision made whilst designing and conducting research, it is important to reflect upon the possible advantages and disadvantages of using CAQDAS. Lewins and Silver (2009) helpfully outline the questions which qualitative researchers need to ask when considering whether to use a dedicated package and these are summarised in Blaxter et al. (2010: 224). In essence, they encourage reflection on the research study as a whole from its theoretical orientation to anticipated outputs, in addition to considering practical reasons why a researcher should or should not choose a data management project.

CAQDAS is particularly suited to projects which have amassed a large amount of data and it is always surprising how much even a small-scale qualitative study can yield. Often such projects will involve multiple researchers and/or forms of data and dedicated software can enable flexible handling. Whatever approach is adopted the important factor to hold on to is that data management in itself does not constitute analysis. What is not recommended is a situation where the data is carefully stored on the computer but not embedded in the thinking of the researcher.

INTERPRETING THE DATA

The final stage in the data analysis process is referred to as interpretation which has been helpfully summarised as 'the process by which you put your own meaning on the data you have collected and analysed, and compare that meaning with those advanced by others' (Blaxter et al., 2010: 242). This needs to be done judiciously. At this point the focus will be on examining the data for embedded meanings and understandings that the researcher's meticulous indexing of the data will enable them to identify. It will sometimes be important for the researcher to allow themselves space from the data collection phase when tackling this interpretative stage. So whilst analysis should be an ongoing exercise the researcher needs to allow sufficient time for a reflective focus on interpretation in the latter stages of research projects. This, of course, does not preclude the researcher from returning to the field to collect further data (but see the discussion of leaving the field in Chapter 4) and sharing or checking out their interpretations with the research participants (see Box 8.5).

The process of interpretation is far from straightforward. Since the researcher is central to the process, it is important to reflect upon the implications of this. It is problematic to strive for objectivity but at the same time it is worth considering strategies for enhancing the quality of qualitative analysis. Some strategies are listed in Box 8.5.

Box 8.5   Enhancing the quality of qualitative analysis: Suggested strategies

- *Conduct collaborative research*: it is possible others may offer alternative explanations allowing a discussion to take place about which one 'fits' best with the available data rather than which one is correct
- *Adopt a reflexive stance*: reflect carefully on how your identity, background and beliefs may have influenced your interpretation and acknowledge this in published outputs
- *Use different data sources* (but see Chapter 1 for a critical discussion of this approach): different data may yield alternative interpretations and this reflects the complexity of the social world
- *Reflect carefully on data that does not fit*: for example, there may be good reasons for an individual not fitting into a typology which the researcher has developed
- *Avoid the temptation to stick with 'tried and tested' explanations*: it is often reassuring if your conclusions are similar to those who have conducted similar studies but if they are different then consider the reasons why
- *See feedback from research participants (respondent validation)*: for some qualitative researchers this is good practice whilst others are concerned that participants will struggle to make the leap from their experience to the academic analysis
- *Seek feedback from stakeholders*: an alternative to the strategy above is to present the emerging findings to stakeholders, who have not participated in the research but are interested in its findings (see Box 8.1)
- *Take a break*: going back to data with 'fresh eyes' can lead to new ways of seeing the data or make it easier to act as your own critic, revisiting earlier interpretations

---

'WRITING UP' QUALITATIVE RESEARCH

In the final section of this chapter we turn our attention to writing. There is now a substantial literature on writing and qualitative research (Holliday, 2016; Wolcott, 2009; Woods, 2005) and the topic is worthy of more discussion than space allows. Here we need to appreciate that the act of writing itself should be seen as central to the analytic process, a point made strongly by Coffey and Atkinson (1996: 109).

> Writing and representing is a vital way of thinking about one's data. Writing makes us think about data in new and different ways. Thinking about how to represent our data also forces us to think about the meanings and understandings, voices and experiences present in the data. As such, writing actually deepens our level of academic endeavour.

This raises the issue of how findings might be presented and how data might be included in the final 'product'. Typically, qualitative writing is organised around analytic themes which are discussed with reference to extracts of data. Sometimes these can be quite lengthy, particularly if researchers feel that an important role of research is to give a voice to particular groups. The danger of this approach is that data are then presented out of context. This can be addressed in part through providing some contextual material but it leaves qualitative researchers vulnerable to the criticism that they have 'cherry-picked' data to support the argument being advanced. Within a longer publication or thesis, it is possible to present multiple extracts so they become more than one-off illustrations. Crucially, the author needs to convey a sense that their approach to data analysis is systematic and robust. There are exceptions to this oft-used model. For example, Carlen (1985) structures her account of 'criminal women' by presenting their stories individually.

While we are considering writing as an analytic tool at a relatively late stage in this section this is not indicative that it has limited importance. Qualitative researchers need to begin writing at an early stage and, as with analysis itself, see writing as an ongoing process. While some of the earliest efforts at writing may well be discarded such writings provide important foundations for the academic enterprise. Whilst the final stage of research is often referred to as 'writing up', this in many respects is a misnomer.

Increasingly, as we explored in Chapter 2, criminologists are encouraged to disseminate their findings to different audiences and Box 8.6 describes a research project which did this very successfully. Typically, this is in a written form. There are now plentiful opportunities in our digital age to disseminate research findings widely but this requires not only being more concise but adopting a different style. Fortunately, there is a great deal of advice available (see for example, Richardson [1990] who focuses specifically on 'writing up' qualitative research). Crucially as Blaxter et al. (2010) encourage, authors need to reflect upon their voice (i.e. how they tell their 'story') and their style (i.e. how they structure their 'story').

Box 8.6   Writing for different audiences: Disseminating research on the 2011 summer riots

Shortly after the 2011 summer riots in the UK, Tim Newburn (Professor of Criminology at the London School of Economics) undertook a collaborative research project with *The Guardian* newspaper funded by the Joseph Rowntree Foundation and the Open Society Foundation. The large research team was able to draw upon both expertise in journalism and academic writing to produce an accessible research report (Lewis et al., 2011); a series of articles in leading criminology journals including *Theoretical Criminology* (Newburn, 2016) and *Policing and Society* (Newburn et al., 2016); and offer extensive newspaper coverage comprising of a series of articles released over one week with the theme 'Reading the Riots' (see www.theguardian.com/uk/series/reading-the-riots).

The research was included as an impact case study in the 2014 Research Excellence Framework (see Chapter 2).

CONCLUDING COMMENTS

In this chapter we have reflected upon the analytic process, emphasising throughout that attention to analysis should begin at the outset of the research project and be revisited throughout. Our focus has been on the principles underpinning qualitative data analysis; namely, that it is iterative, inductive and centred around the researcher. Appreciating that data are a precious resource, we have reflected upon the need to plan carefully how data will be collected, stored, managed and interpreted. We have explored strategies to avoid feeling daunted by what can sometimes seem a voluminous amount of data and hope that these will prevent feelings of being overwhelmed and put students on the road to concurring with Coffey and Atkinson's (1996) view that analysis should be a positive and rewarding experience.

Exercises

1   Draw up a short schedule for a semi-structured interview which will last approximately 10 minutes and interview a fellow student, friend or family member. Choose a non-sensitive topic such as media coverage of crime. Record the interview and transcribe it. Read through the data gathered and identify at least four analytic themes.

2   Conduct a short period of observation and write up your field notes. For example, you could observe policing in action, for example at a football match, or the operation of security in a shopping centre. Read through the data gathered and identify at least four analytic themes.

3   Obtain some qualitative data in the form of a document, for example the Justice or Home Secretary's latest speech. Read through the data gathered and identify at least four analytic themes.

Once you have completed all the tasks reflect upon which form of data was the easiest to analyse and why.

FURTHER READING

- Chamberlain, J. (2013) *Understanding Criminological Research: A Guide to Data Analysis*. London: Sage.

  This book outlines the range of approaches which can be used for qualitative and quantitative data against a backdrop of their emergence in criminology. This is accompanied by a call for criminologists to justify their analytic approach.

- Coffey, A. and Atkinson, P. (1996) *Making Sense of Qualitative Data*. London: Sage.

  Using a single dataset, the authors explore different approaches to transforming data into something useful. Whilst the authors explain that it is not a 'cookbook', the text provides a wealth of practical advice.

- Harding, J. (2013) *Qualitative Data Analysis from Start to Finish*. London: Sage.

  Drawing upon the author's own experiences of analysing data, this text lays out the different stages in qualitative data analysis, demystifying a process which is so rarely discussed.

- Richards, L. (2014) *Handling Qualitative Data: A Practical Guide*, 3rd edn. London: Sage.

  Combining practical advice with recognition of the need for a theoretical understanding of the processes of data collection and analysis, this book explores how best to manage, reflect upon and make sense of the rich data which qualitative approaches should yield.

- Silverman, D. (2015) *Interpreting Qualitative Data*, 5th edn. London: Sage.

  Offering 'hands-on' guidance, this text walks those new to qualitative data analysis through the basics. It is supported by a companion website with additional teaching and learning resources.

PART III
BEING A QUALITATIVE RESEARCHER

RESEARCHING WOMEN'S EXPERIENCES OF ELECTRONIC MONITORING

ELLA HOLDSWORTH

This chapter reflects upon research conducted for my PhD thesis on women's experiences of electronic monitoring. My study looks at women who have been convicted of an offence and have been given an electronically monitored curfew as a community order, either on its own or alongside other community requirements. At the time of writing, fieldwork has been completed and I am immersed in data analysis and 'writing up'. The choice of topic draws upon my interest in female offenders in the criminal justice system which I developed during my MA studies in criminology. I was struck by how little gender is recognised within criminal justice policy and practice and this influenced my decision to conduct research in this area. In addition, the focus on electronic monitoring allows an in-depth look at how women experience community sentences; a relatively neglected area within the growing literature on gender and criminal justice. Electronic monitoring (known colloquially as tagging) is a particularly interesting sentence to research because although it is familiar to policy-makers, the media and the public, very little is actually known about how it functions, and how it is experienced by those subject to such monitoring. Research which does exist focuses predominantly on men (Hucklesby, 2008, 2009). Given my choice of topic, it is in some respects inevitable that feminist theory would play a part in shaping the project overall. To conduct research into female offenders and not consider the ever-increasing body of feminist literature would leave a great deal of unanswered questions and would result in research which is theoretically weak. Therefore, I chose my research topic fully expecting that feminist research and theory would feature heavily in the literature review, the theoretical basis and the methods and methodology.

This account is intended to highlight challenges the researcher might face when working with female offenders and to offer some indication of how best to respond to them. The first section explores the background to the research before outlining the aims and methods used. Following this, two issues that were dealt with during interviewing will be discussed in more detail. These relate to impression management and interviewing in the homes of the participants.

OVERVIEW OF THE RESEARCH PROJECT

Little academic research on women's experiences of electronic monitoring had been conducted at the time this study began and this had an impact on the research design. Previous studies of electronic monitoring in England and Wales did not include samples of women which were large enough to be able to draw conclusions about how women might experience electronically monitored curfews (Hucklesby, 2008, 2009). Furthermore, although studies had been conducted in other countries which focused on women's experiences in particular (King and Gibbs, 2003; Maidment, 2002), the different ways in which electronic monitoring is used mean that the findings may not provide an accurate indication of women's experiences of electronic monitoring in England and Wales. Previous research on electronic monitoring in this jurisdiction concentrated on how it functioned (Dodgson et al., 2001; Mair and Nee, 1990; Mair and Mortimer, 1996), and was largely 'shaped' by Home Office research agendas (Mair, 2007).

In addition to contributing to an understanding of electronic monitoring, the study also aims to add to what is known about how women experience community sentences. This area of research has become important over the last decade following the publication of the Corston report (Corston, 2007). This report was commissioned in response to several self-inflicted deaths by female prisoners within one year, adding to concerns about the impact of prison for women who largely commit non-violent offences and pose little risk to the public. Therefore, studying alternative sentences to imprisonment, such as electronic monitoring, is important.

CHOOSING A RESEARCH DESIGN

When it came to devising the methodology, I encountered some issues that I had not envisaged. I was expecting to conduct my research using qualitative methods, as they are commonly used in feminist research and they appeared to offer the best methodological 'fit' for my purposes. This will be discussed in more detail below, but it is important to note that a methodology with feminist underpinnings does not determine the choice of methods (Gelsthorpe, 1990). However, looking further into methodological literature, I realised that there was an impasse between researching offenders and researching women, with relatively few accounts of interviewing female offenders (see Davies, P. [2000] for an exception). The problem with this was that neither accounts of researching women nor offenders seemed to offer an accurate account of the situations I was expecting to encounter when conducting fieldwork. Although I wanted to adopt a feminist approach to research, most notably through the use of semi-structured interviews which would provide women with a voice, I found that the majority of the reflexive accounts failed to provide any realistic guidance to help me prepare for my fieldwork experiences. One particular issue that was present in the research was that I interviewed female offenders about their experiences of electronic monitoring in their homes. While it might be advantageous for the women to be interviewed in their homes where they might feel most comfortable, there were also safety concerns that needed to be addressed, which did not fit in with feminist accounts of researching women.

Given the context in which the research was conducted, it was important to design an exploratory study. Although previous studies had given indications of how women might experience electronic monitoring, this was not sufficient to be able to establish precisely what might be covered; hence an exploratory approach was adopted. The research questions were devised to cover five areas. Firstly, the research analyses which women received an electronically monitored curfew requirement as part of a community order, in terms of their demographic backgrounds, their criminogenic needs and their self-reported criminal careers. Secondly, it explores women's expectations of electronically monitored curfews at the start of their sentences and the factors which influenced these expectations. Thirdly, the research reflects upon the impact that women consider electronic monitoring to have on their lifestyles, attitudes and behaviour during the curfew period. Fourthly the study attempts to appreciate women's relationships with the (private sector) electronic monitoring company plus criminal justice and other agencies they had contact with. Finally, the study considers the ways in which women felt being subject to an electronically monitored curfew had impacted on their lifestyles, attitudes and behaviour, and the likely impact following the end of the curfew period.

The research design was chosen on the basis that it would generate the data required to answer the research questions. The method chosen needed to produce data about women's experiences of electronic monitoring which was in-depth and captured the views of the women themselves. As a result, a qualitative approach was selected with semi-structured interviewing felt to be the most appropriate method. Interviews were conducted with 31 women in North England between April 2012 and May 2013. The majority of these interviews were conducted in interviewees' homes. Access was sought and granted by the private company that carried out electronic monitoring services in the area at the time. The sampling criteria were kept deliberately simple due to the low numbers of women who were electronically monitored as a community sentence, which meant that the sample would be difficult to obtain. Therefore, the monitoring company identified women who were over the age of 18 who had been monitored as part of a community sentence for at least four weeks and who were fluent in English (since funds were not available for interpreting). Women who met the criteria were identified at the end of their period of electronic monitoring, and I accompanied members of staff from the monitoring company on their visit to remove the tag and equipment. It was not possible to inform the women that I would be present beforehand because I was not able to obtain any information which related to any woman subject to electronic monitoring without their consent. This meant that I was unable to invite women to take part in the research in advance. Furthermore, I decided that it would be problematic for others, such as staff at the monitoring company, to invite women for interview on my behalf. This would mean I would have little control over how the research was presented to prospective participants and would be unable to ensure it had been effectively explained. As a consequence, the women did not know I would be accompanying the officer and I was not given any details about the women beforehand.

This meant that women were recruited shortly before interviews were conducted and required the process to be thought through very carefully to ensure that the research was being conducted ethically. It was imperative that informed consent was sought from the women, that they understood what they were being invited to do and that they were able to make a free choice whether or not to take part in the interviews.

Collecting data in this way raised a number of further issues, two of which will now be discussed in more detail. We will begin by considering the importance of impression management in my interactions with participants and how this was affected by the presence of a monitoring officer when the research was conducted, followed by a discussion of conducting research in the homes of the participants.

RECRUITING PARTICIPANTS: CHALLENGES AND CONSIDERATIONS

The decision made to accompany electronic monitoring officers (when they were collecting equipment at the end of a curfew order) and ask women at this point whether they would be willing to participate was a practical one. Although it would have been desirable to allow women time between initial approach and conducting the interviews, there was no satisfactory method of contacting them prior to this. I was unable to have access to their names and contact details and it was unreasonable for me to expect the monitoring company to invite women on my behalf. Furthermore, had this happened I would not have had any understanding of how the women were recruited or how the research was explained, resulting in a situation where women may have given their consent without being fully informed about the project. In addition, risk issues needed to be carefully thought about, which led to the decision that I would have to be accompanied when conducting the interviews. The participants were all women who had been convicted of a criminal offence. While this in itself did not indicate the level of risk of the women, it laid open the potential that some participants had received convictions for very serious offences, including violent offences. Indeed, some women interviewed had been convicted for offences including grievous bodily harm and affray.

Furthermore, although the monitoring company had some information about risk relating to prospective participants, these were not always used as grounds not to visit women or invite them to take part in the research. For example, the monitoring officers held records of all previous visits and telephone interactions between themselves and the people who were electronically monitored. On occasions, incidents where women had been verbally abusive to staff on a previous visit were documented but these were not always used as grounds to discount women from taking part in the research. It was possible that such incidents related to the fact that women had received an electronically monitored curfew and their accounts would be very valuable to the research project.

The presence of a monitoring officer created implications for how I represented myself as a researcher, both to the officers and to the women themselves. With reference to the former, it was important to ensure that relationships were maintained during the research process. This has been defined as part of maintaining access or 'staying in'. This is an important point in any research project: access might be granted initially but there is a process involved whereby relationships with those who provide access must be maintained to ensure that all the necessary data can be collected. However, it was also vital to maintain relationships in this research project because the officers were present when I introduced myself to prospective participants and invited them to take part in the interviews. It had been envisaged that, apart from exceptional circumstances when issues of risk meant I could not be left in the address alone, the officers would wait while I conducted the interview out of earshot. Fortunately, there were no circumstances where it was necessary for the officers to be present when the interviews took place. Although I invited women in 'higher risk' situations, they declined to take part in the research. This was usually when a large number of people were present in the house, and it was decided in subsequent conversations between the officer and I that I would not have been able to remain in the address alone. However, by being present before the interviews commenced, officers could have had an impact on how I presented myself to participants. Accompanying an officer to invite women to be interviewed often meant that the officers introduced me to the women first, and subsequently the women's first impressions may have been affected by how I was represented by the officers. Thus, over the course of inviting over 80 women to take part in the research, I was introduced as a 'colleague', 'a student doing a project or questionnaire', or perhaps even worse, 'doing a PhD and very clever'! None of these introductions helped me to present myself to potential participants as I would have wished.

The issue of researchers presenting themselves to participants has gained attention from feminist researchers, who emphasise the significance of the way in which interviews are conducted and the level of disclosure by the women during the interview (Finch, 1993; Oakley, 1981; Reinharz, 1992). Specifically, the way in which a researcher presents themselves contributes to the development of rapport, which is regarded as a necessary feature of semi-structured interviewing. The notion of rapport and the implications of this for conducting research from a feminist perspective have been discussed by Oakley (1981). Oakley criticises traditional methodological approaches for their position on rapport, in particular the caution in ensuring that the researcher does not become too friendly in attempting to develop a rapport with an interviewee, as this might have a negative impact on the reliability and validity of the data. She also rejects the traditional position of the researcher remaining neutral during the interview, in order to avoid 'bias' in the data, which extends to exercising caution in answering questions directed towards the researcher. Finch (1993) asserts that female researchers will inevitably be better placed to interview women and that the interview should revolve around the shared identity of being female. Furthermore, she also argues that women may be more willing to engage in the interview and answer questions. Finch (1993) relates this willingness to talk back to the inferior position of women and society. As a result of this, women may be more accustomed to intervention from outside agencies in their lives and answering their questions.

Such accounts of interviewing women from a feminist perspective were appealing, especially as I wanted to incorporate feminist methods of conducting research into my study. However, from the outset I considered it over optimistic to assume that these approaches could be easily replicated. There were several reasons why I could not rely purely on being female in order to develop rapport. Firstly, the interviews were being conducted on experiences of electronic monitoring within the context of the criminal justice system. I was unable to draw from personal experience to develop rapport as a consequence. It is suggested that Finch's (1993) account of interviewing women does not entirely reflect the experience of interviewing offenders because it is more likely that the lives of the researcher and the participants are markedly different from each other and the factors they have in common are fewer than the differences.

Reflecting on interviewing women in prison, Pamela Davies (2000) discussed the anticipation and the anxiety that comes with interviewing known offenders that in her case had done something serious enough to warrant a custodial sentence. Although during my research, interviewing female offenders did not invoke feelings of anxiety, despite the fact that the women had committed serious crimes, other emotions were present, including feeling sympathy towards women due to the situations they had found themselves in. It is questionable, though, how appropriate it is to openly display sympathy with female offenders, particularly when discussing the nature of the offences. There is a risk that sympathy could be translated into condoning criminal activity, which would leave a researcher in a difficult ethical situation.

Despite these differences, it is not suggested that researchers consider offenders as 'different' from the researcher. Instead, I endeavoured to be open-minded about the similarities between the participants and myself, and common ground was found wherever this was possible. However, there were limits to the extent that similarities could be drawn upon to develop rapport, even in situations when it was present. Several researchers have asserted that interviews which adhere to feminist principles require the researcher to disclose details about herself in the interviews. Indeed, Finch (1993) argues that this is the only way that research can avoid being unethical or exploitative. This extends to instances when participants ask questions of the researcher, and introduces doubt over whether interviews should only contain discussions related to the interview schedule or whether it is appropriate for the researcher to answer unrelated questions or discuss unrelated issues. Reinharz (1992) asserts that self-disclosure will produce a more comfortable environment for the participants and will enable them to be relaxed and possibly discuss matters in more detail than they would have done. In this study, the use of shared identity may be problematic.

Although in principle, this appeared to be a valid way to conduct interviews with women, it became apparent that there were limits to how useful this approach would be. For example, in several instances, it was possible to draw from the experience of being a parent as common ground with which to build up rapport. However, although in principle this might have been a good way to build rapport with participants, there were limits to how well this could function. As a researcher, it was important to think about how much personal information I wished to divulge, and how much it was wise for me to disclose. What might start off as a light conversation about children might develop into a situation where I would not be comfortable disclosing information that was innocently being asked by a participant, such as the names of children or the school they attend. This leaves an awkward situation where both parties are reminded of the purpose of the conversation, which is to conduct an interview rather than 'make friends'.

CHOOSING A RESEARCH LOCATION: ENGAGING PARTICIPANTS

Out of the 31 interviews that were conducted, 25 were conducted where women lived. The remaining interviews were conducted in a number of probation offices in the North of England. Using the homes of participants as a setting to conduct research raised specific issues. Before the interviews began, it was not possible to know the living circumstances of the women, in terms of what type of residence they lived in (whether it was their own home, temporary housing, hostel accommodation), and who they lived with (such as partners, children, relatives or people they did not know). The potential differences in the living arrangements of the women made it necessary to consider the issues before the interviews took place.

Some researchers have argued that conducting research in the homes of women assists in conducting the interviews by making them feel comfortable as they are in familiar surroundings (Finch, 1993). This could be said to assist with the concerns that researchers adopting feminist principles have about power relations between researchers and the researched (Finch, 1993; Letherby, 2003; Oakley, 1981). The argument is that conducting research in an environment which is familiar to the women may help to dissipate power from the researcher to the 'researched' woman so that the power imbalance is addressed. This may well be the case with other research topics in which women are interviewed in different circumstances, but it is questionable whether this applies to research with female offenders. When accompanying officers to invite women to take part in the research, I visited a wide variety of residences. It was anticipated that this would include visits to hostels; however, this turned out not to be the case. Nevertheless, it would be unwise to assume that women who did live in their own place of residence had a safe and secure setting. Some women lived in situations which were far from ideal, such as in problematic and insecure living arrangements. In addition, some women reported complex relationships with partners and relatives, where issues such as alcoholism, mental health problems and in one case, violence, were present. A number of women described their homes as temporary accommodation and were hoping to move as soon as possible. Furthermore, some women who lived in a poor standard of privately rented accommodation explained that they were embarrassed about where they were living, and were hoping to move somewhere better in the near future.

Rather than positively addressing power relations between the researcher and participants, women in these positions may have felt more uncomfortable being interviewed in their own homes than in another setting. Being interviewed in their homes may have made some women more ashamed of their living circumstances or judged or intruded upon as a result of taking part in the research, thus emphasising the power relations rather than dissipating them. For these reasons it cannot be assumed that conducting research in the homes of female offenders will always be advantageous to them, and I was aware that it may have invoked a variety of responses from the participants. As a result, I was mindful of these issues during interviewing, and ensured that I conducted the interviews sensitively.

There was also a possibility that other people were present during the interviews, which had implications for the research. This might include partners, family members, friends or children. This also had implications for how the interviews were conducted. This required a particular need for the interviews to be conducted with care and sensitivity. Hoyle (2000) researched domestic violence by interviewing women in their home and considered the implications that the research may have on the family and the well-being of the participant once the researcher has left. In Hoyle's (2000) study, the perpetrator of the violence was often present during the interview, and due to the sensitive nature of the interview and the potential for harm to the researcher and the victim who was there to be interviewed, a decoy was planned whereby the accompanying police officer took the perpetrator into a separate room where he was interviewed, and told that his partner was being asked the same questions. While nothing of this nature was necessary or appropriate for this study, it was important to be aware of the implications of conducting the research on the women, and to conduct the interviews with due care, particularly because women were being asked to disclose information about their lives.

WHAT I LEARNED

Before the research began, I set out with ideals about conducting research from a feminist perspective. What I quickly learnt is that it is not always possible to replicate an approach when the circumstances differ significantly. However, researchers should not view negatively a situation where data are collected in circumstances which are different to what was envisaged. It is important to be flexible, and while an ideal situation may never be achieved, it is beneficial to consider what such a situation may look like and how it might be approximated in practice. It is also helpful to consider in detail the research process before any data are collected. Issues such as impression management and building rapport may be easy to overlook initially, but it was vital to think about such issues before I began to invite women to take part in the research, as they have an impact on how well the interviews are conducted and subsequently, the quality of the data collected.

TIPS FOR INTERVIEWING FEMALE OFFENDERS IN THEIR PLACES OF RESIDENCE

1. Consider how you will build up rapport with female offenders in advance. Have an idea of how you will approach situations where the conversation may lead you to disclosing more personal information than is desirable.

2. Finding some things to chat about before the interviews take place will help to set your participants at ease and will help to produce a better interview.

3. Be aware of your surroundings at all times, particularly bearing in mind people who arrive at the property after the interview has started. Accept that interruptions to the interviews are likely and try not to let these affect the flow.

4. Do not rely on the use of a voice recorder as there will be some situations where this is not possible, such as where there is a large amount of background noise. Be prepared to take notes and write them up as soon as possible after the interview.

5. Be prepared, as much as you can be, to interview in different environments. Accept that the interviews may take place in homes that you may not wish to spend a lot of time in, but do not allow this to be a distraction from the interview.

6. Be risk-aware at all times but try not to discount interviewing in homes just because they are unpleasant environments as this could produce a sampling bias. Try not to judge people's living conditions.

7. Consider what your course of action will be if you see or hear something of concern during the interview.

8. Similarly, be prepared for criminal acts to be divulged during interviews and decide in advance how you will respond to these.

9. Keep your use of language plain and straightforward.

10. Do not assume that your participants will have literacy skills: be prepared to read out all written information provided, including information sheets and consent forms.

Exercises

1   What factors may affect the development of rapport between researchers and participants, and how might they be managed?

2   How might gatekeepers (see Chapter 4 if you need a reminder of what this term means) play a role in shaping how participants perceive researchers?

3   What issues must be considered when deciding where to conduct interviews?

FURTHER READING

- Davies, P. (2000) 'Doing interviews with female offenders', in V. Jupp, P. Davies and P. Francis (eds), *Doing Criminological Research*. London: Sage.

  Davies shares her experiences of using semi-structured interviews to gather data for a study of women who committed offences for economic gain. She reflects upon the actual interview as well as the before and after stages.

- Hoyle, C. (2000) 'Being a "nosy bloody cow": Ethical and methodological issues in researching domestic violence', in R. King and E. Wincup (eds), *Doing Research on Crime and Justice*. Oxford: Oxford University Press.

  Hoyle's account of interviewing female victims of domestic violence raises some interesting ethical issues, and highlights the issues of conducting interviews in the homes of participants and the possible roles of gatekeepers.

- Worrall, A. (1990) *Offending Women: Female Lawbreakers and the Criminal Justice System*. London: Routledge.

  Worrall discusses some of the issues in relying on gatekeepers to identify female offenders for interview.

USING FOCUS GROUPS TO EXPLORE YOUNG PEOPLE'S PERCEPTIONS OF FASHION COUNTERFEITING

10

JOANNA LARGE

This chapter is based on an empirical doctoral research project that sought to develop a criminological understanding of the consumption of fashion counterfeit goods (Large, 2011). The broader aim of that research was to deconstruct counterfeiting in terms of the various cultural, legal, social and economic conceptualisations of it that were in existence. The research took a mixed methods approach which involved a quantitative survey and a series of qualitative interviews and focus groups with consumers. The idea behind the research was to contextualise fashion counterfeiting within the broader literature about consumption and fashion and begin to develop a more thorough knowledge base about the subject within a criminological framework. This chapter will reflect upon the methodological approach used for that project and, specifically, it will examine the use of focus groups as a research method with young people. A general overview of, and justification for, the methodology adopted is provided, but the primary focus in this discussion is on critically exploring two specific research issues that this project faced: (1) conducting focus groups within a school setting; and (2) getting young people to take part and engage with the focus groups.

OVERVIEW OF THE RESEARCH PROJECT

The inspiration for the doctoral research can be traced back to a European Union (EU) funded project – *Project Couture: Public and Private Partnership for Reducing Counterfeiting of Fashion Apparels and Accessories* (Large and Wall, 2007a, 2007b) – on which I was employed as a research assistant. *Project Couture* was focused on assessing the enforcement of counterfeiting regulation in the UK, France and Italy and in completing the fieldwork it became very clear that there was a gap in the criminological knowledge base about counterfeiting, and intellectual property crime more generally (Wall and Large, 2010). At the time, this topic was thought to be important to research since, although the 'problem' of counterfeiting had become recognised increasingly as a serious crime problem – with its perceived links to 'organised' crime, economic crime and even terrorism (ACG, 2008) – it had yet to attract significant attention in the criminological world. Even now, despite a more recent growth in academic interest, Yar's (2005: 23) claim that intellectual property crime is a 'relatively neglected research area in academic sociology and criminology' remains valid.

In terms of offering some brief context, despite increased enforcement activities that seek to tackle counterfeiting and remove counterfeit products from the market, policing agencies are hindered by numerous difficulties whilst trying to do so (Wall and Large, 2010). Alongside these enforcement activities, a consumer-based initiative has also developed. This approach attempts to 'educate' consumers about the 'dangers of buying fakes' (AIM, 2005: 4) and is loosely based on the premise that if consumers are educated about the 'harms' of counterfeiting then they will cease purchasing – at least in terms of knowingly purchasing – counterfeit products and thus a reduction in demand will cause a reduction in supply. The importance of the consumer role is emphasised in the *Intellectual Property Crime Report* (IPCG, 2007: 5) which states that 'the biggest hurdle to overcome is to educate the general public'. One of the starting assumptions from existing policy and literature on counterfeiting that my research sought to challenge was the idea that 'educating' consumers about the dangers of counterfeiting would be sufficient to convince them not to buy fashion counterfeits. This was felt to be problematic: it fails to take account of the additional complexities of fashion and consumption and much of what we know about people's interactions with fashion counterfeit goods is based upon stereotypical preconceptions which, although informed to an extent by academic research, tends to be from marketing and brand management perspectives. Therefore, rather than looking at this issue from an enforcement or policy point of view, the decision was made in the PhD to take a 'bottom up' approach to gain a clearer understanding of consumer interaction with counterfeit fashion goods so as to explore the assertion that counterfeit consumers are not 'different' or 'other'; rather, they are no different to those who follow 'routine and situated practice' (Rutter and Bryce, 2008: 1150).

The project sought to answer the following overarching research question: what perceptions do consumers have about fashion counterfeiting and how do these relate to their fashion purchasing and assumptions underpinning anti-counterfeiting policy? To unpack this question, a series of sub research questions were also posed:

1. What perceptions and understandings do consumers' have about fashion counterfeiting?
2. How do consumers' perceptions about fashion counterfeiting relate to their consumption patterns?
3. Who buys counterfeit fashion items and who does not?
4. Why do people buy fashion counterfeit items or not?
5. What are the different consumption patterns in buying fashion and/or fashion counterfeit items?
6. What factors shape consumers' behaviour and attitudes towards buying fashion counterfeit items?

7. a) What are the key assumptions about fashion counterfeiting that currently inform policy and b) how do these assumptions relate to consumer perceptions and behaviours?

CHOOSING A RESEARCH DESIGN

Stemming from an 'interpretivist paradigm' (Sarantakos, 2012: 118), my research project was exploratory and interdisciplinary in nature. When reflecting upon designing this research project, it is worth noting that initially it was perceived that this would be a wholly qualitative research project, and follow strictly in the qualitative epistemological tradition. However, as the research proposal progressed into a feasible project, it became clear that due to the lack of existing data in this area a quantitative approach would enable a much broader picture to be gained to generate some initial exploratory data (Bryman, 2008). However, on the other hand, it was felt that gathering only quantitative data would be insufficient in exploring the overall research aim and therefore the methodology naturally progressed into one which took a multi-methodological approach. In what has been described by Sarantakos (2012: 48) as a 'successive paradigm triangulation', this project sought to use a quantitative method to provide a sense of context followed by qualitative methods to provide a more in-depth understanding. Therefore, three research methods, which worked in conjunction with each other, were selected – (1) a survey strategy in the form of a self-completion questionnaire; (2) semi-structured interviews; and (3) focus groups – which would provide data that was 'mutually illuminating' (Bryman, 2008: 603).

It is worth pausing for a moment and reflecting upon the use of mixed methods to collect both qualitative and quantitative data (see also Chapter 1). There is a longstanding debate within the social research literature as to whether it is possible – or even desirable – to use methods which come from separate epistemological backgrounds in the same research project, with a significant number of theorists arguing that they simply are not compatible (such as Smith, 1983; see Bryman, 2008). To place oneself in one epistemological tradition implies that one follows the presumption that quantitative and qualitative approaches are both intrinsically different and can be clearly separated (Bryman, 2004: 454). However, there is an increasing body of literature which argues that care should be taken when identifying them as separate and opposing traditions. Indeed, Hammersley (1996: 164) goes further and argues that to reduce the differences between the approaches to a 'bare dichotomy' will result in a 'serious distortion'. Indeed, there is a growing body of researchers who recognise the value of integrating quantitative and qualitative methods through recognising their 'differences' but at the same time 'recognise their compatibility' (Sarantakos, 2012: 48). Therefore, this research project followed the presumption that different methods are capable of exploring 'different layers of social reality' and together provide complementary insights (Walklate, 2008: 325).

Since my research was exploratory and multi-method in its approach, I needed to select a theoretical approach which aligned with this design, and 'adaptive theory' (Layder, 1998) appeared the most appropriate since it has a number of key characteristics enabling an inductive approach. Notably in adaptive theory there is an acknowledgement that no research is 'theory neutral' and an acceptance of fluid movement between collecting data and developing findings and going back to more data collection without findings being fixed in stone. Further, adaptive theory also allows a wide search for relevant data which was important for an interdisciplinary research project such as this. Finally, but essentially, it permits 'a genuine willingness to utilise appropriately both quantitative and qualitative data sources' (Bottoms, 2008: 98–99).

RECRUITING PARTICIPANTS: CHALLENGES AND CONSIDERATIONS

Originally a series of general focus groups was planned to take place after a preliminary analysis of all other data had taken place, with their purpose being to explore some of the key issues and findings. However, as the research progressed it was decided that this would be unnecessary due to the large amount of qualitative data already gathered through the interviews. Further, due to the diverse nature of respondents it was thought that the actual practical difficulties of setting up and carrying out these groups would not warrant any worthwhile findings (see Barbour, 2007). Despite this, after having carried out 27 semi-structured interviews, it was felt that the sample lacked a voice from people under 20 years of age. An opportunity arose through contact with a local sixth form college to access young people who fell within this age group, and it was felt that this was something really important to do; not only to add breadth to the sample but also due to some of the findings which were coming out of the survey and the interviews, highlighting that age was often an important factor in relation to consumption, particularly in terms of counterfeit fashion. Focus groups are a useful way to gather group opinions via group discussions and, of particular importance for this study, they provide the ability to explore earlier data collection findings further as well as generating new insights into a topic (see Barbour, 2007; Matthews and Ross, 2010).

The sample for the focus groups was gained through making use of a personal contact, the gatekeeper, who was the Head of a Sociology department within a local sixth form college. Following an initial meeting with the gatekeeper to discuss the purpose of the research and the practicalities of conducting it such as when would be the most suitable time, the focus groups were arranged. One of the difficulties in negotiating access to participants through a school setting is identifying appropriate people to participate and a suitable time to conduct the research. The gatekeeper agreed that taking part in an actual research project would be useful for students studying Sociology and allowed the focus groups to be set up during time allocated for a social research methods class. This in itself had implications for the nature of the focus groups: on the one hand, students were likely to have a relatively good understanding of what research was about and about research ethics so they may be keen to take part (thus boosting the numbers of willing research participants) and have some level of understanding of issues such as voluntary consent and their right to not participate. However, on the other hand, these 'positives' also had the potential to be negatives, especially with regard to how the students interacted as part of the focus group. Despite the initial set up of the focus groups and access, it was important to ensure that students could voluntarily attend the focus groups and did not feel compelled to do so. Thus the focus groups were timetabled at the end of term after all compulsory teaching sessions had ended. Students were told about the research project and invited to take part in the focus groups in advance by the gatekeeper but were assured that it was entirely their decision whether or not they wanted to attend as attendance would not be monitored by the tutor. In addition, the focus groups were open to any student within the sixth form college and an advert was placed on the school electronic notice boards inviting all students to take part. Although students were all informed about the research in advance by the gatekeeper, on the day of the actual focus group they were also told more about the purpose of the research, what the focus group would be about and, prior to the focus group taking part, were offered the opportunity to leave if they had changed their minds. Permission was sought from individual focus group participants and discussions were recorded digitally and transcribed. Prior to starting the activities, the participants were asked to complete a short questionnaire which asked for some key descriptive data (age, gender, ethnicity, sources of income [this was in addition to the questions from the original questionnaire to find out where young people who are still in full time education receive their income from], average spend per month on fashion, why they buy fashion goods and whether or not they had ever bought a counterfeit).

One of the disadvantages of accessing participants in this way was that no previous knowledge about the potential participants was available other than that they would be aged between 16 and 20 and were likely to be from a diverse range of ethnic backgrounds (this information was provided by the gatekeeper). There was also no way of controlling for any aspects of the demographics of the sample or indeed for a minimum/maximum number of participants; this was entirely dependent on relying on the gatekeeper to inform potential participants about the research and hope that some would turn up on the day. It was also likely that most of the students would know each other (from being in the same class) although the focus groups were open for anyone who attended the college to take part.

In the end, two focus groups were carried out in June 2010 with young people from the sixth form college. The participants were all aged between 16 and 18 years, with a mean age of 17 years. In reflection of the sampling process, there was a heavy gender imbalance within the groups with Focus Group 1 (FG1) consisting of females only and Focus Group 2 (FG2) consisting of two males and six females. This was mostly likely down to the fact that despite the wider invitation to all pupils, only Sociology students opted to participate. In addition, the nature of the topic may also have added to this bias. The focus groups, however, were ethnically diverse; this was a reflection of the nature of the ethnic make-up of the school (the gatekeeper estimated that approximately one in five of the school's pupils were from a minority ethnic background). In terms of the amount participants spend on average per month on fashion goods, there was a clear difference in terms of average spend for the focus group participants compared to the average spend of the survey and interview participants (the focus group participants having a much more diverse range within the smaller spend brackets). Notably, in line with the earlier interview and survey work, the focus group participants were almost equally split in relation to whether they had ever previously bought a fake or not. This was an important finding, highlighting the importance of conducting these focus groups with young people, as the focus groups recognised the need to challenge the existing presumption that young people are the most likely group to purchase counterfeits.

CHOOSING A RESEARCH LOCATION: ENGAGING PARTICIPANTS

Conducting focus groups is different from conducting group interviews (see Bryman, 2008: 473) since a core feature of focus groups is to generate interaction between participants with the researcher acting as moderator. One of the advantages of focus groups is that rather than simply interacting with the researcher as in a group interview situation, participants will drive the conversation themselves and interact as a group (see Barbour, 2007). It was therefore necessary to design a schedule which would be suitable for the purpose and would add to the existing dataset collected whilst being flexible enough to capture new insights. Through having already completed the analysis of the survey and a preliminary analysis of the 27 interviews, it was possible to be quite specific in terms of the aims of the focus groups and therefore add to the existing data and explore issues that had arisen rather than merely repeat it.

In order to ensure that the focus groups had a clear focus driven by the research aims although at the same time allowing group interaction to drive the discussions, it was decided that the focus groups would be based around three topics: (1) shopping; (2) style; and (3) fashion counterfeits. As with the earlier interviews that had been conducted the focus groups followed a structure which identified key points to cover and prompts, but were designed to allow flexibility and flow from the group dynamics. In order to assist the flow, a number of visual aids were used to encourage participation and prompt ideas. For the topic of shopping, posters were made which had pictures of different shops around the city, ranging from market stalls to high street retailers to luxury shops. For style, a montage of different magazines was made using pictures of celebrities and fashion features. For counterfeits, posters were used in conjunction with pictures associated with counterfeiting – such as market stalls selling counterfeits, police officers and internet websites – to stimulate discussions further. Throughout the focus groups, the participants were encouraged to annotate these visual aids, either through writing directly on them or by sticking on post-it notes with their comments and thoughts. This was in place of researcher notes which can be disruptive to the flow of focus groups and were also useful for stimulating debate within the groups.

The natural setting of the focus groups in an environment which the students felt comfortable in and familiar with was seen as an important contributor to encouraging the students to confidently share and discuss their views. The general lively nature of the group-based discussions also highlighted agreements and differences of views between the young people. However, the danger of focus groups is that some participants may feel uncomfortable in speaking their views

(Sarantakos, 2012) or some group dynamics may be less positive resulting in more strained discussions and this can have an impact on the data generated. Therefore, despite attempts to mitigate these risks through conducting the focus groups in the students' natural 'habitat' (their classroom), it was still notable, especially in the second focus group, that a few participants remained reluctant to contribute. Additionally, the members of the second group were less talkative and whilst discussion was still stimulated and maintained, it was more reliant on researcher prompts and questioning. This was also where the visual aids played an important role; they encouraged and stimulated discussion within the groups, helped to ensure a shared understanding of topics and issues, but also allowed for debate when there were disagreements on how something might be interpreted. Importantly, they allowed the participants who were more reluctant to verbally participate to share their thoughts.

Counterfeiting as a term is itself problematic, and there are a variety of other terms such as fake, imitation, copy, pirate and look-a-like which are often used interchangeably or in association with counterfeit. A number of people have tried to distinguish the differences and similarities between the uses of these terms yet frequently each of them have slightly different meanings to different people. For example, Wilke and Zaichkowsky (1999: 9) discuss the differences between 'counterfeiting' and 'imitating' and suggest that the term 'counterfeiting' means 'a direct copy', whereas 'imitating' can indicate that only part of the original is copied. In terms of researching this topic, Bosworth and Yang (2002) raise a note of caution regarding the differing interpretations of consumers of the term counterfeiting, and thus this was something which had to be considered throughout the research. Gauging some sense of understanding of what terms such as fake and counterfeit meant to participants was very important for the exploratory nature of this research – and for understanding consumer views and behaviours in relation to fashion counterfeiting – and the visual aids really allowed these discussions to develop. However, another important advantage of using the visual aids was it helped to engage those who were less confident, or felt less comfortable, speaking aloud. Although buying of counterfeit fashion goods is not an illegal activity, there certainly can be social stigma and stereotyping surrounding consuming fashion counterfeits which was reflected in the findings of the earlier stages of the research. Thus this increased the risk that some of the focus group participants may have felt uncomfortable in giving their view or talking about their own behaviour for fear of judgement from their peers. Through providing the visual aids and encouraging the participants to write on these, or stick their thoughts on them via post-it notes, it was hoped that the views from all of the participants would be captured. Indeed, the visual aids seemed to provide a really positive addition to the focus groups; the participants were keen to annotate the posters and the pictures enabled discussions to be focused. They were also a great help for ensuring a shared understanding and exploring participants' differing points of view. As a practical research tool, the visual aids served as a useful addition to the transcribed verbal data gleaned from the focus groups as they provided a written record and written insights of some of the main points of discussion.

WHAT I LEARNED

Due to the inductive and exploratory nature of this research project, it was essential that a flexible and iterative approach to methods was taken and the mixed methodology allowed for this. The use of focus groups with young people, whilst having certain limitations with sample size and population representation, added a fascinating and important insight to the research. By targeting an under-represented group within the existing research in this way, young people's views could be heard and provided an interesting angle to consider some of the older interviewees' reflections on their own, younger self. Despite the disadvantages mentioned before, and the difficulties of focus groups particularly in terms of their planning, design and management, the fact that these were conducted during the latter stage of the fieldwork enabled a clear focus for the groups. Indeed, the small number of groups conducted minimised the time-consuming nature of conducting, transcribing and analysing such data (see Bryman, 2008). The focus groups had a specific purpose and were well placed to add to the qualitative data collection which had already been gathered by the interviews, and develop the findings generated by the survey, as well as generating further insights. Upon reflection, approaching the focus groups in this way was the right thing to do within the limitations and constraints of the research project. The use of visual aids was essential to the successful engagement of young people in this project and, despite the potential disadvantages of relying on a gatekeeper to negotiate access and how this influenced the sample of participants, the use of the gatekeeper within the school environment also worked in the research's favour. Of course, in an ideal world – where money, time and deadlines are not an issue – to be able to repeat these focus groups with other young people in different settings (for example, at youth centres or the premises of youth groups) would have further strengthened the research but realistically the data gathered from the two focus groups which did take place supported the project's exploratory aim, allowed further investigation into the preliminary findings from the earlier stages of the research and gave an opportunity for young people to have a voice within a project they had previously not been captured within.

TIPS FOR CONDUCTING FOCUS GROUPS WITH YOUNG PEOPLE

1. Discuss the purpose of your research and what you intend to cover with your focus group with the (potential) gatekeeper in advance. This can help reduce any worries or concerns they might have about your research and whether or not to allow you access.
2. Be aware that using a gatekeeper to gain access can have implications for whether your participants feel like they can give voluntary informed consent. Plan in advance how you will manage this.
3. Be prepared to explain and discuss your research before you start with your (potential) participants. Answer any queries they might have and provide them with an opportunity to leave if they are not comfortable continuing.

4. Consider in advance if you want to collect any demographic information about your participants – if yes, consider preparing a brief self-completion questionnaire for this.

5. Discuss confidentiality with your participants at the start – encourage them to respect each other's opinion (even if they disagree) and to remember that what is discussed during the focus group should remain confidential.

6. If you are going to be discussing crime, or sensitive topics, ease your participants in to the discussion with a more general conversation at first.

7. Ensure that you carefully plan your focus group so that it runs smoothly – prepare a topic schedule with prompts to help you keep on track but take a flexible approach in how you facilitate your session to allow for group dynamics.

8. Remember that you are a facilitator and not an interviewer – allow natural discussions to emerge within the focus group.

9. Consider using visual aids to encourage participation in your focus groups and help elicit ideas.

10. Even if you are audio recording, make time to take detailed notes following your focus group – note down any main points which were discussed, group dynamics and how the discussion went.

Exercises

1   What are the difficulties with conducting focus groups? What other techniques could be used to encourage participants to engage in discussions?

2   Why might conducting focus groups with young people offer opportunities over using other qualitative research methods?

3   What are the particular issues associated with conducting focus groups with young people in a school setting? How might these issues be overcome?

FURTHER READING

- Barbour, R. (2007) *Doing Focus Groups*. London: Sage.

  This book provides practical advice on designing and conducting focus groups, alongside guidance on how to make sense of focus group data.

- Merryweather, D. (2010) 'Using focus group research in exploring the relationships between youth, risk and social position', *Sociological Research Online* 15(1)2. Available at: www.socresonline.org.uk/15/1/2.html.

  This article reflects specifically on conducting focus groups with young people. Whilst cognisant of the limitations of focus groups, the author argues that this method was able to generate narratives which provided an invaluable means for developing a rich and nuanced account of the relations between youth and risk.

- Peek, L. and Fothergill, A. (2009) 'Using focus groups: Lessons from studying daycare centers, 9/11 and Hurricane Katrina', *Qualitative Research*, 9(1): 35–59.

  Drawing upon their experiences of using focus groups for three research projects, this article offers a reflective account of the value and practicalities of using this method for social research. They suggest that the methods are particularly suited to research with marginalised, stigmatised or vulnerable groups.

RESEARCHING WITH YOUNG PEOPLE WHO ARE VULNERABLE AND 'DIFFICULT TO REACH'

KATHY HAMPSON

11

This chapter is designed to give an insight into the difficulties and ethical considerations which arose when researching a particularly vulnerable and 'difficult to reach' participant group, namely young offenders. After outlining the context of my study, I will explain how the research design was shaped by my awareness of working with young offenders, and the ensuing difficulties which arose. Towards the end I have translated the lessons learnt from this fieldwork experience into a list of tips, which might save the novice researcher some time and difficulties. I have also included two case studies illustrating some of the difficulties encountered and how I responded, along with some questions for further reflection. Should you wish to research a similar group I recommend that you take up some of the further reading suggestions at the end.

OVERVIEW OF THE RESEARCH PROJECT

My research project, which was completed for a part-time PhD, explored whether the emotional intelligence (EI) of young people who commit offences was related in any way to their offending (and their other criminogenic risk factors). This came out of my work with young people as Youth Justice Worker with a Youth Offending Team (YOT), working with convicted young people who had been given court orders. EI, in this context, was defined as the ability to perceive, use, understand and manage emotions (Mayer et al., 2000: 109–110; Salovey and Grewal, 2005: 2), which I felt was an important factor in why many young people end up in trouble. I was therefore concerned that EI does not form part of any assessment criteria, when youth justice practitioners work with young people arrested for offences committed through loss of temper or as a result of breakdowns in relationships. I wanted to find out firstly how well EI could be assessed in these young people, and secondly where any links lay. All children and young people are vulnerable, but this group are particularly so as they often come from a background of deprivation and difficulty (please take note of Tip 1 at the end concerning confidentiality). Many will have been excluded from mainstream school, had social care referrals, experienced difficulties with substance use, and may have experienced being in custody with the ensuing difficulties that will have brought. Most of them will have had a vast number of different professionals working with them and their families, and may therefore find it difficult to engage with yet more people, resulting in poor levels of attendance at arranged appointments. This is why I have described them as 'difficult to reach'.

In order to conduct this research project, I worked with young people between the ages of 10 and 18 who were on current Supervision Orders. This was negotiated as a separate piece of work from my 'day job', to be conducted extra to work hours and requirements, but the participants were 'accessed' through the same YOT. Putting this in place as an official agreement also helped to separate the research from my paid role. My plan was to utilise a questionnaire designed to assess the EI of young people with as many of those on Supervision Orders as was possible within reasonable time constraints. For this I gained the support of senior managers, so I could encourage colleagues to use the questionnaire with the young people on their caseload.

CHOOSING A RESEARCH DESIGN

I decided to use both quantitative and qualitative approaches, as I felt to use either as a stand-alone methodology would have been to miss out on a substantive amount of available data and provide a narrow perspective. I also wanted to check the questionnaire 'results' by having the facility to triangulate with the interview data (Tashakkori and Teddlie, 1998: 80). As I was looking at young people who had offended, I wanted to give them a voice in the research, which could only be gained by conducting in-depth interviews. Using quotes from the interview also added a human face to the project (Johnson and Onwuegbuzie, 2004: 14). The quantitative dataset comprised all young people on Supervision Orders, initially to be gathered over the period of 12 months, up to a total of 200 participants. Each young person's own worker was to use the specified questionnaire (a series of questions with a 5-point Likert scale answer system attached to them). Although this seemed to be a simple system to use, the reality caused some difficulties, which are discussed later, and increased the importance of the data from the interviews. The quantitative dataset then served to build the sample for the interviews along four areas of interest: young people scoring in the top and bottom deciles, young people who are looked after by the local authority, and young people with a low age of first offending (aged 12 and below). This enabled me to look in far more depth at specific areas of interest from previous research, specifically young people who first offended at a very young age, and those looked after by the local authority. These young people were all interviewed by me, using a semi-structured interview schedule. All interviews were recorded (with the young person's permission) and transcribed later.

One of the major challenges for my research study was the vulnerability of the participants as both offenders and under 18 years of age. Their well-being was of paramount importance in this process, so procedures needed to be put in place to ensure that this was safeguarded. There was an extra element to this, however, given that the young people were on court orders which compels their attendance at appointments, on threat of being returned to court for any failure to comply. It had to be made clear that young people should neither be required to complete the questionnaire nor attend an interview with me. However, this also needed to be balanced with ensuring that the young people were not being asked to attend above their normal level of contact, which might have affected their ability to comply with their orders in the future. Therefore, an agreement was reached (and communicated to case-holders) whereby the young people completed a consent form first, at which point they could decline to take part with no penalty, and then the questionnaire was completed with them, which they could also decline to complete at any point. The young people were also given the option to request that their completed questionnaire was not included in the dataset. It should be recognised that merely giving someone a consent form does not mean they are able to give informed consent to the process in hand. With vulnerable young people in particular, there is inevitably a power imbalance between researcher and potential participant which might impede their perceived ability to decline consent (see Tip 2). In practice very few young people declined to take part, but the few who did demonstrated to a certain degree that refusal was an acceptable option for them. I decided at the start not to include any young people who were currently in custody at the time of the project, partly because their ability to give consent freely might have been even more compromised than those in the community and partly because of the logistical difficulties of accessing young people in custody, and using recording devices in custodial settings.

The interviews posed further difficulties in terms of safeguarding the young person's well-being. The interviewees were not (for ethical reasons) young people with whom I had worked previously which meant that they were being asked to discuss potentially difficult subject areas with a complete stranger. There was also a potential conflict relating to their own perceptions of their ability to decline to take part given that I, and their case-holder (who would have originally asked them to participate) were workers within the YOT (a perceived position of power from the young person's perspective), which might have made it more difficult for them to decline to participate (which is also true of the consent for the questionnaires). This posed the question of how valid the notion of 'informed consent' was in this context. In discussion with senior managers, it was decided that since parental consent had been obtained for the young people to complete their court orders, and since the research would only really cover areas they could reasonably be expected to talk about in any case, that separate consent from parents would not be necessary. Both consent forms included information about the research project, what would be done with this information, and how their identity would be protected. Only questionnaires and interviews with completed affirmative consent forms were included in the dataset. It was a potential weakness that the young people may have felt compelled to attend an interview, as part of their court order, which may have reduced levels of engagement. This may have been the case with 'Ivan' (see the end of the chapter for a description of the process of interviewing him), who signed a consent form, turned up for the interview, but clearly did not feel comfortable answering questions (see Tip 3 at the end of the chapter for dealing with non-attendance at interview). Fortunately, this did not occur frequently, possibly because of the way the interviews were structured.

SPECIAL DESIGN CONSIDERATIONS: INTERVIEWING YOUNG PEOPLE

The interview structure included young people talking about their offence (for which they were on the Supervision Order), and then questions about their own feelings, and their perception of others' feelings about the incident. It was designed to see how sophisticated their communication of emotions was, including basic emotional language, and then investigate their ability to apply emotional understanding to the victims of their offences. These were potentially difficult areas for the young people to discuss with me: they may have felt awkward at discussing their offence with someone other than their worker, they may have found it difficult to talk about potentially sensitive situations, and also may have found it invasive to talk about their own feelings, especially if this is not something with which they were familiar. Once I had devised the questions for the semi-structured interview, I discussed them with senior managers to ensure that they were happy for me to proceed. They authorised its use, based on the fact that it only contained questions they could reasonably be expected to talk about on their order. Young people on court orders are required to talk about what happened and as the young people on Supervision Orders are usually recidivists, it is something with which they would have been familiar. However, this brings its own difficulties as they could already be suffering from repetition fatigue, which might detract from their ability or desire to go into this difficult subject matter yet again. Young people are also required on their order to look at victim empathy so to do so on this occasion would not have been to cover anything different to a normal supervision session. However, this familiarity might have led me to assume that they would comprehend terminology around victims when it may never have been explained properly, which did prove to be important. It became evident that the structure of the interview was going to be very important, both in ensuring that the young people could cope with the level of the conversation, and encourage the fullest responses (see also Becker and Greer, 2004: 248). I had an advantage over many researchers in that I talk to young people about these issues on a daily basis through my work so was confident that I could draw responses out of them sensitively and with a realistic chance of gaining a beneficial answer. Other researchers may find this more difficult with this client group given the reputation teenagers have for being uncommunicative!

It was important to introduce the interview in a non-threatening manner, but also to revisit the consent form, ensuring that the young people knew what they had agreed to giving them an option to opt out at that point. I always ensured that each conversation began with some light banter about something completely irrelevant like the weather, what football team they supported, or what they got up to that weekend. Having started the conversation, the next stage of the interview was much easier to move into (see Tip 4). I began each one with a short empathy questionnaire, which was partly to gain some insight into their ability to understand others' emotions beforehand, partly as a gentle introduction before more personal questions, and partly to help them to begin thinking about emotional issues. After the questionnaire, I asked them to tell me about their offence. Again, I feel that I had an advantage over others in that I am required to ask young people about their offences during interviews for court reports, and so was able to communicate a non-judgemental attitude which is crucial for an honest conversation to develop. I tried not to lead them too much through their description of what happened, because I wanted them to be able to take themselves back there in their mind, which would help them also to be able to identify how they might have been feeling at the time (due to a slow court process, some of the offences were quite historic). On the other hand, some young people glossed over what happened in a few sentences, which required further gentle questioning to help them remember more details. Having talked through the details of what happened, I then wanted them to talk about how they felt, both then and now, about what had happened. This was a potentially difficult part of the process, particularly if young people were beginning to express regret for their actions. The conversation then moved to whom the victims of their actions were, and how they might have been affected (see Tips 5–9 for more about interviewing young people). I rewarded them at the end of the interview with a bar of chocolate but did not withdraw this if they decided (as one young person did) that they did not want to proceed further after the first question. This was to ensure that the chocolate did not become a tool of coercion. Non-attendance at an agreed interview was taken to be a withdrawal of consent, and young people were merely given a new appointment to return to the youth offending service as required by their Supervision Order, rather than given any consequence for not attending the interview.

RECRUITING PARTICIPANTS: CHALLENGES AND CONSIDERATIONS

In practice, some unanticipated difficulties occurred, although more with colleagues than the young participants! I had originally (and optimistically!) aimed for 200 young people on Supervision Orders completing the questionnaire within a 12-month period. This was realistic in terms of the number of young people receiving the order, but not so where I was relying on colleagues to gather the data. I launched the project at a regular meeting which is held for the whole YOT, giving an overview of the aims of my research, and also some practical advice for practitioners using the questionnaires. At the time, our YOT was made up of four area teams. The responses were fairly good from my own team, with a steady stream of questionnaires being returned. However, receiving a completed questionnaire from the other teams was rare! I used subsequent YOT events to encourage participation by entering every worker who had submitted a questionnaire into a prize draw. This increased the participation rate somewhat but my original target was clearly going to be unrealistic. I had the full support of managers for this project, which was useful because they supported the completion of the questionnaire with workers in supervision, and challenged them regarding eligible young people whom they had not asked. Even given these encouragement tactics, I only managed to gain 100 responses over a period of more than two years. It is important to keep revising research plans to ensure they are still achievable and make alterations when circumstances prove otherwise. One of the disadvantages of having lots of different practitioners complete the questionnaires with the young people was inconsistency in relation to the level of assistance given. This resulted in some clear misunderstandings on the part of the young people, particularly where questions were phrased in the negative (in a questionnaire, it is good practice to phrase some questions negatively, for example 'I don't …' rather than 'I do …', to stop people selecting similar answers throughout). Without clear guidance, the young people were obviously confused as to which end of the Likert scale they intended their answer to be. In hindsight, I would have spent much more energy ensuring that all the practitioners used the same approach which would have resulted in much better consistency.

The interviews were largely much easier in practice than anticipated with the young people responding well to the questions, and often talking very freely about their thoughts. This was possibly because more of the potential difficulties had been successfully anticipated, and therefore addressed in advance. I ended up interviewing 13 young people, each falling into one of the four categories outlined earlier, with the exception of one young person convicted of a sex offence. He was interviewed because previous research has implied that people who have committed sex offences were more likely to have an extremely inhibited level of EI, which I wanted to investigate further. It was sometimes difficult to draw out responses from young people who claimed they could not remember what had happened, and sometimes difficult to keep young people on the subject in hand. A little digression was not a problem, but long-winded story telling made transcription difficult! When conducting semi-structured interviews, which could end up being quite long, it is worth remembering that it all has to be transcribed before use. It was tempting to edit what the young people said when using quotations in my thesis but in the end I was persuaded that in order to give the young people a voice in the research, I needed to keep true to what had actually been said, even if this resulted in the occasional swear word! I found that in reality they did not pepper their responses with swearing, but sometimes used it to express something they found difficult to communicate in any other way, thus making it more important to include in this type of study.

WHAT I LEARNED

There are complexities in using a mixed methods approach: How should the two datasets be analysed? How should the two aspects be combined within the analysis? Should one dataset produce the other, or should they be entirely separate? Although thought needs to be given to all these different questions and more prior to the data gathering process, many of the answers were in this project a pragmatic response to the question 'What works?' I decided that to stick with quantitative data, I would not get a flavour of the young people about whom this research was concerned, which seemed not only to miss vital information, but also to do those young people a disservice. I was able to start the interviews before the questionnaires were completed, which was just as well given the time it took to gather 100 responses, because I had already identified which types of young people I wanted to interview. Therefore, the interview sample was selected using the questionnaire responses (those scoring in the top and bottom deciles) and the demographic information I had gathered. The analysis was interesting because the differences in the responses of the young people with their questionnaire scores highlighted what I had already suspected – that the questionnaires had been completed very inconsistently, an issue discussed earlier. Therefore, those who had achieved higher questionnaire scores were not necessarily those demonstrating higher levels of emotional intelligence. In this way, one dataset was used to comment on the other, enabling 'checks and balances' to be performed to identify through the qualitative interview data the problems of gathering quantitative data through self-completion questionnaires.

Of course, the joy of semi-structured interviews is that although certain themes have been identified in order to devise the questions for interview, other themes can emerge through the conversational style (see Tip 10). In this case, it became clear that many of the young people interviewed saw themselves as being victims in a variety of ways, which is not something I had anticipated in my rationale for setting up the interviews (see the discussion of interviewing 'Anna' on page 175, who was much more vocal when she could express her feelings of victimisation). This gave me further themes to explore when analysing the transcribed interviews. New themes can be buried within the data and will therefore only emerge through repeated reading of the transcribed interviews in a way which puts aside the preconceived ideas of what might emerge from the data. New themes may provide questions for further research. In many respects, good qualitative research opens up as many questions as it answers.

TIPS FOR INTERVIEWING VULNERABLE AND 'DIFFICULT TO REACH' YOUNG PEOPLE

1. Think about confidentiality before you start – you cannot promise to keep what they say confidential if they tell you something which puts either them or someone else in danger. Be careful also about inviting confessions to crimes which have not yet been dealt with through the criminal justice system. If any of these things happen in an interview you will need to pass it on so make sure your interviewees know that to begin with.
2. Be aware that you may be deemed by interviewees to be in a position of authority over them and the implications this might have for the validity of informed consent.

3. Young people sometimes find it difficult to refuse consent for something but may communicate this through non-attendance. Ensure that if missed interviews are being rearranged that informed consent is not being compromised as a result.

4. Have some small talk ready to use initially, rather than launching straight into the main body of the interview. If you can have a laugh with them before you start, the results will be better.

5. Ensure that your language is accessible.

6. Be non-judgemental in your approach. Even if you are talking about something like a crime they have committed, remember that they have already been punished!

7. Try not to interrupt their responses, although it might help to have some encouraging phrases at hand ('tell me more about that', 'what happened after that?').

8. Use active listening techniques. Try not to be so intent on your next question that you miss out on helping them expand on something they have just said. Reflect back to them what they have said to make sure you know what they mean.

9. Be careful not to dismiss swearing as inappropriate; it may be saying something about their communication.

10. Allow young people to express their views and opinions, even if this is not strictly within the interview remit, as this might allow new themes to emerge.

Exercises

Read through the reflexive accounts of the interviews conducted with Ivan and Anna (pseudonyms rather than real names) and answer the questions.

Ivan

As with all of the young people I interviewed, consent was gained from Ivan to interview him for the research project by his case worker, who went through a consent form with him. His case is illustrative of the difficulties which may lie in this process, especially when there is an imbalance of power between the person asking for consent and the person giving it. Ivan attended the appointment with me (which was allowed to count towards the appointments he had to keep for his court order, but was not one which would have resulted in any consequences had he missed it), and I began by revisiting the consent form with him. He was not very communicative but did not say he wanted to withdraw consent. He began the interview reasonably enthusiastically, completing the empathy questionnaire with no difficulties. However, when I tried to talk to him about his offence, he was very vague and evasive, even though I tried several different ways of trying to draw him out. It was clear that he did not want to talk about this, so we moved on to a different question, but his earlier enthusiasm had evaporated and he no longer wanted to take part. I clarified this with him and he agreed that he did not want to continue with the interview.

It could be the case that Ivan had felt unable to refuse consent with his worker, who was clearly in a position of authority over him. He may also have found it difficult to say to me at the start that he no longer wanted to take part given that I also worked for the YOT and therefore was perceived as in a position of authority.

However, interpretation of his body language and diminishing responses was a much clearer message, which I was able to then clarify with him and subsequently stop the interview process.

Questions for discussion

1   How valid do you think Ivan's signed consent form was?

2   Why do you think he agreed to be interviewed when it was made clear to him at the time that he did not have to take part?

3   Ivan was only 11 when the interview took place. Do you think his age had an impact on what happened?

Anna

I interviewed Anna at the hostel where she was living because this was most convenient for her and encouraged her to feel more comfortable. For most of my interviews I used a digital recorder so I could more accurately use the words of the young people. This was specified on the consent form, but Anna did not want to be recorded, so I wrote notes for her interview instead.

Anna was one of those young people who claimed not to be able to remember what had happened during the offence, because it occurred some time ago. Whether this was the truth or not, Anna was not giving me her consent to discuss this in detail, so I had to move on to other aspects of the interview. She was much more vocal when discussing how she had been affected, which added to the emerging theme which I discovered, that the young people seemed to see themselves as victims in many different ways. Although some of her interview was a frustrating process, it added valuable detail to the themes I had wanted to discuss.

As with all the young people, Anna's name had been changed for the purposes of the discussion, and no identifying features were retained.

Questions for discussion

1   Why do you think Anna declined to be recorded?

2   Why do you think she agreed to take part in the interview?

3   Do you think Anna gained anything by taking part?

FURTHER READING

- Alderson, P. and Morrow, V. (2011) *The Ethics of Research with Children and Young People: A Practical Handbook*. London: Sage.

   This detailed text covers ethical issues at every stage of the research process, arguing that ethical questions are at the centre of research with children and young people.

- Shaw, C., Brady, L. and Davey, C. (2011) *Guidelines for Research with Children and Young People*. London: National Children's Bureau. Available at www.nfer.ac.uk/nfer/schools/developing-young-researchers/NCBguidelines.pdf.

These helpful guidelines are produced by researchers based at the National Children's Bureau, a UK-based charity. They also explore the policy and practice background to the involvement of children and young people in research and the benefits of doing so.

- Tisdall, K., Davis, J. and Gallagher, M. (2008) *Researching with Children and Young People: Research Design, Methods and Analysis*. London: Sage.

Aimed in particular at postgraduate students and practitioners, this text goes beyond exploring the issues raised when researching children and young people and considers how they become research collaborators or conduct their own research.

CONCLUSION: BECOMING A QUALITATIVE RESEARCHER

Reflecting on the future of their topic of interest is a favourite past time of criminologists. Students of criminology are likely to encounter a multitude of these reflections as they dip into the burgeoning criminological literature. In this short concluding chapter, I will follow in this tradition and look to the future in two different ways. First, I will remind readers of the different research methods available to criminologists and consider new developments. Second, I will argue for a greater focus on the quality of criminological research through reflecting on the criteria which might be used to evaluate qualitative studies. Finally, I will end by offering (I hope!) some brief words of encouragement and wisdom to criminologists contemplating using qualitative methods. This should be read in conjunction with the excellent texts available (see for example, Bell and Waters, 2014) to support those taking their first steps on a journey to becoming independent researchers, often in the context of completing academic or professional training courses.

EMBRACING QUALITATIVE APPROACHES

In previous chapters we have reflected upon a wide range of qualitative approaches. Criminologists have made extensive use of qualitative interviews, and some have deployed ethnographic techniques despite the many challenges of doing so. But the criminological community has been slow to realise the full potential of conducting research using the ever-increasing number of documentary sources available to them and to date there has been little attempt to make use of secondary qualitative data. Many criminologists – myself included – tend to have their favoured method which they naturally gravitate towards but I want to encourage a more considered approach. Ultimately the choice of method is the outcome of a balancing act between academic considerations (for example, theoretical positioning, nature of the research questions) and practical ones (for example, time and resources) and the researcher will need to make a judgement call. They also need to be mindful of the context in which research takes place (see Chapter 2), the need for it to be conducting ethically (see Chapter 3) and accessibility of the desired data (see Chapter 4). These different considerations will influence research strategy and design. As I have argued elsewhere (King and Wincup, 2008: 35) 'research is an art (or at least a craft) as well as a science and a great deal depends on the professional judgement and experience of the craftsperson'.

In order to consider the full range of approaches and their relative strengths and weaknesses criminologists need to remain in touch with important methodological developments. In earlier chapters in this book we noted that new forms of technology offer opportunities for collecting, recording and analysing data. Arguably the internet and associated technology provides one of the most exciting prospects for researchers, allowing qualitative data to be collected in this virtual environment. These opportunities might prove particularly useful to novice researchers with limited, if any, budgets but it is important to view online methods as more than a practical solution to the problems which qualitative researchers have typically faced and consider their unique contribution. Conducting qualitative research in this way and reflecting upon practical, methodological and ethical consideration is a 'project under construction'. Crucially we need to assess the quality of the data they can generate.

ASSESSING THE QUALITY OF QUALITATIVE CRIMINOLOGICAL RESEARCH

There is a tendency for qualitative research to be judged using the same criteria as quantitative studies. This not only glosses over the unique strengths of qualitative approaches but unfairly criticises qualitative studies for not achieving something they never set out to do. Qualitative researchers have been accused of producing data that are neither reliable or valid. It has been suggested that reliability is compromised because the approach is far from objective and the researcher influences the data gathered. Similarly, it has been argued that qualitative research lacks validity: since it is not based upon a representative sample it is not possible to rule out alternative explanations and the findings cannot be generalised beyond the unique research context. Arguably these positivist criteria over-emphasise the objective nature of quantitative research but this is not our concern here. Instead, we consider more appropriate ways of assessing the quality of qualitative research.

Over the past three decades, qualitative researchers have invested considerable energy attempting to identify the quality criteria by which qualitative research might be judged. These efforts serve a number of purposes. First, they identify the unique features of qualitative research so that qualitative studies can be judged on their own merits rather than benchmarked against quantitative ones. Second, they serve to improve the quality of qualitative research by allowing individual researchers or others (for example, those tasked with peer reviewing a funding proposal) to reflect systematically on whether the research design developed will yield high quality data which can answer the stated research questions fully. Finally, if sufficiently detailed they can be used to support researchers conducting systematic qualitative reviews, which aim to support evidence-based policy and practice (see Boland et al., 2013). The latter purpose is somewhat controversial because it opens up a debate about whether specific criteria are necessary or desirable (see Hammersley, 2007).

We will adopt the view here that attempts to identify quality criteria that have been useful for educating researchers of the broad aims of qualitative research and therefore how to critically 'appreciate' qualitative studies, either those which have already been conducted or those still at the proposal stage. Lincoln and Guba (1985) make a useful contribution, although critics may question their starting point which is to 'translate' criteria for evaluating quantitative research to qualitative approaches. For Lincoln and Guba (1985) the key criteria for qualitative research are credibility, transferability, dependability and confirmability, all of which are essential to building up a sense of trust in the research study. Essentially what the first two refer to is the importance of designing and conducting a research project which will produce data which can be used to develop a credible account of a research 'problem'; one which has applicability in other contexts (for example, conceptually, methodologically or practically; see Tracy [2010]). The latter two recognise the subjective nature of the research process. Qualitative research may not be objective but those who use this approach can strive towards a degree of neutrality (for example, through a commitment to reflexivity and through transparency at all stages of the research process). Overall, in common with all forms of research, qualitative research needs to be rigorous, ethical and coherent (see Tracy, 2010).

BECOMING A QUALITATIVE CRIMINOLOGICAL RESEARCHER

In the preceding chapters we have explored and celebrated the achievement of qualitative researchers within criminology. We have considered studies on a wide range of topics to illustrate both the flexibility and vitality of the qualitative research tradition. Unsurprisingly given my commitment to qualitative research I recommend it to criminological researchers as an approach which is particularly suited to the study of crime and criminal justice. However, I am neither evangelical in my commitment to qualitative methods nor anti-statistical. The most appropriate methods should be used to answer the research question, and this may involve using a combination of methods, including those which lead to the collection of quantitative data. These type of considerations need to be borne in mind when designing a qualitative criminological research project. Learning to reflect critically on your own research design is an important stage in the qualitative criminological research apprenticeship. It will not only help you to refine your approach but also to recognise the strengths and weaknesses of your chosen design so you can defend it should you need to (for example, in a viva).

Criminologists using qualitative techniques will find their experiences of conducting research both challenging and rewarding. There are many academic rewards for criminologists who select a qualitative approach and these were described in the first chapter. In addition, conducting qualitative research on criminological topics has personal rewards for the researcher. Of course, criminological research also has a 'bleak side' (Baldwin, 2007: 393) and I have been keen to portray an honest account of conducting criminological research by exploring the political sensitivities, ethical dilemmas, access difficulties and encounters with risk, vulnerability and danger faced by criminologists. Any negative aspects are easily outweighed by the academic and personal rewards.

My aim in this text was to convey a little of the realities of conducting qualitative research by grounding the discussion of the research process and methodological issues in my own experience and those of the wider criminological community. I deliberately use the words 'a little' because it has been my intention to demonstrate that the true learning experience comes from *doing* research. In this respect, one of my main aims was to inspire criminologists to conduct qualitative research and to begin to equip them with the necessary 'tools' to undertake high-quality studies. I hope I have been successful.

REFERENCES

ACG (2008) *The Crime of the 21st Century*. High Wycombe: Anti-Counterfeiting Group.

Adams, C. (2000) 'Suspect data: Arresting research', in R. King and E. Wincup (eds), *Doing Research on Crime and Justice*. Oxford: Oxford University Press.

Adams, P. (2016) 'Commentary on INEBRIA's position statement on the alcohol industry', *Journal of Studies on Alcohol and Drugs*, 77(4): 540.

Adler, P. and Adler, P. (1995) 'The demography of ethnography', *Journal of Contemporary Ethnography*, 24(1): 3–29.

Aiello, M. (2014) 'Policing the masculine frontier: Cultural criminological analysis of the gendered performance of policing', *Crime Media Culture*, 10(1): 59–79.

AIM (2005) 'Faking it: Why counterfeiting matters', briefing paper, April. Brussels: Association des Industries de Marque, European Brands Association.

Anderson, S. (2016) 'Recreating recovery through collage: Using creative, embodied methods to explore meanings and processes of recovery', poster presented at *Meanings of Recovery: A Dialogue Across the Sociologies of Mental Health, Physical Illness, Injury and Addiction*, University of Surrey, 11–12 July.

Arksey, H. and Knight, P. (1999) *Interviewing for Social Scientists*. London: Sage.

Asquith, L. (2015) 'Life after genocide: A Bourdieuian analysis of the post migratory experience of genocide survivors', unpublished PhD thesis, University of Huddersfield.

Atkinson, P. (1992) *Understanding Ethnographic Texts*. London: Sage.

Atkinson, P., Coffey, A. and Delamont, S. (2003) *Key Themes in Qualitative Research: Continuities and Change*. Walnut Creek, CA: AltaMira Press.

Back, L. (2002) 'Dancing and wrestling with scholarship: Things to do and things to avoid in a PhD career', *Sociological Research Online*, 7(4).

Baldwin, J. (2007) 'Research on the criminal courts', in R. King and E. Wincup (eds), *Doing Research on Crime and Justice*, 2nd edn. Oxford: Oxford University Press.

Baldwin, J. and McConville, M. (1977) *Negotiated Justice*. London: Martin Robinson.

Banks, C. (2012) 'The other cultural criminology: The role of action research in justice work and development', in D. Gadd, S. Karstedt and S. Messner (eds), *The SAGE Handbook of Criminological Research Methods*. London: Sage.

Banks, J. (2013) 'Edging your bets: Advantage play, gambling, crime and victimisation', *Crime Media Culture*, 9(2): 171–187.

Banks, J. (2014) 'Online gambling, advantage play, reflexivity and virtual ethnography', in K. Lumsden and A. Winter (eds), *Reflexivity in Criminological Research: Experiences with the Powerful and Powerless*. Basingstoke: Palgrave Macmillan.

Barbour, R. (2007) *Doing Focus Groups*. London: Sage.

Bartels, L. and Richards, K. (eds) (2011) *Qualitative Criminology: Stories from the Field*. Annandale, NSW: The Federation Press.

Barton, A. (2004) *Fragile Moralities and Dangerous Sexualities: Two Centuries of Semi-Penal Institutionalisation for Women*. Aldershot: Ashgate.

Barton, A. and Johns, N. (2012) *The Policy Making Process in the Criminal Justice System*. Abingdon: Routledge.

Becker, H. (1963) *Outsiders: Studies in the Sociology of Deviance*. New York: Free Press.

Becker, H. (1967) 'Whose side are we on?', *Social Problems*, 14(3): 239–247.

Becker, H. and Greer, B. (2004) 'Participant observation and interviewing', in C. Seale (ed.), *Social Research Methods*. London: Routledge.

Bell, J. (1999) *Doing Your Research Project: A Guide for First Time Researchers in Education and the Social Sciences*, 3rd edn. Buckingham: Open University Press.

Bell, J. and Waters, S. (2014) *Doing Your Research Project: A Guide for First Time Researchers in Education and the Social* Sciences, 6th edn. Buckingham: Open University Press.

Belur, J. (2014) 'Status, gender and geography: Power negotiations in police research', *Qualitative Research*, 14(2): 184–200.

Bishop, L. (2007) 'A reflexive account of reusing qualitative data: Beyond primary/secondary dualism', *Sociological Research Online*, 12(3).

Blaxter, L., Hughes, C. and Tight, M. (1996) *How to Research*. Buckingham: Open University Press.

Blaxter, L., Hughes, C. and Tight, M. (2010) *How to Research*, 4th edn. Buckingham: Open University Press.

Bloomfield, S. and Dixon, L. (2015) *An Outcome Evaluation of the Integrated Domestic Abuse Programme (IDAP) and Community Domestic Violence Programme (CDVP)*. London: Ministry of Justice.

Bloor, M., Frankland, K., Thomas, M. and Robson, K. (2001) *Focus Groups in Social Research*. London: Sage.

Boland, A., Cherry, G. and Dickson, R. (2013) *Doing a Systematic Review: A Student Guide*. London: Sage.

Bonger, W. (1916) 'Criminality and economic conditions', abridged extract in E. McLaughlin, J. Muncie and G. Hughes (eds) (2003), *Criminological Perspectives: A Reader*. London: Sage.

Bosworth, D. and Yang, D. (2002) 'The economics and management of global counterfeiting', paper submitted to the Sixth World Congress on Intellectual Capital and Innovation. Available at: www.ulb.ac.be/cours/solvay/vanpottelsberghe/resources/resources/rsaem_39.pdf.

Bottomley, K. and Pease, K. (1986) *Crime and Punishment: Interpreting the Data*. Milton Keynes: Open University Press.

Bottoms, A. (2008) 'The relationship between theory and research in criminology', in R. King and E. Wincup (eds), *Doing Research on Crime and Justice*, 2nd edn. Oxford: Oxford University Press.

Bourque, L. and Fielder, E. (2002) *How to Conduct Telephone Surveys*, 2nd edn. Thousand Oaks, CA: Sage.

Brewer, J. (2000) *Ethnography*. Buckingham: Open University Press.

Briggs, D. (2013) *Crack Cocaine Users: High Society and Low Life in South London*. Abingdon: Routledge.

British Society of Criminology (2006) *Code of Ethics for Research in the Field of Criminology*. London: British Society of Criminology.

British Sociological Association (2002) *Statement of Ethical Practice for the British Sociological Association*. Durham: British Sociological Association.

Brookman, F. (1999) 'Accessing and analysing police murder files', in F. Brookman, L. Noaks and E. Wincup (eds), *Qualitative Research in Criminology*. Aldershot: Ashgate.

Brookman, F., Noaks, L. and Wincup. E. (2001) 'Access to justice: Remand issues and the Human Rights Act', *Probation Journal*, 43(3): 195–202.

Brown, K. (2015) *Vulnerability and Young People: Care and Social Control in Policy and Practice*. Bristol: The Policy Press.

Brown, T. (2016) 'Afterword' in S. Sedley, *Missing Evidence: An Inquiry into the Delayed Publication of Government-commissioned Research*. London: Sense about Science.

Bruce, J. (2013) 'Understanding "back stage" and "front stage" work in restorative justice conferences: The benefits of using ethnographic techniques', *Current Issues in Criminal Justice*, 25(1): 517–526.

Bryant, A. and Charmaz, K. (2010) *The SAGE Handbook of Grounded Theory*. Thousand Oaks, CA: Sage.

Bryman, A. (2004) *Social Research Methods*, 2nd edn. Oxford: Oxford University Press.

Bryman, A. (2008) *Social Research Methods*, 3rd edn. Oxford: Oxford University Press.

Bulmer, M. (1984) *The Chicago School of Sociology, Institutionalization, Diversity and the Rise of Sociological Research*. Chicago: University of Chicago Press.

Burgess, R. (1984) *In the Field: An Introduction to Field Research*. London: Allen and Unwin.

Burns, E. (2010) 'Developing email interview practices in qualitative research', *Sociological Research Online*, 15(4).

Butler-Kisber, L. (2007) 'Collage in qualitative inquiry', in G. Knowles and A. Cole (eds), *Handbook of the Arts in Social Science Research*. Thousand Oaks, CA: Sage.

Calvey, D. (2000) 'Getting on the door and staying there: A covert participant observation study of bouncers', in G. Lee-Treweek and S. Linkogle (eds), *Danger in the Field*. London: Routledge.

Campbell, A. (1984) *The Girls in the Gang*. Blackwell: Oxford.

Campbell, D. and Fiske, D. (1959) 'Convergent and discriminant validation by the multitrait-multimethod matrix', *Psychological Bulletin*, 56: 81–105.

Carlen, P. (1985) *Criminal Women*. Cambridge: Polity Press.

Cavadino, M., Dignan, J. and Mair, G. (2013) *The Penal System: An Introduction*, 5th edn. London: Sage.

Chambliss, W. (1975) 'Towards a political economy of crime', abridged extract in E. McLaughlin, J. Muncie and G. Hughes (eds) (1996) *Criminological Perspectives: A Reader*. London: Sage.

Charlesworth, A. (2015) *Data Protection and Research Data*. Bristol: Jisc.

Charmaz, K. (2014) *Constructing Grounded Theory*, 2nd edn. London: Sage.

Cockcroft, T. (1999) 'Oral history and the cultures of the police', in F. Brookman, L. Noaks and E. Wincup (eds), *Qualitative Research in Criminology*. Aldershot: Ashgate.

Cockcroft, T. (2012) *Police Culture: Themes and Concepts*. Abingdon: Routledge.

Coffey, A. (2006) 'Impression management', in V. Jupp (ed.), *The SAGE Dictionary of Social Research Methods*. London: Sage.

Coffey, A. and Atkinson, P. (1996) *Making Sense of Qualitative Data*. London: Sage.

Cohen, S. (1972) *Folk Devils and Moral Panics: The Creation of the Mods and Rockers*. London: Paladin.

Cohen, S. and Taylor, I. (1972) *Psychological Survival: The Experience of Long-Term Imprisonment*. Harmondsworth: Penguin.

Cohen, S. and Taylor, I. (1977) 'Talking about prison blues', in C. Bell and H. Newby (eds), *Doing Sociological Research*. London: George Allen and Unwin.

Coleman, C. and Moynihan, J. (1996) *Understanding Crime Data*. Buckingham: Open University Press.

Coleman, C. and Norris, C. (2000) *Introducing Criminology*. Cullompton: Willan Publishing.

Corston, J. (2007) *The Corston Report: A Report by Baroness J Corston of a Review of Women with Particular Vulnerabilities in the Criminal Justice System*. London: Home Office.

Corti, L. and Bishop, L. (2005) 'Strategies in teaching secondary data analysis of qualitative data', *Forum: Qualitative Social Research*, 6(1): article 47.

Costley, C., Elliot, G. and Gibbs, P. (2010) *Doing Work Based Research: Approaches to Enquiry for Insider Researchers*. London: Sage.

Crace, J. and Plomin, J. (2001) 'Grant aid', *The Guardian*, 17 July.

Croall, H. (2001) *Understanding White Collar Crime*. Buckingham: Open University Press.

Crow, G. (2013) 'Action research', in E. McLaughlin and J. Muncie (eds) *The SAGE Dictionary of Criminology*, 3rd edn. London: Sage.

Davies, C. (2002) 'The dictionary, the reader and the handbook', *Qualitative Research*, 2: 417–421.

Davies, P. (2000) 'Doing interviews with female offenders', in V. Jupp, P. Davies and P. Francis (eds), *Doing Criminological Research*. London: Sage.

De Bie, J. and De Poot, C. (2016) 'Studying police files with grounded theory methods to understand Jihadist networks', *Studies in Conflict and Terrorism*, 39(7–8): 580–601.

Deakin, H. and Wakefield, K. (2014) 'Skype interviewing: Reflections of two PhD researchers', *Qualitative Research*, 14(5): 603–616.

Deegan, M. (2007) 'The Chicago school of ethnography', in P. Atkinson, A. Coffey, S. Delamont, J. Lofland and L. Lofland (eds), *Handbook of Ethnography*. London: Sage.

Delamont, S. (2002) 'Whose side are we on? Revisiting Becker's classic ethical question at the *fin de siecle?*', in T. Welland and L. Pugsley (eds), *Ethical Dilemmas in Qualitative Research*. Aldershot: Ashgate.

Delamont, S. (2003) *Feminist Sociology*. London: Sage.

Delamont, S., Atkinson, P., Coffey, A. and Burgess, R. (2001) *An Open Exploratory Spirit? Ethnography at Cardiff 1974–2001*, working paper series 20. Cardiff: Cardiff School of Social Sciences.

Denscombe, M. (2014) *The Good Research Guide*, 5th edn. Buckingham: Open University Press.

Denzin, N. (1970) *The Research Act in Sociology*. London: Butterworths.

Denzin, N. (1990) 'Researching alcoholics and alcoholism in American society', in N. Denzin (ed.), *Studies in Symbolic Interactionism*, 11: 81–107.

Denzin, N. (1994) 'Postmodernism and deconstructionism', in D. Dickens and A. Fontana (eds), *Postmodernism and Social Inquiry*. London: UCL Press.

Denzin, N. (1997) *Interpretive Ethnography*. Thousand Oaks, CA: Sage.

Dey, I. (1993) *Qualitative Data Analysis: A User-Friendly Guide for Social Scientists*. London: Routledge.

Ditton, J. (1977) *Part-time Crime: An Ethnography of Fiddling and Pilferage*. London: Macmillan.

Dixon, D. (1997) 'Editorial: Ethics, law and criminological research', *Australian and New Zealand Journal of Criminology*, 30(3): 211–216.

Dodgson, K., Goodwin, P., Howard, P., Llewellyn-Thomas, S., Mortimer, E., Russell, N. and Weiner, M. (2001) *Electronic Monitoring of Released Prisoners: An Evaluation of the Home Detention Curfew Scheme*, Home Office research study no. 222. London: Home Office.

Dorling, D., Gordon, D., Hillyard, P., Pantazis, C., Pemberton, S. and Tombs, S. (2008) *Criminal Obsessions: Why Harm Matters more than Crime*. London: Centre for Crime and Justice Studies.

Downes, D. and Morgan, R. (2012) 'Overtaking on the left? The politics of law and order in the "Big Society"', in M. Maguire, R. Morgan and R. Reiner (eds), *The Oxford Handbook of Criminology*, 5th edn. Oxford: Oxford University Press.

Downes, D., Rock, P. and McLaughlin (2016) *Understanding Deviance*, 7th edn. Oxford: Oxford University Press.

Downey, S. and Wincup, E. (2004) 'Are the police "Getting it Right?": Exploring the impact of a crime reduction initiative on primary school-aged children', *Criminal Justice Matters*, 47: 12–13.

Durkheim, E. (1895) 'The normal and the pathological', abridged extract in E. McLaughlin, J. Muncie and G. Hughes (eds) (2003), *Criminological Perspectives: A Reader*. London: Sage.

Earle, R., Drake, D. and Sloan, J. (eds) (2015) *The Palgrave Handbook of Prison Ethnography*. Basingstoke: Palgrave Macmillan.

Eastwood, N., Shiner, M. and Bear, D. (2013) *The Numbers in Black and White: Ethnic Disparities in the Policing and Prosecution of Drug Offences*. London: Release.

Eaton, M. (1993) *Women After Prison*. Buckingham: Open University Press.

Economic and Social Research Council (2015) *Strategic Plan 2015*. Swindon: Economic and Social Research Council.

Economic and Social Research Council (2016) 'What we do'. Available at: www.esrc.ac.uk/about-us/what-we-do/ (accessed 1 November 2016).

Ellis, A., Sloan, J. and Wykes, M. (2012) '"Moatifs" of masculinity: The stories about "men" in the British newspaper coverage of the Raoul Moat case', *Crime Media Culture*, 9(1): 3–21.

Ericson, R. and Carriere, K. (1994) 'The fragmentation of criminology', abridged extract in J. Munice, E. McLaughlin and M. Langan (eds) (1996), *Criminological Perspectives: A Reader*. London: Sage.

Fassin, D. (2013) *Enforcing Order: An Ethnography of Urban Policing*. Cambridge: Polity Press.

Feenan, D. (2002) 'Legal issues in acquiring information about illegal behaviour through criminological research', *British Journal of Criminology*, 42(4): 762–781.

Ferrell, J. (1999) 'Cultural criminology', *Annual Review of Sociology*, 25(1): 395–418.

Ferrell, J. (2013) 'Cultural criminology', in E. McLaughlin and J. Muncie (eds) *The SAGE Dictionary of Criminology*, 3rd edn. London: Sage.

Ferrell, J. and Hamm, M. (1998) *Ethnography at the Edge: Crime, Deviance and Field Research*. Boston, MA: Northeastern University Press.

Ferrell, J., Hayward, K. and Young, J. (2008) *Cultural Criminology: An Invitation*. London: Sage.

Fetterman, M. (1989) *Ethnography: Step by Step*. Newbury Park, CA: Sage.

Fetterman, D. (2010) *Ethnography: Step-by-Step*, 3rd edn. Thousand Oaks, CA: Sage.

Fielding, N. (1982) 'Observational research on the National Front', in M. Bulmer (ed.), *Social Research Ethics: An Examination of the Merits of Covert Participant Observation*. London: Macmillan.

Fielding, N. and Fielding, J. (2000) 'Resistance and adaptation to criminal identity: Using secondary analysis to evaluate classic studies of crime and deviance', *Sociology*, 34(4): 671–689.

Finch, J. (1984) 'It's great to have someone to talk to: The ethics and politics of interviewing women', in C. Bell and H. Roberts (eds), *Social Researching*. London: Routledge and Kegan Paul.

Finch, J. (1993) '"It's great to have someone to talk to": Ethics and politics of interviewing women', in M. Hammersley (ed.), *Social Research: Philosophy, Politics and Practice*. London: Sage.

Fine, G. (ed.) (1995) *A Second Chicago School? The Development of a Post-war American Sociology*. Chicago: University of Chicago Press.

Fleetwood, J. (2014) *Drug Mules: Women in the International Cocaine Trade*. Basingstoke: Macmillan.

Fox, M., Martin, P. and Green, G. (2007) *Doing Practitioner Research*. London: Sage.

Fuller, R. and Petch, A. (1995) *Practitioner Research: The Reflexive Social Worker*. Buckingham: Open University Press.

Garland, D. (2002) 'Of crime and criminals: the development of criminology in Britain', in M. Maguire, R. Morgan and R. Reiner (eds), *The Oxford Handbook of Criminology*. Oxford: Oxford University Press.

Geertz, C. (1973) 'Thick description', in C. Geertz (ed.), *The Interpretation of Cultures*. New York: Basic Books.

Gelsthorpe, L. (1990) 'Feminist methodologies in criminology: A new approach or old wine in new bottles?', in L. Gelsthorpe and A. Morris (eds), *Feminist Perspectives in Criminology*. Buckingham: Open University Press.

Glaser, A. and Strauss, A. (1967) *The Discovery of Grounded Theory*. Chicago, IL: Aldine.

Goodey, J. (2000) 'Biographical lessons for criminology', *Theoretical Criminology*, 4: 473–498.

Gouldner, A. (1975) 'The sociologist as partisan', in A. Gouldner (ed.), *For Sociology*. Harmondsworth: Penguin.

Grinyer, A. (2009) 'The ethics of the secondary analysis and further use of qualitative data', *Social Research Update*, 56.

Hakim, C. (1983) 'Research based on administrative records', *The Sociological Review*, 31(3): 489–519.

Hale, C., Hayward, K., Wahidin, A. and Wincup, E. (eds) (2013) *Criminology*, 3rd edn. Oxford: Oxford University Press.

Hall, S., Critcher, C., Jefferson, T., Clarke, J. and Roberts, B. (1978) *Policing the Crisis: Mugging, the State and Law and Order*. London: Macmillan.

Hammersley, M. (1995) *The Politics of Social Research*. London: Sage.

Hammersley, M. (1996) 'The relationship between qualitative and quantitative research: Paradigm loyalty versus methodological eclecticism', in J. Richardson (ed.) (1999), *Handbook of Research Methods for Psychology and the Social Sciences*. Leicester: British Psychological Society.

Hammersley, M. (2001) 'Which side was Becker on? Questioning political and epistemological radicalism', *Qualitative Research*, 1(1): 91–110.

Hammersley, M. (2007) 'The issue of quality in qualitative research', *International Journal of Research and Method in Education*, 30(3): 287–305.

Hammersley, M. and Atkinson, P. (2007) *Ethnography: Principles in Practice*, 2nd edn. London: Routledge.

Hayward, K. and Young, J. (2012) 'Cultural criminology', in M. Maguire, R. Morgan and R. Reiner (eds), *The Oxford Handbook of Criminology*, 5th edn. Oxford: Oxford University Press.

Heaton, J. (1998) 'Secondary analysis of qualitative data', *Social Research Update*, 22.

HEFCE (2011) *Assessment Framework and Guidance on Submissions*. Avilable at: www.ref. ac.uk/media/ref/content/pub/assessmentframeworkandguidanceonsubmissions/GOS%20 including%20addendum.pdf (accessed 1 November 2016).

Heidensohn, F. (1968) 'The deviance of women: A critique and an enquiry', *British Journal of Sociology*, 19(2): 160–175.

Heidensohn, F. (1996) *Women and Crime*, 2nd edn. Basingstoke: Macmillan.

Heidensohn, F. and Gelsthorpe, L. (2007) 'Gender and crime', in M. Maguire, R. Morgan and R. Reiner (eds) *The Oxford Handbook of Criminology*, 4th edn. Oxford: Oxford University Press.

Hine, C. (2015) *Ethnography for the Internet*. London: Sage.

Hobbs, D. (1994) 'Professional and organized crime in Britain', in M. Maguire, R. Morgan and R. Reiner (eds), *The Oxford Handbook of Criminology*. Oxford: Oxford University Press.

Hobbs, D. (2000) 'Researching serious crime', in R. King and E. Wincup (eds), *Doing Research on Crime and Justice*. Oxford: Oxford University Press.

Hobbs, D. (2007) 'Ethnography and the study of deviance', in P. Atkinson, A. Coffey, S. Delamont, J. Lofland and L. Lofland (eds), *Handbook of Ethnography*. London: Sage.

Hobbs, D., Hadfield, P., Lister, S. and Winlow, S. (2003) *Bouncers: Violence and Governance in the Night-time Economy*. Oxford: Oxford University Press.

Hobbs, S. and Hammerton, C. (2014) *The Making of Criminal Justice Policy*. Abingdon: Routledge.

Holdaway, S. (1983) *Inside the British Police: A Force at Work*. Oxford: Blackwell.

Holliday, A. (2016) *Doing and Writing Qualitative Research*, 3rd edn. London: Sage.

Hollway, W. and Jefferson, T. (2008) 'The free association narrative interview method', in L. Given (ed.), *The SAGE Encyclopedia of Qualitative Research Methods*. Thousand Oaks, CA: Sage.

Home Office (1974) *Home Office Research Unit: Summary of Research within the Unit and of Research supported by Grant*. London: Home Office.

Hope, T. (2004) 'Pretend it works: Evidence and governance in the evaluation of the Reducing Burglary Initiative', *Criminal Justice*, 4(3): 287–308.

Hope, T. (2013) 'What do crime statistics tell us?', in C. Hale, K. Hayward, A. Wahidin and E. Wincup (eds), *Criminology*, 3rd edn. Oxford: Oxford University Press.

Hope, T. and Walters, R. (2008) *Critical Thinking about the Use of Research*. London: Centre for Crime and Justice Studies.

Howard League for Penal Reform (2016) *The Cost of Prison Suicide: Research Briefing*. London: Howard League for Penal Reform.

Hoyle, C. (2000) 'Being a "nosy bloody cow": Ethical and methodological issues in researching domestic violence', in R. King and E. Wincup (eds), *Doing Research on Crime and Justice*. Oxford: Oxford University Press.

Hoyle, C. (2012) 'Victims, victimisation and restorative justice', in M. Maguire, R. Morgan and R. Reiner (eds), *The Oxford Handbook of Criminology*, 5th edn. Oxford: Oxford University Press.

Hsieh, H.-F. and Shannon, S. (2005) 'Three approaches to qualitative content analysis', *Qualitative Health Research*, 15(9): 1277–1288.

Hucklesby, A. (2008) 'Vehicles of desistance? The impact of electronically monitored curfew orders', *Criminology and Criminal Justice*, 8(1): 51–71.

Hucklesby, A. (2009) 'Understanding offenders' compliance: A case study of electronically monitored curfew orders', *Journal of Law and Society*, 36(2): 248–271.

Hucklesby, A. (2011) 'The working life of electronic monitoring officers', *Criminology and Criminal Justice*, 11(1): 59–76.

Hughes, G. (1998) *Understanding Crime Prevention: Social Control, Risk and Late Modernity*. Buckingham: Open University Press.

Hughes, G. (2011) 'Understanding the politics of criminological research', in P. Davies, P. Francis and V. Jupp (eds), *Doing Criminological Research*, 2nd edn. London: Sage.

IPCG (2007) *Intellectual Property Crime Report*, Intellectual Property Crime Group, UK Intellectual Property Office. Available at: http://webarchive.nationalarchives.gov.uk/20140603093549/http://www.ipo.gov.uk/ipcreport07.pdf.

Israel, M. (2014) *Research Ethics and Integrity for Social Scientists*, 2nd edn. London: Sage.

Janowitz, M. (1972) *Sociological Models and Social Policy*. Morriston, NJ: General Learning Systems.

Jefferson, G. (2004) 'Glossary of transcript symbols with an introduction', in G Lerner (ed.), *Conversation Analysis: Studies from the First Generation*. Amsterdam: John Benjamins.

Jefferson, T. (2013) 'Hegemonic masculinity', in E. McLaughlin and J. Muncie (eds), *The SAGE Dictionary of Criminology*, 3rd edn. London: Sage.

Jennings, W., Gray, E., Hay, C. and Farrell, S. (2015) 'Collating longitudinal data on crime, victimization and social attitudes in England and Wales: A new resource for exploring long-term trends in crime', *British Journal of Criminology*, 55(5): 1005–1015.

Jewkes, Y. (2011) 'The media and criminological research', in P. Davies, P. Francis and V. Jupp (eds), *Doing Criminological Research*, 2nd edn. London: Sage.

Jewkes, Y. (2015) *Media and Crime*, 3rd edn. London: Sage.

Johnson, R. and Onwuegbuzie, A. (2004) 'Mixed methods research: A research paradigm whose time has come', *Educational Researcher*, 33(7): 14–26.

Johnstone, G. (2005) 'Research ethics in criminology', *Research Ethics Review*, 1(2): 60–66.

Joseph Rowntree Foundation (2016) *Annual Report and Financial Statements for the year ended 31 December 2015*. York: Joseph Rowntree Foundation.

Jupp, V. (2013a) 'Appreciative criminology', in E. McLaughlin and J. Muncie (eds), *The SAGE Dictionary of Criminology*, 3rd edn. London: Sage.

Jupp, V. (2013b) 'Triangulation', in E. McLaughlin and J. Muncie (eds), *The SAGE Dictionary of Criminology*, 3rd edn. London: Sage.

Jupp, V., Davies, P. and Francis, P. (2000) (eds) *Doing Criminological Research*. London: Sage.

Kelly, L., Regan, L. and Burton, S. (1991) *An Exploratory Study of the Prevalence of Sexual Abuse in a Sample of 16–21 Year Olds*. London: Child Abuse Studies Unit, Polytechnic of North London

King, D. and Gibbs, A. (2003) 'Is home detention in New Zealand disadvantaging women and children?', *Probation Journal*, 50(2): 115–126.

King, R. (2000) 'Doing research in prison', in R. King and E. Wincup (eds), *Doing Research on Crime and Justice*. Oxford: Oxford University Press.

King, R. and Wincup, E. (2000) (eds) *Doing Research on Crime and Justice*. Oxford: Oxford University Press.

King, R. and Wincup, E. (2008) 'The process of criminological research', in R. King and E. Wincup (eds), *Doing Research on Crime and Justice*. Oxford: Oxford University Press.

Kirkwood (2014) 'Desistance in practice: Interaction in criminal justice groupwork', *Discovering Desistance*, 20 May. Available at: www.blogs.iriss.org.uk/discovering desistance/2014/05/20/desistance-in-practice-interaction-in-criminal-justice-group work/ (accessed 20 August 2016).

Kozinets, R. (2015) *Netnography: Redefined*, 2nd edn. London: Sage.

Large, J. (2011) 'Criminality, consumption and the counterfeiting of fashion goods', unpublished thesis, University of Leeds.

Large, J. and Wall, D. (2007a) 'First report on the counterfeiting of fashion apparel in the UK – regulation, literature, case studies, counterfeiting drivers', COUTURE Project, unpublished.

Large, J and Wall, D. (2007b) 'Second report on the counterfeiting of fashion apparel in the UK – what factors make a fashion product attractive to counterfeiting?', COUTURE Project, unpublished.

Lavrakas, P. (1993) *Telephone Survey Methods: Sampling, Selection, and Supervision*, 2nd edn. Thousand Oaks, CA: Sage.

Layder, D. (1998) *Sociological Practice: Linking Theory and Social Research*. London: Sage.

LeCompte, M. (2002) 'The transformation of ethnographic practice: Past and current challenges', *Qualitative Research*, 2: 283–299.

Letherby, G. (2003) *Feminist Research in Theory and Practice*. Buckingham: Open University Press.

Leverhulme Trust (2016a) *2015 Annual Review*. Available at: www.leverhulme.ac.uk/ sites/default/files/Publications/LEVERHULME%20AR15%20LO-RES.pdf (accessed 1 November 2016).

Leverhulme Trust (2016b) *Research We Do Not Fund*. Available at: www.leverhulme.ac.uk/ funding/research-we-do-not-fund (accessed 1 November 2016).

Levi, M. (1981) *The Phantom Capitalists: The Organisation and Control of Long-Firm Fraud*. London: Heinemann.

Lewins, A. and Silver, C. (2009) *Choosing a CAQDAS Package*, 6th edn. Available at: www.eprints.ncrm.ac.uk/791/1/2009ChoosingaCAQDASPackage.pdf (accessed 20 August 2016).

Lewis, P., Newburn, T., Taylor, M., McGillivray, C., Greenhill, A., Frayman, H. and Proctor, R. (2011) *Reading the Riots: Investigating England's Summer of Disorder*. London: The London School of Economics and Political Science and The Guardian.

Lewis, S., Vennard, J., Maguire, M., Raynor, P., Vanstone, M., Raybould, S. and Rix, A. (2003) *The Resettlement of Short-term Prisons: An Evaluation of Seven Pathfinders*. London: Home Office.

Liazos, A. (1972) 'The poverty of the sociology of deviance: Nuts, sluts and perverts', *Social Problems*, 20: 103–120.

Liebling, A. (1992) *Suicides in Prison*. London: Routledge.

Liebling, A. (2001) 'Whose side are we on? Theory, practice and allegiance in prisons research', *British Journal of Criminology*, 41: 472–484.

Lightowlers, C. (2011) 'Exploring the temporal dimension between young people's alcohol consumption patterns and violent behaviour', *Contemporary Drug Problems*, 38(2): 191–212.

Lilly, R., Cullen, F. and Ball, R. (2014) *Criminological Theory: Context and Consequences*, 6th edn. Thousand Oaks, CA: Sage.

Lincoln, Y. and Guba, A. (1985) *Naturalistic Inquiry*. Newbury Park, CA: Sage.

Loader, I., Girling, E. and Sparks, R. (1998) 'Narratives of decline: Youth, dis/order and community in an English "Middletown"', *British Journal of Criminology*, 38: 388–403.

Lofland, J. (1987) 'Reflections on a thrice named journal', *Journal of Contemporary Ethnography*, 18: 202–233.

Loucks, N. (2006) *No One Knows: Offenders with Learning Difficulties and Learning Disabilities. Review of Prevalence and Associated Needs*. London: Prison Reform Trust.

Lowman, J. and Palys, T. (2014) 'The betrayal of research confidentiality in British sociology', *Research Ethics*, 10(2): 97–118.

Maguire, M. (2000) 'Researching "street" criminals', in R. King and E. Wincup (eds), *Doing Research on Crime and Justice*. Oxford: Oxford University Press.

Maguire, M. (2002) 'Crime statistics: the 'data explosion' and its implications', in M. Maguire, R. Morgan and R. Reiner (eds), *The Oxford Handbook of Criminology*, 3rd edn. Oxford: Oxford University Press.

Maguire, M. (2004) 'The Crime Reduction Programme in England and Wales', *Criminal Justice*, 4(3): 213–237.

Maguire, M. (2007) 'Researching "street' criminals", in R. King and E. Wincup (eds), *Doing Research on Crime and Justice*, 2nd edn. Oxford: Oxford University Press.

Maguire, M., Morgan, R. and Reiner, R. (eds) (2012) *The Oxford Handbook of Criminology*, 5th edn. Oxford: Oxford University Press.

Maidment, M. (2002) 'Toward a "woman-centred" approach to community based corrections: A gendered analysis of electronic monitoring in Eastern Canada', *Women and Criminal Justice*, 13(4): 47–68.

Mair, G. (2007) 'Research on community penalties', in R. King and E. Wincup (eds), *Doing Research on Crime and Justice*, 2nd edn. Oxford: Oxford University Press.

Mair, G. and Nee, C. (1990) *Electronic Monitoring: The Trials and their Results*, Home Office research study no. 120. London: Home Office.

Mair, G. and Mortimer, E. (1996) *Curfew Orders with Electronic Monitoring*, Home Office research study no. 163. London: Home Office.

Malinowski, N. (1926) *Crime and Custom in Savage Society*. New York: Harcourt, Brace and Company.

Manning, P. (1987) 'The ethnographic conceit', *Journal of Contemporary Ethnography*, 16: 49–68.

Maruna, S. (2007) *Making Good: How Ex-Convicts Reform and Rebuild their Lives*. Washington, DC: APA Books.

Mason, J. (2002) *Qualitative Researching*, 2nd edn. London: Sage.

Mass Observation (2016) *History of Mass Observation*. Available at: www.massobs.org.uk/about/history-of-mo (accessed 20 August 2016).

Matthews, B. and Ross, L. (2010) *Research Methods. A Practical Guide for the Social Sciences*. Harlow: Pearson Education Limited.

Matza, D. (1969) *Becoming Deviant*. New Jersey: Prentice Hall.

Mauthner, N., Parry, O. and Backett-Milburn, K. (1998) 'The data are out there, or are they? Implications for archiving and revisiting qualitative data', *Sociology*, 32(4): 733–745.

Mayer, J., Salovey, P. and Caruso, D. (2000) 'Emotional intelligence as zeitgeist, as personality, and as a mental ability', in R. Bar-On and J. Parker (eds), *The Handbook of Emotional Intelligence*. San Francisco: Jossey-Bass.

McEvoy, K. (2001) *Paramilitary Imprisonment in Northern Ireland: Resistance, Management and Release*. Oxford: Oxford University Press.

McKeganey, N. and Barnard, M. (1996) *Sex Work on the Streets: Prostitutes and their Clients*. Buckingham: Open University Press.

Mhlanga, B. (1999) *Race and Crown Prosecution Service Decisions*. London: Home Office.

Mhlanga, B. (2000) 'The numbers game: Quantitative research on ethnicity', in R. King and E. Wincup (eds), *Doing Research on Crime and Justice*. Oxford: Oxford University Press.

Millman, M. (1975) 'She did it all for love: a feminist view of the sociology of deviance', *Sociological Inquiry*, 45 (2–3): 251–279.

Monaghan, M. (2011) *Evidence vs Politics: Exploiting Research in UK Drug Policy Making*. Bristol: The Policy Press.

Moore, J. (2013) 'Social media: The next generation of archiving', *FCW*, 25 November. Available at: www.fcw.com/articles/2013/11/25/exectech-social-media-archiving.aspx (accessed 20 August 2016).

Morgan, D. (1997) *Focus Groups as Qualitative Research*, 2nd edn. Thousand Oaks, CA: Sage.

Morgan, R. and Hough, M. (2007) 'The politics of criminological research', in R. King and E. Wincup (eds), *Doing Research on Crime and Justice*, 2nd edn. Oxford: Oxford University Press.

Morrow, V., Boddy, J. and Lamb, R. (2014) *The Ethics of Secondary Data Analysis*. University of Southampton: National Centre for Research Methods.

Mulgan, R. (2014) *Making Open Government Work*. Basingstoke: Palgrave Macmillan.

Muncie, J. (2013) 'Positivism', in E. McLaughlin and J. Muncie (eds), *The SAGE Dictionary of Criminology*, 3rd edn. London: Sage.

Newburn, T. (2016) 'Reflections on why riots don't happen', *Theoretical Criminology*, 20(2): 125–144.

Newburn, T., Diski, R., Cooper, K., Deacon, R., Burch, A. and Grant, M. (2016) '"The biggest gang"? Police and people in the 2011 English Riots', *Policing and Society*. Available at: www.tandfonline.com/doi/full/10.1080/10439463.2016.1165220 (accessed 20 August 2016).

Noaks, L. (1988) 'The perception and fear of crime and its implications for residents in the Bettws community', unpublished MSc(Econ) thesis, Cardiff University.

Noaks, L. and Wincup, E. (2004) *Criminological Research: Understanding Qualitative Approaches*. London: Sage.

Nuffield Foundation (2015) *Nuffield Foundation Trustees' Report and Financial Statements 2014*. London: Nuffield Foundation.

Oakley, A. (1981) 'Interviewing women: A contradiction in terms', in H. Roberts (ed.), *Doing Feminist Research*. London: Routledge.

O'Connell Davidson, J. and Layder, D. (1993) *Methods, Sex and Madness*. London: Routledge.

O'Connor, H., Madge, C., Shaw, R. and Wellens, J. (2008) 'Internet-based interviewing', in N. Fielding, N.R. Lee and G. Blank (eds), *The SAGE Handbook of Online Research Methods*. London: Sage.

Ofcom (2016) *Facts and Figures*. Available at: www.media.ofcom.org.uk/facts/ (accessed 20 August 2016).

Office for National Statistics (2016) *Internet Access – Households and Individuals: 2016*. Available at: www.ons.gov.uk/peoplepopulationandcommunity/householdcharacteristics/homeinternetandsocialmediausage/bulletins/internetaccesshouseholdsandindividuals/2016 (accesed 1 November 2016).

Open University (2016) *Crimes of the Powerful*. Available at: www.open.edu/openlearn/people-politics-law/crimes-the-powerful/content-section-0 (accessed 25 July 2016).

O'Reilly, K. (2011) *Ethnographic Methods*, 2nd edn. Abingdon: Routledge.

Parker, H. (1996) 'Young adult offenders, alcohol and criminological cul-de-sacs', *British Journal of Criminology*, 36: 282–298.

Parry, O. and Mauthner, N. (2004) 'Whose data are they anyway? Practical, legal and ethical issues in archiving qualitative research data', *Sociology*, 38(1): 139–152.

Parry, O. and Mauthner, N. (2005) 'Back to basics: Who re-uses qualitative data and why?', *Sociology*, 39(2): 337–342.

Payne, B. (2016) *White-collar Crime: The Essentials*, 2nd edn. Thousand Oaks, CA: Sage.

Pearson, G. (1993) 'Talking a good fight: Authenticity and distance in the ethnographer's craft', in D. Hobbs and T. May (eds), *Interpreting the Field: Accounts of Ethnography*. Oxford: Oxford University Press.

Phillips, N. and Strobl, S. (2006) 'Cultural criminology and kryptonite: Apocalyptic and retributive constructions of crime and justice in comic books', *Crime Media Culture*, 2(3): 304–331.

Pink, S., Horst, H., Postill, J., Hjorth, L., Lewis, T. and Tacchi, J. (2015) *Digital Ethnography: Principles and Practice*. London: Sage.

Player, E. and Jenkins, M. (1993) *Prisons after Woolf: Reform through Riot*. London: Routledge.

Plummer, K. (2001) *Documents of Life 2: A Invitation to Critical Humanism*, 2nd edn. London: Sage.

Polsky, N. (1971) *Hustlers, Beats and Others*. Harmondsworth: Pelican.

Punch, M. (1979) *Policing the Inner City*. London: Macmillan.

Putt, J. (2013) 'Community studies using ethnographic techniques: Still relevant to criminology?' *Current Issues in Criminal Justice*, 25(1): 475–489.

Quetelet, A. (1842) 'Of the development of the propensity to crime', abridged extract in E. McLaughlin, J. Muncie and G. Hughes (eds) (2003), *Criminological Perspectives: A Reader*. London: Sage.

Rawlinson, P. (2000) 'Mafia, methodology and "alien" culture', in R. King and E. Wincup (eds), *Doing Research on Crime and Justice*. Oxford: Oxford University Press.

Raynor, P. (2004) 'The Probation Service "Pathfinders": Finding the path and losing the way?', *Criminal Justice*, 4(3): 309–325.

Reiman, J. (1979) 'Research subjects, political subjects and human subjects', in C. Klockars and F. O'Connor (eds), *Deviancy and Decency: The Ethics of Research with Human Subjects*. London: Sage.

Reiner, R. (2010) *The Politics of the Police*, 4th edn. Oxford: Oxford University Press.

Reiner, R. and Newburn, T. (2007) 'Police research', in R. King and E. Wincup (eds), *Doing Research on Crime and Justice*, 2nd edn. Oxford: Oxford University Press.

Reinharz, S. (1992) *Feminist Methods in Social Research*. New York: Oxford University Press.

Renzetti, C. (2013) *Feminist Criminology*. Abingdon: Routledge.

Richardson, L. (1990) *Writing Strategies: Reaching Diverse Audiences*. Newbury Park, CA: Sage.

Robson, C. and McCartan, K. (2015) *Real World Research*, 4th edn. Chichester: Wiley.

Rock, P. (1994) 'The social organisation of British criminology', in M. Maguire, R. Morgan and R. Reiner (eds), *The Oxford Handbook of Criminology*. Oxford: Oxford University Press.

Roseneil, S. (1993) 'Greenham revisited: Researching myself and my sisters', in D. Hobbs and T. May (eds), *Interpreting the Field: Accounts of Ethnography*. Oxford: Oxford University Press.

Rutter, J. and Bryce, J. (2008) 'The consumption of counterfeit goods: "Here be pirates"', *Sociology*, 42(6): 1146–1164.

Salovey, P. and Grewal, D. (2005) 'The science of emotional intelligence', *Current Directions in Psychological Science*, 14(6): 281–285.

Sarantakos, S. (2012) *Social Research*, 4th edn. Basingstoke: Palgrave Macmillan.

Schneider, J. (2006) 'Professional codes of ethics: Their role and implications for international research', *Journal of Contemporary Criminal Justice*, 22(2): 173–192.

Scott, J. (1990) *A Matter of Record*. Cambridge: Polity Press.

Sedley, S. (2016) *Missing Evidence: An Inquiry into the Delayed Publication of Government-commissioned Research*. London: Sense about Science.

Seymour, L. (2010) *Public Health and Criminal Justice: Promoting and Protecting Offenders' Mental Health and Wellbeing*. London: Centre for Mental Health.

Shaffir, W. (1991) 'Managing a convincing self-presentation: Some personal reflection on entering the field', in W. Shaffir and R. Stebbins (eds), *Experiencing Fieldwork: An Insider View of Qualitative Research*. Newbury Park, CA: Sage.

Shaffir, W. and Stebbins, R. (eds) (1991) *Experiencing Fieldwork: An Insider View of Qualitative Research*. Newbury Park, CA: Sage.

Shaffir, W., Stebbins, R. and Turowetz, A. (eds) (1980) *Fieldwork Experience: Qualitative Approaches to Social Research*. New York: St. Martin's Press.

Sharpe, K. (1998) *Red Light, Blue Light: Prostitutes, Punters and the Police*. Aldershot: Ashgate.

Sharpe, K. (2000) 'Mad, bad and (sometimes) dangerous to know: Street corner research with prostitutes, punters and the police', in R. King and E. Wincup (eds), *Doing Research on Crime and Justice*. Oxford: Oxford University Press.

Shaw, C. (1930) *The Jack-roller: A Delinquent Boy's Own Story*. Chicago: University of Chicago Press.

Shaw, C. and McKay, H. (1942) *Juvenile Delinquency and Urban Areas*. Chicago: University of Chicago Press.

Silver, C. and Lewins, A. (2014) *Using Software in Qualitative Research: A Step-by-Step Guide*, 2nd edn. London: Sage.

Silverman, D. (1985) *Qualitative Methodology and Sociology*. Aldershot: Gower.

Silverman, D. (1998) 'Qualitative/quantitative', in C. Jenks (ed.), *Core Sociological Dichotomies*. London: Sage.

Skeggs, B. (2001) 'Feminist ethnography', in P. Atkinson, A. Coffey, S. Delamont, J. Lofland and L. Lofland (eds), *Handbook of Ethnography*. London: Sage.

Smart, C. (1976) *Women, Crime and Criminology: A Feminist Critique*. London: Routledge and Kegan Paul.

Smith, C. and Wincup, E. (2000) 'Breaking in: Researching criminal justice institutions for women', in R. King and E. Wincup (eds), *Doing Research on Crime and Justice*. Oxford: Oxford University Press.

Smith, C. and Wincup, E. (2002) 'Reflections on fieldwork in criminal justice institutions' in T. Welland and L. Pugsley (eds), *Ethical Dilemmas in Qualitative Research*. Aldershot: Ashgate.

Smith, C. and Wincup, E. (2009) 'Gender and crime', in C. Hale, K. Hayward, A. Wahidin and E. Wincup (eds), *Criminology*, 3rd edn. Oxford: Oxford University Press.

Smith, J. (1983) 'Quantitative versus qualitative research: An attempt to clarify the issue', *Educational Researcher*, 12(3): 6–13.

Smithson, H., Ralphs, R. and Williams, P. (2013) 'Used and abused: The problematic usage of gang terminology in the United Kingdom and its implications for ethnic minority youth', *British Journal of Criminology*, 53(1): 113–128.

Snow, D. (1980) 'The disengagement process: A neglected problem in participant observation research', *Qualitative Sociology*, 3: 100–122.

Social Policy Association (2009) *Guidelines on Research Ethics*. London: Social Policy Association.

Social Research Association (2003) *Ethical Guidelines*. London: Social Research Association.

Socio-Legal Studies Association (2009) *Statement of Principles of Ethical Research Practice*. London: Socio-Legal Studies Association.

Stacey, J. (1988) 'Can there be a feminist ethnography?', *Women's Studies International Forum*, 17: 417–419.

Stanley, L. and Wise, S. (1993) *Breaking Out: Feminist Consciousness and Feminist Research*. London: Routledge and Kegan Paul.

Statista (2016) *Number of Monthly Active Twitter Users Worldwide from 1st Quarter 2010 to 2nd Quarter 2016 (in millions)*. Available at: www.statista.com/statistics/282087/number-of-monthly-active-twitter-users/ (accessed 20 August 2016).

Stern, N. (2016) *Building on Success and Learning from Experience: An Independent Review of the Research Excellence Framework*. London: Department for Business, Energy and Industrial Strategy.

Stevens, A. (2011) 'Telling policy stories: An ethnographic study of the use of evidence in policy-making in the UK', *Journal of Social Policy*, 40(2): 237–256.

Stokoe, E. (2010) '"I'm not gonna hit a lady": Conversation analysis, membership categorization and men's denials of violence towards women', *Discourse and Society*, 21(1): 59–82.

Strauss, A. (1987) *Qualitative Analysis for Social Scientists*. Cambridge: Cambridge University Press.

Sumner, C. (1994) *The Sociology of Deviance: An Obituary*. Buckingham: Open University Press.

Surette, R. (2014) *Media, Crime and Criminal Justice: Images, Realities and Policies*, 5th edn. Stamford, CT: Cengate Learning.

Sutherland, E. (1949) *White-collar Crime*. New York: Holt, Rinehart and Winston.

Tashakkori, A. and Teddlie, C. (1998) *Mixed Methodology*. Thousand Oaks, CA: Sage.

Taylor, I., Walton, P. and Young, I. (1973) *The New Criminology: For a Social Theory of Deviance*. London: Routledge and Kegan Paul.

Taylor, S. (1991) 'Leaving the field: Research, relationships, and responsibilities', in W. Shaffir and R. Stebbins (eds), *Experiencing Fieldwork: An Insider View of Qualitative Research*. Newbury Park, CA: Sage.

Tesch, R. (1990) *Qualitative Research: Analysis, Types and Software Tools*. London: Falmer.

Tombs, S. and Whyte, D. (2013) 'White collar crime', in E. McLaughlin and J. Muncie (eds), *The SAGE Dictionary of Criminology*, 3rd edn. London: Sage.

Tong, S. and Du, J. (2014) *Media Victimisation, Risk and Fear: A Grounded Theory Analysis of Media Content in Hong Kong*, working paper series 3(1). Available at: www.speed-polyu.edu.hk/workingpaperseries2014no3.php (accessed 20 July 2016).

Tonkiss, F. (1998) 'Civil/political', in C. Jenks (ed.), *Core Sociological Dichotomies*. London: Sage.

Tracy, S. (2010) 'Qualitative quality: Eight "big-tent" criteria for excellent qualitative research', *Qualitative Inquiry*, 16(10): 837–851.

Travers, M. (2001) *Qualitative Research through Case Studies*. London: Sage.

Travers, M., Putt, J. and Howard-Wagner, D. (2013) 'Special issue on ethnography, crime and criminal justice', *Current Issues in Criminal Justice*, 25(1): 463–469.

Treadwell, J. and Garland, J. (2011) 'Masculinity, marginalisation and violence: A case study of the English Defence League', *British Journal of Criminology*, 51(4): 621–634.

Trotter, C. (2006) *Working with Involuntary Clients: A Guide to Practice*. London: Sage.

Truman, C. (2003) 'Ethics and the ruling relations of research production', *Sociological Research Online*, 8(1).

UK Data Archive (2016) *About our Data*. Available at: www.ukdataservice.ac.uk/get-data/about (accessed 20 August 2016).

Van Maanen, J. (2011) *Tales of the Field: On Writing Ethnography*, 2nd edn. Chicago: University of Chicago Press.

Walklate, S. (2007) *Understanding Criminology: Current Theoretical Debates*, 2nd edn. Buckingham: Open University Press.

Walklate, S. (2008) 'Researching victims', in R. King and E. Wincup (eds) *Doing Research on Crime and Justice*, 2nd edn. Oxford: Oxford University Press.

Wall, D. and Large, J. (2010) 'Jailhouse frocks: Locating the public interest in policing counterfeit luxury fashion goods', *British Journal of Criminology*, 50(6): 1094–1116.

Walters, R. (2008) 'Government manipulation of criminological knowledge and the politics of deceit', in W. McMahon (ed.), *Critical Thinking about the Uses of Research*. London: Centre for Crime and Justice Studies.

Wardhaugh, J. (2000) 'Down and outers: Fieldwork amongst street homeless people', in R. King and E. Wincup (eds), *Doing Research on Crime and Justice*. Oxford: Oxford University Press.

Wax, R. (1971) *Doing Fieldwork: Warnings and Advice*. Chicago: University of Chicago Press.

Webb, E., Campbell, D., Schwartz, R. and Sechrest, L. (1966) *Unobtrusive Measures: Nonreactive Research in the Social Sciences*. Chicago: Rand McNally College Publishing Company.

Weber, M. (1949) *The Methodology of the Social Sciences*. Glencoe, IL: The Free Press.

Whyte, D. (2000) 'Researching the powerful: Towards a political economy of method', in R. King and E. Wincup (eds), *Doing Research on Crime and Justice*. Oxford: Oxford University Press.

Whyte, W. (1943) *Street Corner Society: The Social Structure of an Italian Slum*. Chicago: University of Chicago Press.

Wiles, R., Pain, H. and Crow, G. (2010) *Innovation in Qualitative Research Methods: A Narrative Review*. Southampton: ESRC National Centre for Research.

Wilke, R. and Zaichkowsky, J. (1999) 'Brand imitation and its effects on innovation, competition and brand equity', *Business Horizons*, November/ December: 9–18.

Williams, B. (2006) 'Meaningful consent to participate in social research on the part of people under the age of eighteen', *Research Ethics*, 2(1): 19–24.

Williams, M. (2007) 'Cybercrime and online methodologies', in R. King and E. Wincup (eds) *Doing Research on Crime and Justice*, 2nd edn. Oxford: Oxford University Press.

Williams, M. and Burnap, P. (2016) 'Cyberhate on social media in the aftermath of Woolwich: A case study in computational criminology and big data', *British Journal of Criminology*, 56(2): 211–238.

Williams, M. and Wall, D. (2013) 'Cybercrime', in C. Hale, K. Hayward, A. Wahidin and E. Wincup (eds), *Criminology*, 3rd edn. Oxford: Oxford University Press.

Wincup, E. (1997) 'Waiting for trial: Living and working in a bail hostel', unpublished PhD thesis, Cardiff University.

Wincup, E. (1999) 'Researching women awaiting trial: Dilemmas of feminist ethnography', in F. Brookman, L. Noaks and E. Wincup (eds), *Qualitative Research in Criminology*. Aldershot: Ashgate.

Wincup, E. (2001) 'Feminist research with women waiting trial: the effects on participants in the qualitative research process', in K. Gilbert (ed.) *The Emotional Nature of Qualitative Research*. Boca Ratpn, FL: CRC Press.

Wincup, E. (2013) *Understanding Crime and Social Policy*. Bristol: The Policy Press.

Wincup, E., Bayliss, R. and Buckland, G. (2003) *Youth Homeless and Substance Use: A Report to the Home Office Drugs and Alcohol Unit*. London: Home Office.

Wincup, E. and Hucklesby, A. (2007) 'Researching and evaluating resettlement', in A. Hucklesby and L. Hagley-Dickinson (eds), *Prisoner Resettlement: Policy and Practice*. Cullompton: Willan Publishing.

Winlow, S. (2001) *Badfellas: Crime, Tradition and New Masculinities*. Oxford: Berg.

Wolcott, H. (2009) *Writing up Qualitative Research*, 3rd edn. Thousand Oaks, CA: Sage.

Wolf, D. (1991) 'High risk methodology: Reflections on leaving an outlaw society', in W. Shaffir and R. Stebbins (eds), *Experiencing Fieldwork: An Insider View of Qualitative Research*. Newbury Park, CA: Sage.

Woods, P. (2005) *Successful Writing for Qualitative Researchers*, 2nd edn. London: Routledge.

Worrall, A. (1990) *Offending Women*. London: Routledge.

Yar, M. (2005) 'A deadly faith in fakes: Trademark theft and the global trade in counterfeit automotive components', *Internet Journal of Criminology*. Available at: www.internet journalofcriminology.com/Yar%20-%20A%20Deadly%20Faith%20in%20Fakes.pdf.

Yeomans, H. (2014) *Alcohol and Moral Regulation: Public Attitudes, Spirited Measures and Victorian Hangovers*. Bristol: The Policy Press.

Young, K., Ashby, D., Boaz, A. and Grayson, L. (2002) 'Social science and the evidence-based policy movement', *Social Policy and Society*, 1(3): 215–222.

INDEX